Global Heritage Assemblages

T0270858

UNESCO aims to tackle Africa's under-representation on its World Heritage List by inscribing instances of nineteenth- and twentieth-century modern architecture and urban planning there. But, what is one to make of the utopias of progress and development for which these buildings and sites stand? After all, concern for 'modern heritage' invariably—and paradoxically it seems—has to reckon with those utopias as problematic futures of the past, a circumstance complicating intentions to preserve a recent 'culture' of modernization on the African continent.

This new title in Routledge's Studies in Culture and Development series introduces the concept of 'global heritage assemblages' to analyze that problem. Based on extensive anthropological fieldwork, it describes how various governmental, intergovernmental, and nongovernmental actors engage with colonial and postcolonial built heritage found in Eritrea, Tanzania, Niger, and the Republic of the Congo. Rausch argues that the global heritage assemblages emerging from those examples produce problematizations of 'the modern', which ultimately indicate a contemporary need to rescue modernity from its dominant conception as an all-encompassing, epochal, and spatial culture.

Christoph Rausch is an assistant professor in the Humanities and Social Sciences at University College Maastricht, the Netherlands.

Routledge Studies in Culture and Development
Paul Basu, Wayne Modest, and Tim Winter, Series Editors

There is a burgeoning interest among academics, practitioners and policy-makers in the relationships between 'culture' and 'development'. This embraces the now well-recognized need to adopt culturally sensitive approaches *in* development practice, the necessity of understanding the cultural dimensions *of* development, and more specifically the role of culture *for* development. Culture, in all its dimensions, is a fundamental component of sustainable development, and throughout the world we are seeing an increasing number of governmental and non-governmental agencies turning to culture as a vehicle for economic growth, for promoting social cohesion, stability and human wellbeing, and for tackling environmental issues. At the same time, there has been remarkably little critical debate around this relationship, and even less concerned with the interventions of cultural institutions or creative industries in development agendas. The objective of the Routledge Studies in Culture and Development series is to fill this lacuna and provide a forum for reaching across academic, practitioner and policy-maker audiences.

The series editors welcome submissions for single- and jointly authored books and edited collections concerning issues such as the contribution of museums, heritage and cultural tourism to sustainable development; the politics of cultural diplomacy; cultural pluralism and human rights; traditional systems of environmental management; cultural industries and traditional livelihoods; and culturally appropriate forms of conflict resolution and post-conflict recovery.

Global Heritage Assemblages

Development and Modern
Architecture in Africa

Christoph Rausch

Routledge
Taylor & Francis Group

LONDON AND NEW YORK

First published 2017 by Routledge

2 Park Square, Milton Park, Abingdon, Oxfordshire OX14 4RN
52 Vanderbilt Avenue, New York, NY 10017

Routledge is an imprint of the Taylor & Francis Group, an informa business

First issued in paperback 2018

Copyright © 2017 Christoph Rausch

The right of Christoph Rausch to be identified as author of this work has been asserted by him in accordance with sections 77 and 78 of the Copyright, Designs and Patents Act 1988.

All rights reserved. No part of this book may be reprinted or reproduced or utilised in any form or by any electronic, mechanical, or other means, now known or hereafter invented, including photocopying and recording, or in any information storage or retrieval system, without permission in writing from the publishers.

Notice:
Product or corporate names may be trademarks or registered trademarks, and are used only for identification and explanation without intent to infringe.

British Library Cataloguing in Publication Data
A catalogue record for this book is available from the British Library

Library of Congress Cataloging in Publication Data
A catalog record for this book has been requested

ISBN: 978-1-138-21947-2 (hbk)
ISBN: 978-0-367-19305-8 (pbk)

Typeset in Sabon
by Apex CoVantage, LLC

Dedicated to my daughter Nora with whom I gladly share today and who gives meaning to my recent past and near future.

In loving memory of Nora's mother Karen (1977–2012)

Contents

Acknowledgments

Ideas occur to us when they please, not when it pleases us. [. . .] In any case, ideas come when we do not expect them, and not when we are brooding and searching at our desks. Yet ideas would certainly not come to mind had we not brooded at our desks and searched for answers with passionate devotion.

—*Max Weber, 1918*[1]

This book is the outcome of a long research process and could not exist without the 'collaboratory' I have found in the global heritage assemblages that it features. I heartily thank all of my contacts and interviewees, whose names and details are listed in the appendix. Also, this publication would have been impossible without support from my personal and professional heritage assemblages, which—for better or for worse—are not at all global.

In Maastricht and Delft I am grateful to have had the pleasure of working together with Marieke Kuipers, who has been a reliable and kind PhD supervisor throughout. I also thank Tom Avermaete, Mia Fuller, Valentina Mazzucato, Peter Pels, and Renée van de Vall for their positive assessment of my dissertation, on which this book is based, as well as for their constructive criticism during my public PhD defense. Mia Fuller I especially thank for her invitation to spend time as a visiting researcher at the University of California, Berkeley; I much appreciate her support and reassurance. In Berkeley, James Holston and Aihwa Ong have generously granted time and advice, and of course, I am obliged and thankful to Paul Rabinow for not hesitating to meet and to engage in *Wissensarbeitsforschung* with me.

Many of the arguments brought forward in this book were first presented at seminars and conferences in Europe. I have benefited most from debates at the venues mentioned below and hereby thank all their organizers and participants, particularly the individuals listed, for their helpful feedback: research seminar at BTU Cottbus, Magdalena Droste and Regina Göckede, research seminar at Maastricht University, Valentina

Mazzucato; research seminar at Delft University of Technology, Tom Avermaete; conference "The Heritage Theater" at Rotterdam Erasmus University, Marlite Halbertsma, Alex van Stipriaan and Ferdinand de Jong; the 2010 conference of the European Association of Social Anthropology (EASA) at the University of Dublin, Maynooth, panel "The Anthropology of International Organizations", Jens Adam, Christoph Brumann, Michael Lidauer and Cris Shore; EASA 2012 conference at Université de Paris, Nanterre, panel "Affect and Knowledge: Inquiry, Breakdown, Disquiet", Gaymon Bennett, Frédéric Keck, Meg Stalcup, Anthony Stavrianakis and Mattias Viktorin; 14th Annual Heritage Seminar on "Heritage Scapes" and 16th Annual Heritage Seminar on "African Heritage Challenges" at Cambridge University, Britt Baillie, Paul Basu, Leanne Philpot, and Marie-Louise Stig Sørensen.

It makes me proud that the Boekman foundation and the Dutch Organization for Scientific Research together have chosen my dissertation to be among the three best theses published in the Netherlands in the fields of art, culture, and related policies between 2012 and 2014. Also, it was an honor to be invited to present my work as a guest scholar at the Max Planck Institute for Social Anthropology in Halle, where I thank Christoph Brumann for his sponsorship.

For making Maastricht University my academic home, I am grateful to my colleagues and students, especially at University College Maastricht, as well as to my collaborators at the Maastricht Centre for Arts and Culture, Conservation and Heritage. Furthermore, I decidedly do not want to miss mentioning dear friends, many of whom will never read this book because they are otherwise meaningfully engaged. And I thank my extended family in Germany, Estonia, and the Netherlands; especially Maria-Anna Rausch, Karl-Heinz Rausch, Anna Meyer, Martin Rausch, Krista Karolin-Kattenbeld, Koit Pärna, and Josef Schenten whose hospitality to the dogs and me at his estate in the Eifel-mountains provided motivation and solace more than once.

Finally and most of all, I give thanks and credit to my best friend and dear wife Karen Pärna, whose love and care—both intellectual and in every other way—has made this a better book. I cannot begin to put into words how very much it pains me that Karen did not live to read these lines of acknowledgment. And it pains me even more to contemplate that she does not live to see our, *her* beloved daughter Nora grow up and learn to read them too.

Note

1. Max Weber, "Science as a Vocation," *Daedalus* 87, no. 1, Science and the Modern View (1958). 113.

Part I

Prologue
A Cult of Heritage

Since 1972, the UNESCO *Convention Concerning the Protection of the World Cultural and Natural Heritage* is the gospel of what the historians Françoise Choay and David Lowenthal independently from each other call a cult of heritage: "a newly popular faith whose shrines and icons daily multiply and whose praise suffuses public discourse".[1] An epiphanic moment in this cult of heritage was the construction of the Aswan High Dam in Egypt.

The Aswan High Dam is a modern development project that could be said to be archetypical of the 20th century. Gamal Abdel Nasser, the second president of Egypt since it gained its independence in 1952, made the decision to once and for all tame the floodings of the river Nile immediately following his inauguration in 1956. Aiming to add on to dams built by the British colonial powers in 1889, 1912 and 1933, Nasser commissioned the new dam in order to produce the hydroelectric power deemed necessary for the industrial development of a newly independent nation-state. A large reservoir would ensure access to drinking water across the country, as well as feed a new system of agricultural irrigation.

In 1954, the Egyptian government had already made a request for a loan from the World Bank for a planned dam. The World Bank, however, cut off this funding when Egypt nationalized the Suez Canal in 1956. In turn, Nasser accepted assistance to build the Aswan High Dam from the Soviet Union, raising Cold War tensions in the region. Still, neither the military invasion of Egypt by the United Kingdom, France and Israel in the wake of the Suez crisis nor the 1967 Six-Day War or the War of Attrition between Israel and Egypt between 1969 until 1970 stopped the Egyptian government from pursuing efforts to build the new dam. Construction of the Aswan High Dam was completed on July 21, 1970, shortly before Nasser's death in September that year.

By 1976, the Aswan High Dam was to create an enormous artificial lake—Lake Nasser. This, however, did not only mean the promise of autonomous economic development for Egypt, the rise of the Nile waters also meant environmental devastation, the inundation of human settlements and the displacement of their populations. Moreover, the reservoir threatened to destroy ancient monuments. Indeed, Lake Nasser would eventually be as wide as 25 kilometers in some areas, flooding the Nile valley over 300 kilometers up into Egyptian Nubia and even some 200 kilometers into Sudanese Nubia. As a result, its waters would submerge dozens of temples and historic sites, the cultural value of which had been cemented by centuries of colonial archaeology.

Soon the Egyptian and Sudanese governments realized the importance of the Nubian monuments for their purposes of nation building. For example, Nasser stated,

> We pin our hopes on the High Dam for the implementation of our plans of economic development; but likewise we pin our hopes on the preservation of the Nubian treasures in order to keep alive monuments which are not only dear to our hearts—we being their guardians—but dear to the whole world which believes that the ancient and the new components of human culture should blend in one harmonious whole.[2]

Thus, in 1959, the Egyptian ministry of culture approached the young United Nations Educational, Scientific and Cultural Organization (UNESCO, founded in 1946) with a request for "active material, technical and scientific assistance in the design and execution of projects to save the monuments of Nubia".[3] The Sudanese ministry of education joined this call for "the judgment of history" when it submitted its own appeal for international cooperation in the same year.

At the time, UNESCO was already active in Egypt as, immediately following political independence, the intergovernmental organization had established the *Documentation and Study Centre for the History of Art and Civilization of Ancient Egypt* in Cairo. This center of expertise—a legatee of colonial archeological services—focused on the photographic and photogrammetric documentation of the Nubian monuments.[4] In the face of looming material destruction, however, UNESCO deemed exclusive documentation insufficient. When it became clear that the Aswan High Dam was definitely going to be built, the appeals by the Egyptian and Sudanese governments to devise measures to save the "stone treasures"[5] of Nubia from the floods saw a swift response from the UNESCO member states.

In 1960, shortly after the official inauguration of the construction works on the Aswan High Dam's foundations, UNESCO's director general Vittorino Veronese presented the 55th session of UNESCO's Executive Board with a proposal to safeguard the ancient Nubian monuments. In dramatic prose, Veronese's appeal explains his perception of the dilemma at stake:

> Work has begun on the Aswan dam. Within five years, the Middle Valley of the Nile will be turned into a vast lake. Wondrous

structures, ranking among the most significant on earth, are in danger of disappearing beneath the waters. The dam will bring fertility to huge stretches of desert, but the opening of new fields to the tractors, the provision of new sources of power to future factories, threatens to exact a terrible price.[6]

Veronese viewed the inundation of Nubia as a special challenge for modern development, stating, "It is not easy to choose between a heritage of the past and the present well-being of people, living in need in the shadow of one of history's most splendid legacies; it is not easy to choose between temples and crops."[7]

UNESCO was convinced that "[m]odern needs and modern technology may compel and produce the [Aswan High Dam] but the Present cannot afford to squander the Past".[8] Its monthly magazine, *UNESCO Courier*, maintained that

[t]he twentieth century has become an age of startling transformation, and its changes everywhere on the planet threaten the heritage of the past on which man's cultural life depended. [. . .] But, in protecting our common artistic heritage, there must be a worldwide feeling of responsibility.[9]

Veronese called for "services, equipment and money" to "save the threatened monuments" of Nubia in their material authenticity.[10] He urged the member states of his international body to consider that "treasures of universal value are entitled to universal protection".[11] It was "now or never", as the *UNESCO Courier* headlined: Social and economic progress was to be paired with "cultural and spiritual progress".[12]

Swiftly following Veronese's appeal, the director general was authorized to set up and chair an International Action Committee. Initially, this committee was split into two, an Executive Committee constituted of formal representatives of 15 member states, as well as an Honorary Committee of Patrons. The latter panel was chaired by King Gustav Adolf VI of Sweden and included Queen Elizabeth of Belgium, Queen Frederika of Greece, Princess Grace of Monaco, Princess Margrete of Denmark, Prince Mikasa of Japan, Mrs. Eleanor Roosevelt, Dag Hammerskjold, André Malraux and Julian Huxley. Soon, however, there were complaints that a legitimate heritage authority had to have scientific expertise in the fields of archaeology, Egyptology, and historic preservation. An additional Consultative Committee was set up in response, as well as an advisory Panel of International Experts. In 1961, UNESCO's Department of Cultural Activities formed a specialist Service for the Monuments of Nubia, which bundled the various initiatives.

Originally, Veronese had identified the challenge of the Campaign to Save the Monuments of Nubia as one of "bringing to light an as yet undiscovered wealth for the benefit of all".[13] Yet, the "generous response" from the UNESCO member states, which Veronese requested in his original appeal to UNESCO's Executive Committee, must be seen against the backdrop of an Egyptian and Sudanese vow to grant unlimited access to foreign archeological expeditions. Veronese literally announced "a new era of marvelous enrichment" in the field of Egyptology:

> In return for the help the world gives them, the governments of Cairo and Khartoum will open the whole of their countries to archeological excavation and will allow half of whatever works of art may be unearthed by science or by hazard to go to foreign museums. They will even agree to the transport, stone by stone, of certain monuments of Nubia.[14]

The internationally orchestrated safeguarding campaign would mark a new era of enrichment indeed, as particularly the collections of European and American museums, already filled with colonial trophy from Egypt, would see valuable new additions.[15]

Nevertheless, the multimillion-dollar Nubia campaign was in the "donor states" above all advertised as a humanist mission to preserve cultural heritage *in situ*. As a consequence, the UNESCO Campaign to Save the Monuments of Nubia sparked a general interest in the preservation of cultural heritage abroad. A popular travelling exhibition of pharaonic treasures that visited the UK, France, Germany, Norway, Belgium, the USSR, Canada and the US drew thousands of visitors. Press representatives were treated to a Nile cruise that included on-board tutoring on Nubia's archaeology, history and cultural heritage, generating substantial media coverage in the process. The challenge taken on by an international team of engineers to raise the whole temple of Abu Simbel by 200 feet in order to save it from the raised water level particularly fascinated a foreign audience.[16]

Upon the definite flooding of Nubia in 1964, René Maheu, Veronese's successor as UNESCO director general, celebrated the Nubia campaign as a "victory for cultural co-operation", as well as an affirmation of mankind's "profound spiritual unity". In the *UNESCO Courier*, he stated,

> This is not the first time that mankind has reacted generously to a noble cause. But this is the first time that international fellowship has found expression on so large a scale in matters of culture, and that governments have committed their States to such an undertaking. It is also the first time that this same fellowship has invoked the principle that certain religious, historical, and artistic monuments, in which mankind has expressed its deepest convictions and highest aspirations, belong to the whole human race and are part of its common heritage, regardless of when they came into existence or the place where they happen to be. Culture, an essential element of

the intellectual and moral solidarity of mankind has thus been recognized by States, for all the world to see, as an important factor in their co-operation for the promotion of peace by the spirit to which members of UNESCO have pledged themselves. That is the significance of this event, which will itself make history.[17]

And indeed, UNESCO still considers the International Campaign to Save the Monuments of Nubia as "undoubtedly the single UNESCO action that has made the greatest impression on public opinion worldwide".[18]

In 1980, the Campaign to Save the Monuments of Nubia officially came to an end. At the closing ceremony, UNESCO's director general Amadou-Mathar M'Bow referred to the campaign as a striking example of a "new awareness". According to him, the Nubia campaign had been "marked throughout by a spirit of the widest possible co-operation" and had "attained all the objectives originally assigned to it". In closing, M'bow claimed that the campaign "will be numbered among the few major attempts made in our lifetime by the nations to assume their common responsibility towards the past so as to move forward in a spirit of brotherhood towards the future".[19]

In fact, when M'Bow spoke these words, UNESCO had already codified this new awareness of a need for international cooperation to preserve cultural heritage of "outstanding universal value to humanity".[20] In 1972, halfway through and inspired by the International Campaign to Save the Monuments of Nubia, the organization had introduced its Convention Concerning the Protection of the World Cultural and Natural Heritage.

Today, UNESCO's World Heritage Convention remains "one of the most successful international conventions ever drafted" and is regarded as "truly a landmark document, not only in the history of UNESCO, but in history more generally".[21] By now, 190 states have ratified the convention, and together they have inscribed hundreds of cultural monuments and sites on the World Heritage List. Arguably then, the widespread acceptance of a notion of world heritage has elevated Amadou-Mathar M'Bow's belief in a "common responsibility to the past" and René Maheu's confidence in a "profound spiritual unity of mankind" to a kind of popular faith. In this sense, the construction of the Aswan High Dam and the resultant Campaign to Save the Monuments of Nubia initiated a cult of heritage that would reverberate and resonate the world over.

Notes

1. David Lowenthal, *The Heritage Crusade and the Spoils of History* (London: Viking, 1997). Also compare: Francoise Choay, *The Invention of the Historic Monument* (Cambridge: Cambridge University Press, 2001).
2. "Abu Simbel: Now or Never," *UNESCO Courier*, 1961. 6.

3. Fekri A. Hassan, "The Aswan High Dam and the International Rescue Nubia Campaign," *African Archeological Review* 24, no. 3 (2007). 73–94.
4. UNESCO, "Records of the 8th UNESCO Conference in Montevideo, 1954," http://unesdoc.unesco.org/images/0011/001145/114586E.pdf.
5. Pol-Droit, *Humanity in the Making: The Intellectual History of UNESCO* (Paris: UNESCO, 2005). 132.
6. 8 March 1950, Veronese's address quoted in Ibid., 132–133.
7. Ibid.
8. "Abu Simbel: Now or Never." 10.
9. Ibid., 6.
10. Pol-Droit, *Humanity in the Making: The Intellectual History of UNESCO*. 132–133.
11. Veronese quoted in Ibid., 132–133.
12. "Abu Simbel: Now or Never." 6.
13. "Appeal launched on 8 March 1960 by Mr. Vittorino Veronese, Director General of UNESCO," http://www.itnsource.com/shotlist//RTV/1960/03/08/BGY503240109/?s=buries.
14. Ibid.
15. For instance, the Temple of Taffeh temple ended up at the Dutch National Museum of Antiquities in Leiden.
16. Torgny Save-Soderbergh, ed. *Temples and Tombs of Ancient Nubia: The International Rescue Campaign at Abu Simbel, Philae and Other Sites* (London: UNESCO, Thames and Hudson, 1987).
17. Rene Maheu quoted in "Victory in Nubia," *UNESCO Courier*, 1964. 4.
18. Pol-Droit, *Humanity in the Making: The Intellectual History of UNESCO*.
19. "Victory in Nubia: The Greatest Archeological Rescue Operation of All Times." *UNESCO Courier*, February/March 1980. 4.
20. UNESCO, "1972 Convention Concerning the Protection of the World Cultural and Natural Heritage," http://whc.unesco.org/en/conventiontext/.
21. Pol-Droit, *Humanity in the Making: The Intellectual History of UNESCO*.

Introduction
World Heritage as Event

The emergence of the notion of world heritage in reaction to an arche-typical modern development project on the African continent that I described in the Prologue is an event that can be understood as prob-lematizing modernity itself. In 1960, the construction of the Aswan High Dam in Egypt was perceived as a symbol of modernization, and as such as an immediate threat to the ancient monuments of Nubia. Although the Egyptian president Gamal Abdel Nasser acknowledged that "the preser-vation of the legacy of mankind is no less important than the construc-tion of dams, the erection of factories and the greater prosperity of the people", the dominant ideology of modern development for which the Aswan High Dam stood remained fundamentally at odds with the pres-ervation of ancient Nubian heritage.

The International Campaign to Save the Monuments of Nubia then effectively reinterpreted this understanding of modernization as an exclu-sive peril to cultural heritage. UNESCO claimed that in Nubia "a princi-ple has been established, put into practice, tested in the fire of action: the principle that cultural wealth, wherever it may be found, belongs to and enriches all mankind, and that all mankind should therefore participate in its preservation".[1] In fact, with the International Campaign to Save the Monuments of Nubia, as well as with the ensuing World Heritage Convention of 1972, UNESCO introduced the terms *culture* and *the past* as modern development tools in their own right: Assuming moderniza-tion to be inevitable in every society, the intergovernmental organization considered the importance of cultural heritage to be "a vector of develop-ment and social stability, both for present and for future generations".[2]

This invocation of cultural heritage for progress and development argu-ably amounted to what Foucault would call a "breach of self-evidence" concerning classifications, practices and things modern.[3] Though the Egyptian and Sudanese governments would perhaps have claimed the construction of the Aswan High Dam demanded a radical sacrifice of the past to ensure a better, more modern future, the International Cam-paign to Save the Monuments of Nubia flipped this argument around, pointing to the preservation of that very past as a significant resource for this future. Consequently, UNESCO's original appeal to a world heritage of "outstanding universal value to humanity" constituted both a fundamental critique of, *and* a program for, modernization. It is precisely this problematization of progressive modernity that defines the emergence of the notion of world heritage as an event.

UNESCO still struggles to reconcile heritage preservation and modern development. It for example promoted the preservation of world heritage as a means to achieve the United Nations Millennium Development Goals (MDGs), which sought to free people everywhere from conditions of extreme poverty by 2015.[4] According to UNESCO, the MDGs cannot be reached without "cultural heritage resources", and although the organization is not very clear on how exactly these resources should contribute, it warns that they often remain "underutilized" in the "fight against poverty", above all on the African continent.[5]

UNESCO laments that African authorities remain disinterested in the study of cultural heritage, though this would enable them "to better understand today's world and to better prepare for the future".[6] Whereas UNESCO commends "the rich diversity of African heritage" as a contribution of "unique wealth" to world heritage, it is concerned that "very few" on the African continent are even aware of its World Heritage Programme, claiming that "we can legitimately talk here of a 'split' which, as is the case for other sectors of the economy and society, puts Africa at risk of being marginalized".[7] And indeed, UNESCO notes a deplorable African "gap" on its World Heritage List.[8]

Already at the turn of the millennium, UNESCO commissioned the International Council on Monuments and Sites (ICOMOS) to assess its list's representativeness. The main product of ICOMOS's assessment is a 2004 advisory report, *The World Heritage List: Filling the Gaps—An Action Plan for the Future*. This report evaluates the composition of the World Heritage List in terms of a so-called Chronological-Regional Framework that classifies cultural heritage into several sections referring to various regions of the world and to "the historic timeline relevant to each region".[9] Significantly, one of ICOMOS's conclusions is that UNESCO's list makes very little reference to Africa "and some major cultures have not yet been recognized".[10] Most importantly, ICOMOS noted that Africa was completely unrepresented on the list in one "special category" of ICOMOS's framework, a thematic category it refers to as "modern heritage".[11]

Following ICOMOS's analytical frame of reference, cultural monuments and sites are thematically classified as modern heritage if they relate "to the period of 'globalisation' since the First World War". And in contrast to ICOMOS's Chronological Regional Framework's other categories, its modern heritage category is meant to cover "all regions" of what "has been called the 'modern world'", a misleadingly geographical meaning that now spans the surface of the earth.[12] Arguably then,

ICOMOS's introduction of a special modern heritage category as well as of Africa as a regional gap to be filled on the World Heritage List only add to the problematization of modernity familiar from the International Campaign to Save the Monuments of Nubia. In any case, considering that more than half a century ago the emergence of the very notion of world heritage was a reaction to an archetypically modern development project on the African continent—the construction of the Aswan High Dam—ICOMOS's appeal to preserve modern world heritage intrigues, especially when it entails pleas for progress and development in Africa.

Lately, UNESCO's aim, also with an eye on achieving the UN Millennium Development Goals, is to implement a "global strategy for a representative, credible and balanced World Heritage List".[13] To this end, UNESCO borrows from ICOMOS's report, aiming to tackle Africa's underrepresentation on the World Heritage List and, more specifically, that continent's lack of modern heritage inscriptions. Rather than just protecting Africa's ancient past, preserving its recent past as world heritage has now also become one of UNESCO's explicit objectives.

But, if UNESCO originally promoted the "rescue" of ancient Nubian heritage from a perceived *threat* of modernization in the form of the Aswan High Dam while at the same time advertising the preservation of cultural heritage as an *instrument* of modern progress and development, then how does the resultant problematization of progressive modernity affect UNESCO's present call for the preservation of modern heritage in Africa? And what is one to make of the utopian promises of a better future inherent to such projects of modernization? After all, any concern for a 'modern heritage' invariably—and paradoxically it seems—should have to engage those better futures as problematic futures of the past? Essentially, these questions do not only complicate UNESCO's intention to protect as world heritage a recent 'culture' of modernity on the African continent, they also point toward a larger and considerably unstable problem space around classifications, practices and things modern that emerged along with the notion of world heritage as an event. With this book I attempt to study precisely this problem space.

My goal is to contribute to an anthropology of the contemporary by describing cultural heritage practices under current conditions of globalization. More specifically, I analyze how different heritage actors approach modern architecture and urban planning on the African continent. However, although I inquire into how the colonial and postcolonial built environment in Africa comes to figure as modern heritage, I expressly do not offer this book as a regional study *of* Africa. Rather, one of my main claims is that contemporary heritage practices cannot adequately be understood globally without studying Africa as a historically and socially constructed category and "place-in-the-world".[14] In fact, I understand cultural heritage to be made up of contingent practices that may culminate in what I call global heritage assemblages: groupings of administrative apparatuses, technical infrastructures and value regimes that revolve around contested notions of cultural heritage, and that—despite being deeply and historically entwined with colonial and postcolonial nation-building projects on the African continent—have begun to transcend the actual borders and categories of the nation-state.[15]

While cultural heritage is often taken to be a material reality—monumental architecture, for instance—this book does not approach heritage exclusively as material culture cast in monumental form. Instead, I take cultural heritage to be human practices in negotiation of certain values. I argue that cultural heritage concerns the creation and recreation of a range of political, technological and ethical relations and meanings regarding the past, present and future. Put otherwise, I understand heritage as something that is being done. In order to analyze the way heritage values are constructed and legitimized today, I thus ask who is doing what, how and why in these global heritage assemblages.

Concretely, I focus on how transnational networks of governmental, intergovernmental, and nongovernmental organizations, as well as private individuals and corporate actors engage with modern heritage in the form of colonial and postcolonial architecture and urban planning found in (1) Asmara, Eritrea; (2) Niamey, Niger, and Brazzaville, Republic of the Congo; and (3) Dar es Salaam, Tanzania. I analyze the formation of global heritage assemblages around these instances of modern heritage and study their relations to problematizations of 'the modern'. I am particularly interested in how different global heritage assemblages problematize the modern when they (a) assert politics of sovereignty and security, (b) contest technologies of authenticity and value, and (c) negotiate ethics of legitimacy and responsibility. This analysis of global heritage assemblages around modern heritage on the African continent today is accompanied by a genealogy of modern architecture and urban planning practices as they are intertwined with conservation and historic preservation practices in the late 19th and early to mid-20th centuries. I show how these practices were integral to broader projects of colonialism and modernization, and argue that this constitutes a problem for contemporary cultural heritage practices in general.

I have structured this book into three parts. Part I includes the Prologue and this Introduction, immediately followed by a number of chapters in which I elaborate my concept work, as well as explain how I have set up my anthropological inquiry into global heritage assemblages. Subsequently, the three chapters that make up Part II present the results of this inquiry. Part III lists my overall conclusion.

In the remaining chapters of Part I, I first define my conception of global heritage assemblages and substantiate its relevance for the study of cultural heritage practices. Second, I diagnose the central problem of this book, modern architectural heritage. I claim that this issue, which already arose in the 19th century, constitutes a significant anthropological problem that still invites fundamental questions about human relations today. Third, this diagnosis leads me to establish a genealogical pathway toward the institutionalization of modern architectural heritage in Africa in the late 20th and early 21st centuries. I claim that this institutionalization explains the urgency of modern heritage, as it reveals an anthropological problem linking the recent past with the near future in global heritage assemblages. Fourth, I reflect further on how and why I have chosen as my empirical points of reference three specific global heritage assemblages and their relations to instances of modern architecture and urban planning on the African continent. I also justify why and how I have conducted multisited anthropological fieldwork around these assemblages and I discuss the choices I made to mediate the results of my research in the particular form of this book. Finally, I project how the global heritage assemblages around modern heritage in Africa that I go on to describe in Part II might figure as attempts to 'rescue' modernity from its conception as an all-encompassing epochal and spatial 'culture', a theme that I pick up again by way of synthesis in Part III of this book.

Notes

1. "Victory in Nubia." 6.
2. Christian Barillet, Thierry Joffroy, and Isabelle Longuet, eds., *Cultural Heritage and Local Development: A Guide for Local African Governments* (CAR-Terre-ENSAG/Convention France, UNESCO, 2006). 9.
3. Foucault quoted in Rabinow, *Anthropos Today: Reflections on Modern Equipment*.
4. UN, "The Millenium Development Goals," http://www.un.org/millennium goals/.
5. Barillet, Joffroy, and Longuet, *Cultural Heritage and Local Development: A Guide for Local African Governments*. 5; 7, also compare: UNESCO, "African Cultural Heritage and the World Heritage Convention—Report of the First Global Strategy Meeting 1995, Harare," UNESCO, http://whc.unesco. org/en/events/594/.
6. Ibid., 9.
7. Ibid. 7; 9.
8. Jukka Jokilehto, *The World Heritage List: Filling the Gaps—An Action Plan for the Future* (Paris: ICOMOS, 2004).
9. Ibid., 23.
10. Ibid., 29.
11. Ibid., 15.
12. Ibid., 23.
13. UNESCO, "Global Strategy for a Representative and Balance World Heritage List," http://whc.unesco.org/en/globalstrategy/.
14. James Ferguson, *Global Shadows: Africa in the Neoliberal World Order* (Durham: Duke University Press, 2006). 5.
15. Aihwa Ong and Stephen J. Collier, eds., *Global Assemblages: Technology, Politics, and Ethics as Anthropological Problems* (London: Blackwell, 2005). 11.

1 Global Heritage Assemblages

Toward an Anthropology of the Contemporary

My conception of global heritage assemblages fundamentally depends on understanding cultural heritage as human practice. According to the anthropologist Lisa Breglia, such an understanding of "heritage-as-practice" is a relatively new approach that opposes the conventional understanding of "heritage-as-artifact".[1] Breglia claims that the "everyday-life"[2] of heritage is not to be found in examining material culture but, rather, in analyzing the actors and interactions involved in the production and reproduction of heritage. Correspondingly, Breglia introduces her concept of "the heritage assemblage", which she refers to as "a multi-sited object of study, through which we may interrogate how ruins and other landscape features become heritage", as well as "for whom and why this is important".[3] In *Monumental Ambivalence: The Politics of Heritage*, Breglia describes how a specific heritage assemblage in Mexico unfolds as ambivalently "composed of national law and policy, institutional practices, sui generis international heritage regimes, global economies and multiple publics".[4] She concludes that a heritage assemblage is "a set of values, meanings, and practices differently constituted at local, regional, national, and international levels".[5]

Though my conception of global heritage assemblages draws on Breglia's conception of the heritage assemblage, it also forms a critical reaction. While Breglia is primarily interested in how "the invention of heritage is an ambivalent process used by the state to create national identity and collective belonging and how citizens, in turn, ambivalently engage in the produced spaces of heritage",[6] I want to show how contemporary cultural heritage practices consist of much more than powerful institutional claims to patrimony issued by a given nation-state or mere reactions to such claims in the form of privatization.[7] I argue that the nascent social scientific study of cultural heritage, advocated by Breglia and others, needs to transcend the predominant focus on the nation-state as a central object of analysis.[8] In this book, I am specifically interested in how contemporary cultural heritage practices are configured *transnationally* in *global* formations. Extending Breglia's use of the concept heritage assemblage, I thus describe the emergence of *global* heritage assemblages.

I base my conception of global heritage assemblages on the work of anthropologists Aihwa Ong and Stephen Collier. In the introduction to their edited volume *Global Assemblages: Technology, Politics and Ethics as Anthropological Problems*, Ong and Collier define global assemblages as sites for the formation and reformation of what they call—drawing on their colleague Paul Rabinow's definition—anthropological problems.[9] Broadly speaking, then, global assemblages are domains in which forms of human existence are at stake in the sense that they are subjected to political, technological or ethical reflection and debate.[10] However, Collier gives a more succinct definition of global assemblages in "Problematizing Global Knowledge—Genealogies of the Global/Globalizations", his contribution to a special issue of the journal *Theory, Culture & Society*.

For him, global assemblages are "the actual configurations through which global forms of techno-science, economic rationalism, and other expert systems gain significance".[11] He explains what he means by global forms by referring to Max Weber's sociological account of the "specific and peculiar" problems posed to human life by the apparently universal validity of a modern rationalism that can neither be reduced to a social structure, nor be culturally relativized.[12] Accordingly, global forms are reflective practices that depend on what the sociologist Anthony Giddens has called "impersonal principles, which can be set out and developed without regard to context".[13] Collier claims that such global forms feature a "distinctive capacity for decontextualization and recontextualization, abstractability and movement, across diverse social and cultural situations".[14] With this, he does not mean that global forms are everywhere, rather that they are fundamentally unstable; they function as a source of tension and dynamism in human relations.[15] Collier considers global assemblages to be spaces in which global forms such as science, technologies of rational calculation, and expert systems are concretely articulated.[16] As such, global assemblages actively structure and restructure global forms through critical contest and intervention.[17]

In the following, I consider contemporary heritage practices as actively constructing the global in the sense suggested by Collier: I analyze how specific heritage practices constitute global forms that figure in global assemblages. Accordingly, what I call global heritage assemblages are the administrative apparatuses, technical infrastructures and value regimes that revolve around contested notions of cultural heritage which—despite being deeply and historically entwined with nation-building projects—begin to transcend the actual borders and categories of the nation-state.[18] In this respect, I do not approach global heritage assemblages as made up of fundamentally new forms but of forms that are globally shifting, in formation, or at stake today.[19]

Despite its insistence on the 'global', my focus on the transnational emergence of global heritage assemblages should stand in marked contrast to the invocations of the global as an all-encompassing spatial level that are frequent in the popular media, in mainstream scholarly discussions of globalization, and—undeniably—cultural heritage discourse. Indeed, cultural heritage is often mentioned as a pivotal example in totalizing accounts of the global as convergence. Michael Di Giovine, for instance, argues in his book *The Heritage-Scape: UNESCO, World Heritage and Tourism* that through the UNESCO World Heritage program

> individuals fuse with collectives, institutions fuse with bureaucracies, local modalities fuse with global infrastructures, narrative fuses with dialogue, culture fuses with politics. Mediating all of these procedures are monumental structures—the World Heritage sites themselves—which act as primary nodes on this intangible heritage-scape, providing materiality, context and localization to an otherwise immaterial, de-contextualized and de-localized global phenomenon.[20]

Earlier in the same book, Di Giovine likens this 'world-heritage-scape' to the flows of the sea, "seemingly limitless, expansive, but always pushing its tidal confines farther onto the shore".[21]

With his concept of a heritage-scape, Di Giovine refers to Arjun Appadurai's widely influential anthropology of "global flows".[22] In his *Modernity at Large: Cultural Dimensions of Globalization*, Appadurai introduced a theory of a series of fluid—scapes that spread around the globe.[23] What Appadurai calls ethnoscapes, technoscapes, financescapes and ideoscapes are historically situated imaginations of individuals and collectives amounting to amorphous landscapes; perspectival constructs that make sense of global flows of persons, technologies, finance, information and ideologies.[24] Appadurai conceives of global flows as essentially disjunctive and calls for "a general theory of global cultural processes" that can meaningfully account for chaos and volatility.[25] His scapes are to be a first step in that direction.

Di Giovine appropriates this terminology when he presents his heritage-scape as a "worldwide imagined community".[26] However, Di Giovine fails to do justice to Appadurai's expressly nonteleological stance. In contrast, he describes a single heritage order converging around the globe. Di Giovine attributes an "overall mission"[27] to his world-heritage-scape, the "ultimate objective"[28] of which is "to foster 'peace in the minds of men' by co-opting and inverting a common process of identity formation that traditionally employs monuments to delineate boundaries predicated on conflictual narratives of difference".[29] Thus, whereas Appadurai cautions that global cultural flow will often result in violent affirmations of difference and has conceived of his scapes to account for such discord, Di Giovine describes a world-heritage-scape seeking to peacefully resolve cultural conflicts.[30]

My account of contemporary heritage practices under conditions of globalization, then, is an alternative to Di Giovine's interpretation of a universalizing heritage-scape. Working with my conception of global heritage assemblages, I aim to be more sensitive to the tensions resulting from, and inherent to, contemporary cultural heritage practices as they occupy common fields in contingent, uneasy, and unstable relationships.[31] To speak with Ong and Collier, I focus on "the actual global", or the global in the space of assemblage, where global implies "broadly encompassing, seamless and mobile" and assemblage "heterogeneous, contingent, unstable, partial and situated".[32]

Just as I am critical of Di Giovine's theory of a convergent world-heritage-scape, I am generally skeptical of Appadurai's theory of globalization as cultural flow, disjunctive or not. In fact, with the anthropologist James Ferguson, I consider flow to be a "strangely" poor metaphor for relevant dynamics of globalization.[33] In his *Global Shadows: Africa in the Neoliberal World Order*, Ferguson claims that, particularly in Africa, "the global does not flow, thereby watering contiguous spaces; it hops instead, efficiently connecting the enclaved points in the network while excluding (with equal efficiency) the spaces that lie between the points".[34] Following Ferguson then, it is unhelpful to speak of heritage practices as flowing or spreading across the globe. Instead, globalization seems to connect and network separate enclaves from point to point, leaving swaths of unconnected, un-networked spaces far behind.[35] As a consequence, when I focus on the actual global, that is on globally assembled contemporary heritage practices, I consider these to "crisscross"[36] the world in transnational networks that are contingent, selective and contested. I aim to show how global heritage assemblages bundle a range of political, technological, and ethical relations and meanings that not only connect and integrate but also, by definition, disconnect and marginalize.[37]

In this respect, my study of global heritage assemblages adds to an already existing body of the anthropology of global connection and disconnection.[38] To refer back to Collier, I hope that my concept of global heritage assemblages can serve as an alternative tool for the development of "a critical global knowledge, though one that diverges from the standard fare of relativizing cultural analyses, sociological reductions to structures of power, or political economic analyses of hegemony that have dominated discussions of globalization".[39] When I describe contemporary heritage practices in global assemblages, I consider them to be basic starting points for inquiry into, and reflection on, the very norms and forms of human existence today. I thus approach global heritage assemblages as multisited fields of experimentation for what Paul Rabinow calls the anthropology of the contemporary: analytical work that helps develop modes of inquiry into underdetermined, emergent and discordant human relations into actual anthropological problems.

Notes

1. Lisa Breglia, *Monumental Ambivalence: The Politics of Heritage* (Austin: The University of Texas Press, 2006). 13.
2. Ibid., 11.
3. Ibid.
4. Ibid., 209.
5. Ibid., 208.
6. Ibid., 14.
7. Ibid., 5; 15.
8. Ibid., 14; also compare, for example, Laurajane Smith, *Uses of Heritage* (London: Routledge, 2006); Marta de la Torre, *Assessing the Values of Cultural Heritage* (Los Angeles: The Getty Conservation Institute, 2002); Arjun Appadurai, *The Social Life of Things* (Cambridge: Cambridge University Press, 1986).
9. Ong and Collier, *Global Assemblages: Technology, Politics, and Ethics as Anthropological Problems*; Appadurai, *The Social Life of Things*.
10. Ong and Collier, *Global Assemblages: Technology, Politics, and Ethics as Anthropological Problems*. 4; compare a different use of the term in Saskia Sassen, *Territory, Authority, Rights: From Medieval to Global Assemblages* (Princeton: Princeton University Press, 2006).
11. Stephen J. Collier, "Global Assemblages," *Theory, Culture, Society* 23 (2006). 400.
12. Ong and Collier, *Global Assemblages: Technology, Politics, and Ethics as Anthropological Problems*. 10.
13. Giddens quoted in Collier, "Global Assemblages."
14. Ibid., 400.
15. Ong and Collier, *Global Assemblages: Technology, Politics, and Ethics as Anthropological Problems*. 10; 12.
16. Collier, "Global Assemblages."
17. Ibid., 400.
18. Ong and Collier, *Global Assemblages: Technology, Politics, and Ethics as Anthropological Problems*. 11.
19. Ibid.
20. Michael A. Di Giovine, *The Heritage-scape: UNESCO, World Heritage and Tourism* (Lanham: Lexington Books, 2009). 403.
21. Ibid., 104.
22. Arjun Appadurai, *Modernity at Large: Cultural Dimensions of Globalization* (Minneapolis: University of Minnesota Press, 1996). 36; Di Giovine, *The Heritage-scape: UNESCO, World Heritage and Tourism*. 6.
23. Appadurai, *Modernity at Large: Cultural Dimensions of Globalization*.
24. Ibid., 33.
25. Ibid., 46; 47.
26. Ibid.
27. Ibid., 112.
28. Di Giovine, *The Heritage-Scape: UNESCO, World Heritage and Tourism*. 403.
29. Ibid.
30. Peter Pels, Birgit Meyer, and Peter Geschiere, eds., *Readings in Modernity in Africa* (London: International Africa Institute, 2008). 2, 5; Arjun Appadurai, "Disjuncture and Difference in the Global Cultural Economy," *Public Culture* 2, Spring (1990); Appadurai, *Modernity at Large: Cultural Dimensions of Globalization*. 15.
31. Ong and Collier, *Global Assemblages: Technology, Politics, and Ethics as Anthropological Problems*. 12.

32. Ibid., 12.
33. Ferguson, *Global Shadows: Africa in the Neoliberal World Order*.
34. Ibid., 47.
35. Ibid.
36. Ibid., 37.
37. Ibid., 40.
38. Anna Lowenhaupt-Tsing, *Friction: An Ethnography of Global Connection* (Princeton: Princeton University Press, 2005).
39. Collier, "Global Assemblages." 400.

2 Diagnosis

Modern Architectural Heritage as an Anthropological Problem

Before I elaborate on the exact focus and structure of my analysis of global heritage assemblages, let me first explain how I relate heritage practices to Paul Rabinow's general notion of an anthropological problem. For Rabinow the question of "how to think about things human is a problem".[1] However, according to him "the form of the problem—and therefore the practices that produce it and that it produces—has not always been the same".[2] Throughout the history of the human sciences there has never been any consensus about the principles, methods, and modes of specifying or verifying the problem of human thought and knowledge, nor has there ever been agreement on appropriate forms of narration. Though reasoned discourse or 'logos', as Rabinow calls it, has always been characterized by fundamental dissonance, "the hope for a positive science, or the end of metaphysics, or the hermeneutical closure of the bible or other authoritative texts, is like a cargo cult, which persists in the face of constant disappointment".[3] Against this background, Rabinow defines an "anthropological problem" as the apparently unavoidable fact that "anthropos is that being which suffers from too many logoi"; there are simply too many reasoned discourses for us to be able to latch on to one, let alone the *right* one.[4]

Rabinow takes the acknowledgment of that 'hetero-logoi', the inevitable plurality of positions in the production and reproduction of knowledge, as the necessary starting point of research and reflection for the human sciences today. Asserting that the "challenge of confronting anthropos" consists of transforming 'logos' into 'ethos' he proposes an experimental mode of "bringing philosophical learning, diagnostic rigor and a practice of inquiry that operates in proximity to concrete situations into a productive relationship".[5] Rabinow thus aims to develop means of observing and analyzing the way different logoi are currently assembled into contingent forms.[6] He calls for inquiry that focuses on an actual historical, economic, political, and social conjecture in which an issue becomes an urgent "anthropological problem".[7] With this book, I contend that such a critical conjecture is at stake in the complex practices crystalizing around the issue of modern architectural heritage, an issue that I attempt to unravel in the following.

The Crystal Palace

At first sight, the phrase *modern architectural heritage* appears to be a paradox. At least this seems to be the case when one understands—as I do throughout this book—modern architecture to consist of 19th- and 20th-century building projects that themselves often wanted nothing to do with architectural heritage, but instead were informed by ideological claims to not only technical, industrial, and stylistic innovation but also economic, political, and social progress and development.[8] Hooked on the idea of radical change, many modern architects and urban planners saw themselves as experts in "social engineering".[9] They literally aimed to construct a better world, and to this end many of them wanted to get rid of traditional built environments and start with a tabula rasa.[10] As a consequence, utopian ideologies of modern architecture and urban planning constituted a real threat to the existing built fabric of human settlements, which is why a simultaneously emergent heritage activism initially considered modern architecture antithetical to its cause of preserving historic monuments. Though in this sense the idea of modern architectural heritage seems paradoxical, I argue that a more accurate diagnosis of the modern architectural heritage issue inevitably renders it a complex heterodoxy rather than a simple paradox.

My diagnosis of how the issue of modern architectural heritage first became an urgent anthropological problem begins with a constitutive event, the 1851 World's Fair in London. First in a series of World's Fair exhibitions and also known as the Great Exhibition, the 1851 World's Fair is emblematic of a particular zeitgeist; though the 19th century has indiscriminately been declared as an age of industrialization and empire, one may just as well be tempted to call it an era of exhibitions. With Victorian Britain at the height of its economic power and dominant imperial expansion, the *Royal Society for the Encouragement of the Arts, Manufactures and Commerce* organized the first World's Fair in London as a celebration of the superiority of modern Western civilization. Here, the European nation-states started a new tradition of exhibiting their cultural and industrial prowess, explicitly juxtaposing it to displays of 'backward culture' from colonies overseas.

Indeed, the Great Exhibition was informed by a teleological belief in progress and development. Certainly Prince Albert anticipated hosting the event in this spirit, as during the 1849 Lord Mayor's Banquet in London he stated,

> Nobody, [. . .] who has paid any attention to the features of our present era, will doubt for a moment that we are living at a period

of most wonderful transition which tends rapidly to the accomplishment of that great end to which indeed, all history points—the realization of the unity of mankind. [. . .] Gentlemen, the Exhibition of 1851 is to give us a true test and a living picture of the point of development at which the whole of mankind has arrived.[11]

As Prince Albert saw it, humankind would acquire divine powers over nature through a combination of science, industry, and art. He continued:

Science [discovers] the laws of power, motion and transformation; industry [applies] them to raw matter which the earth yields us in abundance, but which becomes valuable only by knowledge; [and] art [teaches] us the immutable laws of beauty and symmetry, and [gives] to our productions forms in accordance with them.[12]

The prince would find this combination of applied science and art realized in the architecture of the exhibition hall that housed the Fair at Hyde Park. With a width of 140 meters, a length of 565 meters and a maximum height of 33 meters, the proportions of the building were huge. Still, its construction took only 4 months due to the use of prefabricated steel modules, which were assembled into an impressive hierarchy of structural spans covered by glass. Architect engineer Sir Joseph Paxton had designed an enormous glazed hall that could serve both as an emblem of industrial progress and stylistic innovation.

The translucency of Paxton's design gave his exhibition hall a memorable nickname, the Crystal Palace, and to the public the Great Exhibition also came to be known as the Crystal Palace exhibition. But, despite its popular attention, the building was only meant to have a temporary presence. This was because the British House of Commons had in July 1850 decreed that by the end of the fair, which began in May 1851 and continued through mid-October, the structure had to be removed from Hyde Park. According to plan, then, and facilitated by Paxton's prefabricated modular design, the exhibition hall's existence would only last a mere four-and-a-half months.

The scheduled dismantling of the Crystal Palace provoked criticism from concerned citizens who swiftly founded a so-called Crystal Palace Company in order to save the building. In the end, the Crystal Palace was taken apart but was rebuilt as a museum of applied arts and ethnography at Sydenham in South London, where it stood until a fire destroyed it in 1936.[13]

Interestingly, the 1851 World's Fair and Paxton's exhibition hall constitute examples of how ideals of modern architecture and heritage preservation emerged simultaneously. On one hand, the Crystal Palace served as a backdrop to the display of 'primitive culture' removed from the European colonies for conservation in the metropolis, both during

the World Fair in Hyde Park, as well as in its role as a home to an ethnographic museum in Sydenham. On the other hand, the Crystal Palace
was itself designated for safeguarding immediately following its conception as a temporary home for the Great Exhibition. As a matter of
fact, Paxton's building almost certainly was the first instance of modern
architecture to be put on any preservation agenda, which is particularly
remarkable considering that John Ruskin, a principal protagonist of the
heritage preservation movement nascent in Britain at the time, was one
of the most outspoken critics of the Crystal Palace, including its eventual
translocation.[14]

In 1849, the year of Prince Albert's optimistic speech in anticipation of
the Great Exhibition, Ruskin had published *The Seven Lamps of Architecture*, a book in which he briefly summoned the future development
of a "new system of architectural laws [. . .] adapted entirely to metallic
construction".[15] However, this was before Ruskin had visited Paxton's
Crystal Palace. Afterward, he swiftly abandoned his hope for an architecture made of steel and glass, instead pessimistically contributing to what
developed into a fierce controversy over the merits of the Crystal Palace.[16]
In fact, when the building reopened at Sydenham in 1854, Ruskin held a
much-noted speech titled *The Opening of the Crystal Palace Considered
in Some of its Relations to the Prospects of Art*, in which he criticized the
aesthetic qualities of Paxton's design and derided its architectural value.[17]

In his address, Ruskin expressed a sense of disillusionment with the
new industrial materials and techniques that the Crystal Palace represented: "The great result, the admirable and long-expected conclusion is,
that in the center of the nineteenth century, we suppose ourselves to have
invented a new style of architecture, when we have magnified a conserva-
tory."[18] Indeed, Ruskin considered the Crystal Palace a greenhouse larger
than any greenhouse ever built before. He took its presence as "final
proof that higher beauty was eternally impossible in iron".[19] For him, the
new steel-and-glass architecture was forever "separated from all good
and great things by a gulf which not all the tubular bridges nor engineering of ten thousand nineteenth centuries cast into one great bronze fore-
headed century, will ever over pass one inch of".[20]

Cultivating a nostalgic vision of the gothic, Ruskin favored traditional
craftsmanship over technology. He had originally laid out his opinion of
architecture in *The Seven Lamps*, listing the field's seven most important
principles. One of Ruskin's principles being the "lamp of memory",[21] he
insisted on the principal duty to "preserve as the most precious of inherit-
ances, that of past ages". He was convinced that only architecture that
was itself capable of becoming historical was of any value.[22] Ruskin did
not grant the Crystal Palace this ability to withstand the ages, complain-
ing that it caused a sense of alienation instead. Whether he "hated industry"—as the architectural historian Siegfried Giedion assumed—or not,
Ruskin did see prefabrication and a rational reorganization of labor as

part of a dangerous post-Renaissance trend toward ever-more precarious social foundations of art and architecture.[23]

William Morris, Ruskin's contemporary and foremost brother in arms, similarly referred to modern architecture such as the Crystal Palace as "the monsters of our time clad in plate glass and cast iron".[24] In fact, Morris's and Ruskin's belief in what Alois Riegl a few years later would call the 'age value' of historic monuments, meaning their gaining of significance through old age, was diametrically opposed to that of the promoters of Paxton's Crystal Palace who, like Prince Albert, exalted progress through innovation in architecture.[25] According to Morris and Ruskin, the modern architecture that the Crystal Palace represented, or even the mere modification of historic buildings using modern materials and techniques, would eventually lead to the destruction of unique works of art.

Ultimately, Morris and Ruskin perceived both the success of modern architecture, as well as new restoration techniques that entailed reconstructing imagined elements of past structures by modern means as threats to the physical authenticity of historic buildings.[26] As a consequence, Morris and Ruskin in 1877 institutionalized their concern with historic preservation by cofounding the British Society for the Protection of Ancient Buildings (SPAB), which developed a conserve-as-found mentality—a conservationism that still informs dominant ideologies of heritage preservation today.[27]

However, Morris and Ruskin's resort to memories of the past as their ideal guiding principle of preservation effectively is just as rooted in the specific historical consciousness characteristic of the 19th century as is the ideology of architectural innovation, of which the Crystal Palace is an early manifestation. Indeed, if Paxton's exhibition hall stood for the particular utopia of progress and development that was on display during the Great Exhibition, Ruskin and Morris's criticism of the design principles of the Crystal Palace is just as utopian because it ultimately results from a similarly teleological understanding of history. As the historian Chris Miele has argued, for Morris and Ruskin "the goal of future history was a return to some imagined social order mystically encoded in medieval matter. Stylistic purity [. . .] and authenticity [. . .] allowed them to commune with a utopian dream".[28] For them, nostalgia was "a way into the vision",[29] which is why they both wrote passionately and fought fervently to protect traditional architectural heritage from what they perceived as the destructive effects of modern architecture. Arguably then, the ideologies of modern architecture and heritage preservation, emerging around the time of the 1851 World's Fair and projected on the Crystal Palace, are both products of a heightened awareness of cultural change.

On one hand, Paxton's Palace represents the utopian conviction that in order to ensure future progress and development modern architecture was to separate itself entirely from the old. On the other hand, Ruskin and Morris's opposition to this powerful architectural program is a case in point that hoping for an unproblematic circulation between present and past remained seductive as a solution to the problems posed by the new awareness of history.[30] Both Paxton's embrace of radical architectural innovation as well as Morris's and Ruskin's nostalgic resort to age value were reactions to a newly perceived need to manage the past in order to manage the future.[31]

In this context, it is very important to note that the original design of the Crystal Palace elevated present use value over any potential acquisition of age value. In fact, Paxton's design explicitly preempted Ruskin's criticism that the Crystal Palace would prove incapable of attaining historical value: the building was not even meant to become historical in the first place. Rather, it was fundamentally meant to be of a transitory existence. Accordingly, the building not only negated the past in the present, but also the past in the future; not only did it turn against traditional architectural styles, construction materials and techniques, but it also denied its very own coming of age. Indeed, it was through its fundamental transitoriness that the Crystal Palace symbolized the utopian belief that modern architecture could bring about progress.

Essentially then, the Crystal Palace represented a pronounced antimonumental stance. Nevertheless, it immediately acquired significance as a monument to civilization and development. To Ruskin's chagrin, Paxton's modern architecture became what Lowenthal would call an "instant tradition".[32] While the Great Exhibition invented a tradition of World's Fairs celebrating universal progress and development, the Crystal Palace was preserved in Sydenham as what Octavio Paz would somewhat contradictorily refer to as a "tradition of the new".[33]

A Tradition against Itself

The literary critic Paz coined the expression "tradition of the new" in his book *Children of the Mire: Modern Poetry from Romanticism to the Avant-Garde*. In it, he is specifically interested in what happens when the modern belief of being at the forefront of history that was embodied in 19th-century avant-garde poetry gradually becomes historical. Yet Paz's literary analysis can also be adapted to modern architecture. Applied to the Crystal Palace, Paz's concept of a tradition of the new describes the apparent paradox of modern architectural heritage; it signifies that the negation of the past in the present and in the future can itself only be imagined in a manner devised by the past for its own overcoming. Indeed, the construction, deconstruction, and subsequent reconstruction of the Crystal Palace poses the question of how and why to preserve a tradition of the new, a tradition against itself.[34] In essence, the historicity of the modern avant-garde—whether in literature art or architecture—indicates a "stalemate"[35] between the past and the future, just as preserving the

Crystal Palace as an emblem of a future architecture hints at a very basic struggle with the idea of progress.[36]

Helpful in understanding the issue at stake here is Reinhart Koselleck's conceptual history of progress. In his *Futures Past: On the Semantics of Historical Time*, Koselleck introduces experience and expectation as anthropological preconditions of historical consciousness, arguing that, since the late 18th century, the perception of a difference between past and future, or between experience and expectation, has led to the emergence of a distinctly modern temporality. According to Koselleck, modern temporality is best described with the help of two metaphors, the "space of experience" and the "horizon of expectation". Whereas for him the space of experience entails the present knowledge of a past of historical events that have been recognized and can be remembered, the horizon of expectation refers to present conceptions of the future, of hopes, fears, or rational projections.[37]

Koselleck argues that modern time began when the dominant horizon of expectation changed from an eschatological belief in a better after-life to a belief in progress, or the future improvement of worldly human existence. According to him, our modern faith in political, social, techno-logical and economic development means that the horizon of expectation no longer fully encloses the space of experience, as was the case in pre-modern times. With the onset of modernity, the previously symmetrical relationship between the space of experience and the horizon of expecta-tion became an asymmetrical one of increasing and accelerating temporal differentiation. In effect, Koselleck claims that the modern concept of progress emerged in reaction to a situation at the turn of the 19th century in which the old clashed with the new—a state of affairs of which the debate about the Crystal Palace was symptomatic.[38]

Similarly, in his *Present Past: Modernity and the Memory Crisis*, liter-ary scholar Richard Terdimann reflects on how the 19th century was obsessed with time, arguing that history turned "adverse"[39] back then:

> People's relation to [history] in experience and in theory became a conceptual leapfrog in two dissimilar movements: the first, a regis-tration of the leviathan density of the practices and discourses that oblige us haplessly to relive the past in the present; the second, an intense aspiration to negate these practices and discourses.[40]

Terdimann speaks of a new and disorienting opacity of the past that led to a crisis of diachronicity in the form of a rupture between, on one hand, accounts of modernization, as, for instance, represented in ideolo-gies of architectural innovation and critical historiographies, on the other hand, which theorized and retheorized temporal relations such as appeals to preserve heritage.[41] Because of this crisis of diachronicity, Terdimann claims, time was out of joint in the 19th century.[42] In fact, according to him—and the preservation of the Crystal Palace despite its scheduled short life certainly attests to it—even utopias turned out to be "memory effects" at the time. This was because, as Terdimann notes, the future could be remembered "only as counterdiscourses of the past, regulated by the past in the mode of [. . .] inevitably unidirectional determinations".[43]

The Crystal Palace powerfully reflects this problem. After all, the building's construction, deconstruction, and reconstruction around the Great Exhibition fundamentally complicated notions of progressive change and the opposition between tradition and modernity. Indeed, the reconstructed Crystal Palace hypostasized the past as the radical antinomy of the present and the future: it introduced a need to remember as sites and sources of cultural disquiet the utopias of modern architecture.[44] Ultimately then, the 1851 World's Fair and its venue, the Crystal Palace, shows an apparently simple, paradoxical relation between architectural innovation and heritage preservation, turning it into a rather complex and heterodox anthropological problem and introducing the issue of modern architectural heritage as a Foucauldian problematization of modernity.

Problematizing Modernity

For the philosopher Michel Foucault, a problematization is not simply the way something turns into a problem; it "does not mean the representation of a previous object nor the creation through discourse of an object that did not exist".[45] For him, a problematization is

> [t]he ensemble of discursive and non-discursive practices that make something enter in the play of true and false and constitute it as an object of thought (whether in the form of moral reflection, scientific knowledge, political analysis, etc.).[46]

Foucault explains that problematizations are problematic, unsurprisingly, because "something prior must have happened to introduce uncertainty, a loss of familiarity; that loss, that uncertainty is the result of difficulties in our previous way of understanding, acting, relating".[47]

The issue of modern architectural heritage as it first manifested itself with the Crystal Palace indicates one such problematized domain: it was a nexus of conflicting responses to a historical, economic, political and social situation.[48] In fact, with Paul Rabinow, who draws directly on Foucault, one can say that the issue of modern architectural heritage marked a "space of conditioned contingency" that emerged in relation to, and formed a feedback relation with, a "more general situation, one that is real enough in standard terms but not fixed or static".[49] Clearly then, the more general situation at stake in the construction, deconstruction and reconstruction of the Crystal Palace is that of progressive modernity. Put differently, 19th-century modernity, of which the Great Exhibition in London constituted an emblem, is the historical, economic, political and social conjecture from which the issue of modern architectural heritage emerges, and the significant instability of this conjecture lies in its dimension of emergence, which appears crucial. Indeed, until the Great Exhibition unfolded as described above, the Crystal Palace's fundamental transitoriness could not have been identified as a problem; its solution in the form of the building's translocation and preservation at Sydenham could not have been addressed.[50]

Following Rabinow, "events problematize classifications, practices, things".[51] As an event, the construction, deconstruction and reconstruction of the Crystal Palace problematized modernity because it revealed how different stylized configurations of the modern can assemble into a productive relationship of conflict and tension.[52] In the Crystal Palace, an initial imperative to "make it new"[53] through modern architectural innovation clashed with tradition in the form of an early appeal to heritage preservation. Resulting from this clash is the issue of modern architectural heritage, which—as an anthropological problem—indicates a historically troubled situation. In other words, the issue of modern architectural heritage as it begins to unfold in the 19th century marks time on difference.[54] For one thing, it makes one pause between two different goal-directed modern actions: innovation and preservation. Moreover, it makes one reflect on how vehemently progressive modernity depends on the opposition of the old and the new, as well as on the complex problems that stem from this pertinent juxtaposition.[55]

Notes

1. Rabinow, *Anthropos Today: Reflections on Modern Equipment*. 4.
2. Ibid., 4.
3. Ibid., 6.
4. Ibid., 6.
5. Ibid., 3.
6. Ibid., 15.
7. Ong and Collier, *Global Assemblages: Technology, Politics, and Ethics as Anthropological Problems*. 15.
8. For example, Kenneth Frampton, *Modern Architecture: A Critical History* (New York: Oxford University Press, 1980).
9. James Holston, *The Modernist City: An Anthropological Critique of Brasilia* (Chicago: University of Chicago Press, 1989).
10. Hilde Heynen, "Transitoriness of Modern Architecture," in *Modern Movement Heritage*, ed. A. Cunningham (London: E.F.N. Spon, 1998). 31.
11. "The Speech of H.R.H. The Prince Albert, K.G., F.R.S., at The Lord Mayor's Banquet, in the City of London, October 1849," http://pages.zoom.co.uk/leveridge/albert.html.
12. Ibid.
13. Pieter van Wesemael and George Hall, *Architecture of Instruction and Delight: A Socio-Historical Analysis of World Exhibitions as a Didactic Phenomenon (1798–1851–1970)* (Rotterdam: 010 Publishers, 2001). 203–205.

14. Jukka Jokilehto, *A History of Architectural Conservation* (Amsterdam: Elsevier, 1999). 174.
15. Ruskin quoted in Nikolaus Pevsner and Richard Weston, *Pioneers of Modern Design: From William Morris to Walter Gropius*, rev. ed. (New Haven: Yale University Press, 2005). 134.
16. Ibid.
17. Ibid.
18. Ibid., 146.
19. Ibid., 133.
20. Ibid., 146.
21. John Ruskin, *The Seven Lamps of Architecture* (New York: Dover Publications, 1989).
22. Jokilehto, *A History of Architectural Conservation*. 179.
23. Sigfried Giedion, *Space, Time and Architecture: The Growth of a New Tradition* (Cambridge, MA: Harvard University Press, 1974). 168.
24. Morris quoted in Pevsner and Weston, *Pioneers of Modern Design: From William Morris to Walter Gropius*. 26.
25. Alois Riegl, *Der Moderne Denkmalkultus, sein Wesen, seine Entstehung* (Vienna: Kessinger, 2010).
26. In this Ruskin and Morris turned against an approach of stylistic restoration, for instance, represented by Eugene Viollet-le-Duc's medieval revivalism in France.
27. They also founded the arts and crafts movement, for more on Ruskin in particular see Dinah Birch, *Ruskin's Myths*, Oxford English monographs (Oxford: Clarendon, 1988); Dinah Birch, *Ruskin and the Dawn of the Modern* (Oxford: Oxford University Press, 1999); John Cianci and Peter Nicholls, *Ruskin and Modernism* (Basingstoke: Palgrave, 2001); W. G. Collingwood, *The Life and Work of John Ruskin*, 2nd ed. (London: Methuen & Co., 1893); Kristine Ottesen Garrigan, *Ruskin on Architecture: His Thought and Influence* (Madison, WI, London: University of Wisconsin Press, 1973). Chris Miele, "Conservation and the Enemies of Progress?" in *From William Morris: Building Conservation and the Arts and Crafts Cult of Authenticity, 1877–1939*, ed. Chris Miele (New Haven: Yale University Press, 2005). xi; Chris Miele, *From William Morris: Building Conservation and the Arts and Crafts Cult of Authenticity, 1877–1939*, ed. Chris Miele (New Haven: Yale University Press, 2005).
28. Chris Miele, *From William Morris: Building Conservation and the Arts and Crafts Cult of Authenticity, 1877–1939* (New Haven: Yale University Press, 2005). 54.
29. Ibid., 54.
30. Richard Terdiman, *Present Past: Modernity and the Memory Crisis* (Ithaca: Cornell University Press, 1993). 22.
31. Reinhart Koselleck, *Futures Past: On the Semantics of Historical Time* (New York: Columbia University Press, 2004).
32. Lowenthal, *The Heritage Crusade and the Spoils of History*.
33. Terence Hobsbawm and Terence Ranger, eds., *The Invention of Tradition* (Cambridge: Cambridge University Press, 1983); Octavio Paz, *Children of the Mire: Modern Poetry from Romanticism to the Avant-Garde* (Cambridge, MA: Harvard University Press, 1991).
34. Paz, *Children of the Mire: Modern Poetry from Romanticism to the Avant-Garde*.
35. Osborne quoted *in* Paul Rabinow, *Marking Time: On the Anthropology of the Contemporary* (Princeton: Princeton University Press, 2008).
36. Also compare Marshall Berman, *All That Is Solid Melts into Air: The Experience of Modernity* (London: Verso, 1983).

37. Koselleck, *Futures Past: On the Semantics of Historical Time.*
38. Ibid.
39. Terdiman, *Present Past: Modernity and the Memory Crisis.* 23.
40. Ibid., 50–51.
41. Ibid., 23.
42. Ibid., 23.
43. Ibid., 50–51.
44. Ibid., 52.
45. Quoted in Rabinow, *Anthropos Today: Reflections on Modern Equipment.* 18.
46. Ibid., 18.
47. quoted in Ibid.
48. Ibid., 19.
49. Ibid., 20.
50. Ibid., 41.
51. Ibid., 67.
52. Rabinow, *Marking Time: On the Anthropology of the Contemporary.* 3.
53. Peter Gay, *Modernism: The Lure of Heresy* (New York: WW Norton, 2010).
54. Rabinow, *Marking Time: On the Anthropology of the Contemporary.* vii.
55. Ibid., vii.

3 A Pathway

During the 20th century the problematization of progressive modernity, which the issue of modern architectural heritage highlights only gained in urgency. The practices of modern architecture and heritage preservation both provided more and more powerful strategic responses to the emergent historical problem space that was created by modern temporality. Actually, I contend that over the years the fields of modern architecture and heritage preservation gradually stabilized into what I would like to call the apparatus of modernization.

My use of "apparatus",[1] like "problematization", originally stems from Michel Foucault, who understood an apparatus to be "a resolutely heterogeneous grouping comprising of discourses, institutions, architectural arrangements, policy decisions, laws, administrative measures, scientific statements, philosophic, moral and philantrophic propositions".[2] According to Foucault, this grouping is held together by the apparatus, the fundamentally strategic network that can be established between these elements.[3] In his words an apparatus

> is always inscribed in a play of power, but [. . .] always linked to certain coordinates of knowledge, which issue from it, but to an equal degree, condition it. This is what the apparatus consists in: strategies of relations of forces supporting, and supported by, types of knowledge.[4]

Following this definition, I consider the apparatus of modernization to consist of the stabilized forms of 'power/knowledge', including modern architecture and heritage preservation, that were informed by beliefs in unilinear narratives of progress and development toward the powerful *telos* of a universal civilization, and which were dominant from the 19th at least through the late 20th century.[5]

Foucault's interest in apparatuses was closely tied to his goal to write the "history of the present," that is to trace the genealogies of the problematizations characterizing our present era.[6] In fact, Foucault continuously tried to develop methods of diagnosing and conceptualizing historical problematizations. He considered the history of the present to be an experimental project in which the study of formations of dominant apparatuses from the past would provide a means of showing the contingency of the present and therefore point toward a more open future.[7]

Inspired by Foucault, Paul Rabinow has written such a history of the present. His seminal *French Modern: Norms and Forms of the Social Environment* provides a masterful genealogy of the social modernity apparatus in France and its North African colonies during the 19th and early 20th centuries. In *French Modern*, Rabinow moves conceptually through diverse domains of knowledge and practices of power, also including modern architecture, urban planning and heritage preservation. He demonstrates how a century-long process gradually brings these different domains into a common frame of rationality and eventually turns them into an operative apparatus of modernization characteristic of the modern French welfare state.[8]

Following Rabinow's genealogy, the fields of modern architecture and heritage preservation also contributed distinct rationales to the formation of a specific apparatus of modernization. With the present book, however, I do not attempt to contribute to Foucault's project of writing the history of the present. Though I explicitly acknowledge Rabinow's *French Modern* as an important inspiration for my later analysis of how the issue of modern architectural heritage constitutes an ever more urgent and actual anthropological problem culminating in global heritage assemblages, instead of attempting to write another full-fledged genealogy of the apparatus of modernization, I aim to reduce its historical complexity: I connect a limited set of historical nodes to form what Rabinow elsewhere calls a "pathway".[9]

Paul Rabinow's notion of a pathway is presented as an alternative to Foucault's broader history of the present. Rabinow defines a pathway as a sequence of elements and events from the past that is related within a heterogeneous problem space.[10] According to him, the contextualization of such a problem space by means of a pathway is, for example, capable of orienting anthropological inquiry genealogically in a much more selective and potentially more effective manner than Foucault's history of the present.[11] In this spirit, the pathway that I establish in the following highlights powerful practices and coordinates of institutionalized knowledge from the realms of heritage preservation and modern architecture that I take as at first constitutive of an apparatus of modernization and yet significantly destabilizing of this dominant apparatus later on.

My pathway begins with a review of Morris and Ruskin's conservationist manifesto, after which I describe how, at the beginning of the 20th century, early heritage professionals struggled to reconcile ideologies of architectural conservation with imperatives for stylistic restoration. Subsequently, I portray the field of heritage preservation as initially attempting to define itself as antagonistic to architectural innovation. My account reveals, however, that in the second half of the 20th century modern architects and urban planners successfully promoted ideologies of progress and development, effectively overruling any concerns for the historical built environment. Only when heritage preservation was positioned as an additional ingredient of, as well as an alternative means to, universal modernization did it regain ground and could it—seemingly paradoxically—eventually establish the legacy of modern architecture and urban planning as an important cultural inheritance worthy of protection in its own right. This ultimately leads me to the institutionalization of modern architectural heritage as world cultural heritage at the turn of the 20th century. Based on a recapitulation of the construction of the Aswan High Dam and the UNESCO Campaign to Save the Monuments of Nubia, which I already reflected on in the Prologue and Introduction, I consider how, in the 21st century, the notion of modern heritage in Africa emerges as a distinctly contemporary anthropological problem. I argue that it is as such, and specifically as a problematization of progressive modernity, that modern architectural heritage in Africa effectively leads to a latent transformation of the dominant apparatus of modernization and ultimately to the emergence of contemporary cultural heritage practices as new global forms.

Conservation versus Stylistic Restoration

In their 1877 SPAB manifesto, Morris and Ruskin had vowed to protect any building "which can be looked at as artistic, picturesque, historical, antique, or substantial, any work in short, over which educated people would think it worth while to argue at all".[12] By the early 20th century, their conservationism had become reflected in administrative and legislative measures and was widely shared across Europe and its colonies. On a national level, state services responsible for the inventory and protection of monuments were founded, and on an international level, initiative was taken to cooperate in the safeguarding of historic built environments, most notably by the League of Nations. However, Morris and Ruskin's categorical disapproval of stylistic restoration, which they denounced as at best created "by the tricky hand of some unoriginal and thoughtless hack of today" or, at worst, as "the reckless stripping of a building of some of its most interesting material features", quickly came to be relativized.[13]

For instance, in 1904, the 6th International Congress of Architects in Madrid passed a resolution based on a paper by Belgian architect Louis Cloquet. Its first three articles maintained the following:

1. Monuments may be divided into two classes, dead monuments, i.e. those belonging to a past civilization or serving obsolete purposes,

and living monuments, i.e. those which continue to serve the purpose for which they were originally intended.

2. Dead monuments should be preserved only by such strengthening as is indispensible in order to prevent their falling into ruin; for the importance of such a monument consists in its historical and technical value, which disappears with the monument itself.

3. Living monuments ought to be restored so that they may continue to be of use, for in architecture utility is one of the bases of beauty. [. . .][14]

Clearly, these tenets allowed stylistic restoration on account of preserving use value, which is why they differed markedly from Morris and Ruskin's exclusive emphasis on age value in heritage preservation. But, even if age value remained of central concern to many professionals, the employment of modern architectural materials and technologies, which Morris and Ruskin so abhorred, soon gained acceptance in the field of heritage preservation.

For example, in 1931 the International Museums Office of the League of Nations organized the First International Congress of Architects and Technicians of Historic Monuments. This event brought together heritage specialists from a number of different European countries and resulted in the drafting of the so-called *Athens Charter for the Restoration of Historic Monuments*. Initially, this charter began very much in line with Morris and Ruskin's conservationist ideology. Article I even laid down "general principles" against stylistic restoration:

> The conference heard the statement of the general principles and doctrines relating to the protection of monuments. Whatever may be the variety of the concrete cases, each of which are open to a different solution, the Conference noted that there predominates in the different countries represented a general tendency to abandon restorations *in toto* and to avoid the attendant dangers by initiating a system of regular and permanent maintenance calculated to ensure the preservation of buildings.[15]

Obviously, this tied into the conservationism of Morris and Ruskin's manifesto for the SPAB. In the end, however, the 1931 *Athens Charter* turned against Morris and Ruskin when it in exceptional cases approved of a "consolidation" of ancient monuments under "the judicious use of all the resources at the disposal of modern technique and more especially of re-enforced concrete".[16]

Arguably, this endorsement of the use of modern building materials and techniques was momentous. Not only did it effectively authorize stylistic restoration after all. More significant, it concretely and productively related the field of heritage preservation to modern architectural innovation. In fact, the First International Congress of Architects and Technicians of Historic Monuments noted,

> It should be unnecessary to mention that the technical work under-taken in connection with the excavation and preservation of ancient monuments calls for close collaboration between the archaeologist and the architect.

Thus, the Athens congress called for a fusion of heritage preservation concerns with the innovative practices of modern architecture, a problematic combination to suggest—not only considering Morris and Ruskin's adamant rejection of predominant manifestations of modern architecture as a threat to the authenticity of historic monuments and as the cause of social alienation.[17]

Heritage Preservation versus Architectural Innovation

In the beginning of the 20th century, much of the authority of modern architecture and urban planning rested on its claims of being able to bring social progress through the design of buildings and cities. The practices of modern architecture and urban planning were attributed the potential to procure economic growth and industrial development as factors of political stability. Such claims to modernization by means of architectural innovation were not at all exceptional, nor made in isolation, supported as they were by one of the most influential association of architects and urban planners at the time: the *Congrès Internationaux d'Architecture Moderne* (CIAM).

CIAM was founded by a group of European architects and urban planners during a 1928 meeting in La Sarraz, Switzerland. Until its dispersion in 1959, the group met regularly in different European cities and established an international forum for the development of modern architecture and urban planning. It quickly came to be known as a panel of experts that vehemently regarded and actively promoted the architectural profession as a powerful development tool. Already in 1928, the newly appointed CIAM secretary—the architectural historian Siegfried Giedion, who prominently noted Ruskin's 'hate of industry'—listed CIAM's goals as

> a) to formulate the contemporary program of architecture, b) to advocate the idea of modern architecture, c) to forcefully introduce this idea into technical, economic and social circles, d) to see to the resolution of architectural problems.[18]

And while CIAM was always divided into more or less feuding groups and its numerous manifestos surely need to be read as compromises, judged by its powerful influence CIAM did formulate *the* program of modern architecture and urban planning in the 20th century.

Intriguingly then, CIAM reacted to the 1931 *Athens Charter for the Restoration of Historic Monuments* rather quickly and in style by writing an *Athens Charter* of its own, drafted in 1933 during CIAM's fourth conference held onboard the SS *Patros* sailing from Marseilles to Greece. Significantly, this second Athens Charter listed a 95-point program for the comprehensive and rational planning of human dwellings and settlements, including a number of recommendations regarding the protection of "the historic heritage of cities":[19]

> The life of a city is a continuous event that is expressed through the centuries by material works—lay-outs and building structures—which form the city's personality, and from which its soul gradually emanates. They are precious witnesses of the past, which will be respected, first for their historical or sentimental value, and second, because certain of them convey a plastic virtue in which the utmost intensity of human genius has been incorporated. They form a part of the human heritage, and whoever owns them or is entrusted with their protection has the responsibility and the obligation to do whatever he legitimately can to hand this noble heritage down intact to the centuries to come.[20]

As a consequence, CIAM's 1933 *Athens Charter* principally agreed with its 1931 predecessor that "architectural assets" must be preserved, whether found in isolated buildings or in urban aggregations.[21]

Both Athens charters explicitly responded to the same challenge: An increasing and accelerating, but as of then largely uncontrolled, process of urbanization. For example, the First International Congress of Architects and Technicians of Historic Monuments had in 1931 warned architects and urban planners about the chaotic expansion of cities as an imminent threat to architectural heritage:

> The [First International Congress of Architects and Technicians of Historic Monuments] recommends that, in the construction of [new] buildings, the character and external aspect of the cities in which they are to be erected should be respected, especially in the neighborhood of ancient monuments, where the surroundings should be given special consideration. Even certain groupings and certain particularly picturesque perspective treatment should be preserved. [The congress] specially recommends the suppression of all forms of publicity, or the erection of unsightly telegraph poles and the exclusion of all noisy factories and even of tall shafts in the neighborhood of artistic and historic monuments.[22]

The first *Athens Charter* cautioned against modern industrialization and mechanization, which it presented as harmful to the historical fabric of the city, but CIAM's analysis in the second *Athens Charter* reached further, claiming that recent thrusts of urbanization had shattered the *social* fabric of existing human settlements, above all else.

While both Athens charters showed concern for heritage preservation in a time of perceived urban crisis, when compared to the First International Congress of Architects and Technicians of Historic Monuments, which called for "strict custodial protection"[23] of historic buildings and sites, CIAM was much more worried about the overall condition of the city and its effect on inhabitants:

> By no means can any narrow-minded cult of the past bring about a disregard for the rules of social justice. [. . .] The problem [of heritage preservation] must be studied, occasionally it may be solved through some ingenious solution; but under no circumstances should the cult of the picturesque and the historical take precedence over the healthfulness of the dwelling, upon which the well-being and the moral health of the individual so depend.[24]

CIAM sneered at the First International Congress of Architects and Technicians of Historic Monuments and the latter's explicit promotion of an "aesthetic enhancement of historic monuments",[25] referring disparagingly to "certain people, more concerned for aestheticism than social solidarity", who would "militate for the preservation of certain picturesque old districts unmindful of the poverty, promiscuity and diseases that these districts harbor".[26]

Somewhat analogously to Cloquet's 1904 distinction between dead and living monuments, CIAM claimed that

> [d]eath, which spares no living creature, also overtakes the works of men. In dealing with material evidence of the past, one must know how to recognize and differentiate that which is still truly alive. The whole of the past is not, by definition, entitled to last forever; it is advisable to choose wisely that which must be respected. If the continuance of certain significant and majestic presences from a bygone era proves injurious to the interests of the city, a solution capable of reconciling both points of view will be sought.[27]

CIAM ultimately vowed to protect architectural heritage only if this "does not entail the sacrifice of keeping people living in unhealthy conditions".[28] As it repeatedly pointed out, even the demolition, destruction, transplantation, separation and modification of historic monuments and urban ensembles were sometimes necessary for the higher purposes of modern architecture and urban planning.[29]

The debate thus moved from a certain antagonism between conservation and stylistic restoration to a much more principal opposition of architectural innovation with heritage preservation. I have argued earlier that this basic ideological difference already characterized the debate around the Crystal Palace in the second half of the 19th century. In the early 20th century, then, certain traces of Ruskin's original criticism of modern industry and its effect on architecture still ran through the first *Athens Charter*. CIAM in their *Athens Charter*, however, endorsed a much more positive view of industrialization and mechanization, portraying modern industry not simply as a threat to heritage but also as an important source of architectural innovation and as a catalyst for social progress. CIAM even used industry as a metaphor for its version of the modern city, assuming that only when completely replanned as a kind of "machine for living"[30] would the city achieve its full potential.

CIAM believed that the complexity of modern life, as well as its potential benefits could only be made accessible by totally reordering human settlements as industrial units.[31] In this respect, it linked architectural innovation and social transformation in a utopian mode. As the anthropologist James Holston notes,

> Although [CIAM ideology] considers that innovation develops through a search for architectural forms that 'condense' new types of social experience, it views the relationship between architecture and society as transitive: change the architecture and society will be forced to follow the program of social change that the architecture embodies.[32]

According to Holston, CIAM made a utopian proposition, aiming to regenerate the present by means of an imagined future, which in urban form was to be the beachhead of a new society within the existing order.[33] For such an urban machine for living, the modern architect would cease to design individual buildings but would rather oversee the organization of standardized objects, including a selection of relevant types of architectural heritage, into processes and functions.[34]

Modernization versus Heritage Preservation

CIAM's utopian ideology of modernization through architectural innovation constitutes the backdrop against which its concern for heritage preservation must be projected. CIAM's approach to the transformation of society effectively rested on a "total decontextualization"[35] strategy of the existing built environment, including architectural heritage. It believed that modern buildings and urban areas could serve as enclaves of novel aesthetics and social practices and would result in the colonization of their surroundings.[36] As one of the most distinctive features of CIAM's ideology was that it repudiated established architectural conventions, as well as their social, political and economic conditions, this inevitably led to what Holston calls a "total antagonism" with the city's historical built fabric.[37] CIAM thus took a stand for an absolute break with the past, whether that came in the form of architectural heritage or otherwise. Insistently, it only used the past as an endorsement for its particular projection of the future, when the past was mostly to be swept away.[38] CIAM ideally wanted to start with a tabula rasa in order to be able to construct the modern city from scratch—give or take a couple of historic monuments.

From its inception, CIAM thus promoted a total revision of the urban status quo in order to rectify through centralized urban planning what it considered the contemporary malaise of the city.[39] Yet the political climate of early-20th-century Europe did not generally allow for the implementation of CIAM's apocalyptic approach to architecture and urban planning. After all, as this approach required radical intervention in the built environment, as well as possibly the expropriation of private property, it would have to be state-sponsored. Though some national governments implemented social housing schemes influenced by CIAM ideology, and the Soviet Union incidentally tested a CIAM brand of urban planning, all in all the CIAM blueprint for the modern city was not realized on the European continent on a larger scale until after World War II, when the widespread destruction caused by bombings had literally provided for a level field of experimentation.

By then, CIAM had already appropriated another field of experimentation outside of the European metropolis, however. As a matter of fact, CIAM participants had, before and during the war, successfully exported their conceptions of modern architecture and urban planning to the periphery of the colonies. There, regional colonial governments willingly accommodated CIAM's grandiose schemes of urban planning as they proved valuable instruments and symbols of dominance over indigenous populations, and the different colonial regimes thus provided modern architects and urban planners with many opportunities to put their visions into practice. After all, one could reliably count on modern architectural designs and urban plans to respond to the specific requirements of colonial rule. For instance, CIAM's ideas were easily adaptable to colonial politics of racial segregation and control.[40]

Surprisingly then, CIAM's ideology remained successful there even after political decolonization. This was mainly because CIAM advertised modern architecture and urban planning to the emergent postcolonial nation-states on the Latin American, Asian and African continents as straightforward means to catch up with modernization as independent states.[41] Just as CIAM had sold interventions in the built environment as a governance tool to the European colonizers, it promised the ex-colonies what Holston calls a "development inversion": CIAM believed that through the implementation of a new type of city as a model of national development—instead of the other way around—it was possible not only to promote innovation throughout the new postcolonial nation-states but also to propel their societies into a planned future of social welfare and prosperity.[42] Ultimately, CIAM claimed that modern architecture and urban planning would make it possible for the countries of what came to be known as the Third World to skip the predicted but 'unintended' stages of historical development, for instance the perceived chaos and the inequities of Europe's industrial revolution, and develop directly "into a glittering future of a second machine age".[43] CIAM suggested that it could cause "the most backward of nations to jump directly into the most modern of worlds".[44]

By the late 1940s, CIAM's vision of modern architecture and urban planning for progress and development also became widely subscribed to in Europe and Japan, where the damage of the recent war was most severe. There, architects and planners comprehensively adapted to the CIAM approach in their efforts at rebuilding. CIAM even managed to unite the opposing factions of the Cold War in its cause of reforming the built environment. Despite their dissonant political interests, the US, as well as the USSR, invariably came to rely on modern architecture and urban planning in their domestic and foreign development projects. And last but not least, the new international institutions that crystalized post 1945 and symbolized a worldwide thrust for universal modernization were all housed in buildings designed according to CIAM principles. For example, in 1949, a consortium of CIAM architects began planning the United Nations headquarters in New York. Moreover, CIAM figureheads in the mid 1950s took responsibility for the design of the UNESCO offices in Paris. By the 1960s then, many other influential organizations such as the World Bank and the International Monetary Fund had followed, establishing the image of modern architecture as the face of a "modern internationalism" for peace and development.[45]

By this time, CIAM had managed to establish a considerable consensus about the value of modern architecture and urban planning as an easy road to modern progress and development. It thrived as a so-called Modern Movement of architects and urban planners who prominently advised administrations on how to bring about and accelerate a process of universal modernization through reformation of the built environment. Nevertheless, CIAM's success as a Modern Movement immediately led to the growth of an—equally modern—countermovement of heritage preservation. In fact, the very same governments and institutions that supported a broad implementation of CIAM's principles simultaneously stepped up their efforts to protect cultural heritage.[46]

Toward Heritage Preservation for Modernization

As CIAM had always been a relatively loose network of like-minded practitioners of modern architecture and urban planning professionals, its official breakup in 1959 did not necessarily mean an immediate loss of influence of the association's idealistic core principles. The end of CIAM as a structured organization following its eleventh conference, in the Dutch town of Otterlo, did however constitute a certain caesura. More or less at the same time that the Modern Movement was losing its unified voice in CIAM, heritage preservationists began to associate as an "extensive international movement"[47] in their own right. Indeed, while largely in accordance with CIAM ideology, the widespread destruction of historic city centers in the wake of urban restructuring led the heritage community to issue an emergency call.

In 1957, 25 years after CIAM's *Athens Charter* was published, the first International Congress of Architects and Historic Buildings in Paris urged action "to secure integration of historic buildings into town planning".[48] Though this International Congress in the French capital was heir to the International Congress of Architects and Technicians of Historic Monuments held in Athens in 1931, the 1957 Paris meeting represented a growing awareness that the sole listing and safeguarding of outstanding instances of architectural heritage called for in 1931 was not enough. Instead, the meeting's participants deemed necessary a broader protection of historic city centers. In 1956, a mounting concern that a more comprehensive approach to the preservation of architectural heritage was needed had already led to UNESCO's founding of the International Center for the Study of the Preservation and Restoration of Cultural Property (ICCROM) in Rome. A year later, the heritage experts gathered in France recommended that all countries which still lacked adequate organizations to list and preserve heritage should provide for the establishment of such authorities and that "the creation of an international assembly of architects and specialists of historic buildings should be considered".[49]

Such an international body was duly created on the occasion of the Second Congress of Architects and Specialists of Historic Buildings held in 1964 in Venice, where the foundation of a non-governmental organization, the International Council of Monuments and Sites (ICOMOS), was proposed to cooperate closely with existing international bodies such as the International Council of Museums (ICOM), the ICCROM and UNESCO. The congress in Paris also drafted ICOMOS's mission statement, the *International Charter for the Conservation and Restoration of Monuments and Sites*, which explicitly rejected CIAM's frequent choice to destroy certain historic monuments and urban ensembles for the higher purpose of transforming the modern city. Known as the *Venice Charter*, this document stated that not merely "great works of art" but also "more modest works of the past, which have acquired cultural significance with the passing of time" were unconditionally worthy of heritage preservation. In diametrical opposition to CIAM's 'make it new' approach to the modern city, the *Venice Charter* declared that "wherever

the traditional setting exists, it must be kept. No new construction, demolition, or modification [. . .] must be allowed".[50]

The vehemence with which the Venice Charter demanded the protection of architectural heritage in 1964 also has to be seen in the light of
the prominent UNESCO Campaign to Save the Monuments of Nubia,
which happened simultaneously (see Prologue). In fact, the *Venice Charter* directly referred to the Nubia campaign as an honorable exception to
its general principle of *in situ* preservation, stating,

> A monument is inseparable from the history to which it bears witness
> and from the setting in which it occurs. The moving of all or parts
> of a monument cannot be allowed except where the safeguarding of
> that monument demands it or where it is justified by national and
> international interests of paramount importance.[51]

Thus, the Second Congress of Architects and Specialists of Historic Buildings acknowledged the legitimate translocation of Nubian monuments
to protect them from the inundations caused by the construction of the
Aswan High Dam and Lake Nasser. Just as UNESCO reacted to the construction of the Aswan High Dam by emphasizing the necessity of concil-
iating development and preservation, the *Venice Charter* also demanded
an "international solution" for a "rehabilitation" of historic monuments
and city centers, claiming that the safeguarding of historic city centers
"rapidly" needed to be integrated "with contemporary life".[52]

The *Venice Charter* proposed that a reconciliation of heritage protection with a modernization of the built environment could be achieved
through "close association" between the national and international bodies entrusted with preservation and "the authorities qualified to draw
up schemes of town-planning and land utilization".[53] Respectively, the
Charter included a "Motion Concerning the Contribution of Modern
Big Works to the Knowledge of Ancient Civilizations", which considered

- that works of every kind increasingly interfere with sites contain-
  ing archeological remains of high cultural value and lead to their
  destruction;
- that in consequence a serious responsibility for our cultural heritage
  rests upon the present society;
- that there can be absolutely no question of stopping the execution of
  necessary works; but it is of the greatest importance to be warned in
  good time not only of projects affecting sites of recognized archeological value but also of fortuitous discoveries made during works
  carried out on other sites;
- that it is of paramount importance to preserve *in situ* or in the form
  of graphic and descriptive documents those remains which constitute
  the archives of civilization.

The Second Congress of Architects and Specialists of Historic Buildings thus accepted the reigning imperative for modernization but explicitly *linked* it to an obligation to protect cultural heritage.

In essence, the *Venice Charter* authorized ICOMOS to "coordinate the international effort for the preservation and the appreciation of the world heritage of historic monuments".[54] Arguably then, ICOMOS's official foundation in 1965 was an important step toward UNESCO's institutionalization of a world heritage of "outstanding universal value to humanity", which *through* heritage preservation eventually came to serve as a symbol of universal modernization. In fact, as I have explained in more detail in the Prologue and Introduction, such a coupling of heritage preservation and modernization was also inherent to UNESCO's Campaign to Save the Monuments of Nubia.

For example, the writer and French cultural minister André Malraux in 1960 celebrated UNESCO's decision to launch the Nubia campaign as follows:

> Yours is the first attempt to deploy, in a rescue operation, on behalf of statues, the immense resources usually harnessed for the service of men. And this is perhaps because for us the survival of statues has become an expression of life. At a moment when our civilization divines a mysterious transcendence in art and one of the still obscure sources of its unity, at the moment when we are bringing into a single, family relationship the masterpieces of so many civilizations, which knew nothing of or even hated each other, you are proposing an action which brings all men together to defy the sources of dissolution. Your appeal is historic not only because it proposes to save the temples of Nubia, but because through it the first World civilization publicly proclaims the world's art its indivisible heritage.[55]

Malraux referred to UNESCO's appeal to the protection of cultural heritage as a sign of the emergence of a universal civilization. For him, heritage preservation did not *per se* have to be opposed to social and economic progress and development, as it was in itself a sign of modernization.

Of course, both the *Venice Charter* and the UNESCO World Heritage Convention at first pitted modern development against heritage preservation. The World Heritage Convention, for instance, noted in 1972 that heritage is "increasingly threatened with destruction not only by the traditional causes of decay, but also by changing social and economic conditions which aggravate the situation with even more formidable phenomena of damage or destruction".[56] Significantly, however, the *Venice Charter* already combined such references to a modernizing threat to heritage with an appeal to a progressive future:

> Imbued with a message from the past, the historic monuments of generations of people remain to the present day as a living witness

of their age-old traditions. People are becoming more and more conscious of the unity of human values and regard ancient values as a common heritage. The common responsibility to safeguard them for future generations is recognized. It is our duty to hand them on in the full richness of their authenticity.[57]

As a consequence, when heritage preservationists pointed out the importance of protecting the architectural inheritance of an authentic traditional past, they provided a strong counterpoint to CIAM's pursuit of architectural innovation as the expression of an authentic modern future. For instance, in reference to the Nubia campaign, UNESCO stated that "to safeguard these stones of the past is to preserve the human beings of tomorrow".[58] Ultimately then, both authenticities allegedly manifested in the built environment—authenticities of past and future—relied on similar, essentially unilinear understandings of history and progress, which is why they could coexist in the context of the same apparatus of modernization.

The Institutionalization of Modern Architectural Heritage

As the apparatus of modernization emerged in the second half of the 20th century, the impact of an emergent system of international governance increased. Organizations such as the United Nations, the International Monetary Fund and the World Bank promoted intergovernmental cooperation as the most prudent road to modern progress and development. In fact, as I have earlier pointed out, the foundation of UNESCO's World Heritage Programme also represented this approach.

In 1972, UNESCO called upon the international community as a whole and invited its member states to join a system of international cooperation and assistance for the protection of "cultural and natural heritage of outstanding universal value to humanity".[59] In this respect, I have likened UNESCO's World Heritage Convention to the institutionalization of cult of heritage, describing it as characterized by a belief in the spiritual unity of humanity, a universal modern civilization.[60] UNESCO proclaims this faith in a "world heritage of mankind as a whole"[61] through its Intergovernmental Committee for the Protection of the Cultural and Natural Heritage of Outstanding Universal Value, also known as the World Heritage Committee. Indeed, the World Heritage Committee's primary task is to counsel the assembly of states parties to UNESCO's 1972 Convention on its criteria of "outstanding universal value", as well as on the "test of authenticity" that any property has to meet in order to be eligible for World Heritage status.[62] To this effect, the committee acts as a board of experts regulating the World Heritage List; it drafts, adopts and periodically revises operational guidelines in order to facilitate the implementation of the World Heritage Programme.[63] And while state parties to the World Heritage Convention should strive for "an equitable representation of the different regions and cultures of the world",[64] they are required to choose as their representatives to the World Heritage Committee only qualified heritage professionals.[65] Additionally, permanent seats on the committee are reserved for expert advisors from the International Union for Conservation of Nature and Natural Resources (IUCN), as well as from ICCROM and ICOMOS.

If the World Heritage Committee symbolizes a cult of heritage, it can thus be said also to play host to what Edward Said would call a "cult of expertise".[66] The procedure of inscribing properties to the World Heritage List, for instance, dictates that all national nominations have to be submitted to the committee for approval. However, the World Heritage Committee is always required to consult two nongovernmental organizations (NGOs) for advice before taking a decision: the IUCN is in charge of evaluating nominations from the realm of "natural heritage"; and ICOMOS likewise has an exclusive mandate to review nominations from the realm of "cultural heritage".[67] As a result, the IUCN and ICOMOS are reserved considerable influence on the decisions of the World Heritage Committee, particularly when it comes to the operational guidelines that regulate the implementation of the World Heritage List.

The original draft of the World Heritage Convention already bore marks of these organizations, for instance due to its roots in the 1964 *Venice Charter*. As ICOMOS based its authority as the formal lobby of a self-declared "extensive international movement"[68] in the preservation of cultural heritage on this charter, when UNESCO asked ICOMOS to advise on the definition of cultural heritage for the text of the World Heritage Convention, it proposed the *Venice Charter* as an appropriate model.

As a result, the World Heritage Convention features a definition of culture that corresponds closely to ICOMOS's focus on the historic heritage of the built environment:

> For the purposes of this Convention, the following shall be considered as "cultural heritage":
>
> monuments: architectural works, works of monumental sculpture and painting, elements or structures of an archaeological nature, inscriptions, cave dwellings and combinations of features, which are of outstanding universal value from the point of view of history, art or science;
>
> groups of buildings: groups of separate or connected buildings which, because of their architecture, their homogeneity or their place in the landscape, are of outstanding universal value from the point of view of history, art or science;
>
> sites: works of man or the combined works of nature and man, and areas including archaeological sites which are of outstanding

universal value from the historical, aesthetic, ethnological or anthropological point of view.[69]

Initially, this conception of a world cultural heritage consisting of material artifacts of outstanding universal value was widely shared and taken for granted. However, with the success of the World Heritage Convention in the 1980s, which meant a steady increase of properties inscribed to the World Heritage List, UNESCO soon issued a call to explore ways of further "classifying the World Heritage cultural properties [by] historical or stylistic period, as well as by cultural area [. . .] with a view to establishing the truly worldwide list imagined by the World Heritage Convention".[70]

In 1987, the World Heritage Committee set up a working group for this purpose, which presented its report a year later in 1988. Significantly, the report noted that some regions and cultures were already well represented on the World Heritage List while others were inadequately represented or not represented at all.[71] In order to rectify this situation, it suggested that

> the universal representativity of the List could be promoted by constructing a matrix in which the history of civilization would be on one axis. The other axis would be provided by the various 'cultural entities' that existed at different times in history. There would be a number of ways of defining these 'cultural entities', i.e. in artistic or architectural style, in geographical terms, in terms of shared religion etc. Once the matrix is constructed, it could be filled in with the most outstanding properties corresponding to each cultural entity and different chronological periods. This would provide the universally representative reference list.[72]

The group recommended that ICOMOS should be commissioned to coordinate a global study that would "enable the [World Heritage] Committee to identify the outstanding cultural properties handed down as patrimony to our contemporary world by all the 'cultural entities' that have made up the history of world civilization".[73] It was imagined that "regional and sub-regional workshops and expert meetings"[74] would result in an "international tentative list"[75] that could lead "fairly rapidly to the establishment of a comprehensive World Heritage List as envisaged by the Convention".[76]

Now, as I have argued at some length in the Prologue and Introduction, the origin of the World Heritage Convention lay in a fundamental temporal rupture between tradition and modernity: UNESCO's 1972 Convention was the result of the intergovernmental organization's Campaign to Save the Monuments of Nubia, which reacted to the construction of the Aswan High Dam in Egypt as symbolic of the very urgency of this rupture between tradition and modernity.[77] Indeed, UNESCO formulated its universalizing appeal to preserve the past for a common human future in the wake of its Nubia campaign. The World Heritage Convention was a response to modern development as an imminent threat to traditional cultural heritage, though it then also aimed to reconcile tradition with overriding imperatives for modernization. Somewhat ironically then, in the late 1980s, when the World Heritage Committee launched its global study to ensure the representativeness of the World Heritage List, it effectively expanded the conception of world cultural heritage to include modern architecture and urban planning as one of the categories of culture eligible for World Heritage status. At which point the Committee began to inscribe on the World Heritage List manifestations of the very ideology of modern architecture and urban planning that had earlier made the preservation of a world cultural heritage come to be perceived as an urgent necessity.

In 1987, the first example of modern architecture and urban planning to be granted World Heritage status was Brasília, the newly built capital city of Brazil and the largest city in the world that did not exist at the beginning of the 20th century. Like the Aswan High Dam, the city of Brasilia also constituted an archetypical modern development project. Brasília was designed from scratch, in strict adherence to the CIAM master plan of modern urbanism. Construction of the city was ordered in 1956 by Brazilian president Jucelino Kubitschek who had won the national elections based on a promise to achieve "fifty years of progress in five years of government".[78] Kubitschek hoped that a physical move of the Brazilian seat of government from Rio, on the country's east coast, to a newly established federal district in the central province of Goías would bring regional development to the periphery, in the process engendering a unifying spirit of national identity. As James Holston has noted, for Kubitschek, "the foundation of Brasilia signified nothing less than the refoundation of Brazil itself at a national rather than at a colonial stage of development".[79] And indeed, the city did eventually become a national symbol, if only as a World Heritage site.

From the very beginning, Brasília was criticized for being an unattainable utopia of modernization. Brasília's master plan was even criticized for *reinforcing* inequalities in Brazilian society instead of promoting national equality. The many workers who had participated in the construction of the new capital, for instance, were not allowed to take up residence there. After the official opening of Brasília in 1960, the workers' temporary barracks were destroyed and when they proceeded to erect slums on the outskirts of the city, Kubitschek was determined to protect the integrity of Brasília's modern design.

As Kubitschek feared losing political momentum by sanctioning such illegal construction, the president considered the possibility of declaring Brasília national heritage only two months after his inauguration of the

new capital. He wrote a note to an official from the ministry of education, stating,

> The only protection for Brasilia is the preservation of its pilot plan—
> adding it to the heritage registry would, I think, constitute a safety
> measure, more so than the law in Congress, the passing of which
> I doubt. Would you be so gracious as to study the possibility, even if
> it means slightly forcing the very interpretation of 'heritage'? I con-
> sider this fortification indispensable against destructive assaults that
> already seem vigorous.[80]

But such a *pro forma* classification of Brasília as architectural heritage
never became a reality during Kubitschek's term of office, and under the
military regime that was to follow his presidency in the late 1960s and
1970s the city's master plan further lost currency. Only in 1981 did a
national working group for "the preservation of the historical and cultural heritage" of Brasília pick up Kubitschek's idea and urged the safeguarding of the city as "an urban ideal".[81]

It was not until or—depending on the point of view—already in 1986
that the Brazilian government nominated Brasília as world heritage,
describing the city as a landmark in the modern history of planning:

> Urban planner Lucio Costa and architect Oscar Niemeyer intended
> that every element—from the layout of the residential and adminis-
> trative districts (often compared to the shape of a bird in flight) to
> the symmetry of the buildings themselves—should be in harmony
> with the city's overall design. The official buildings, in particular, are
> innovative and imaginative.[82]

In 1987, the World Heritage Committee advised UNESCO's General
Assembly to officially inscribe Brasilia on the World Heritage List on
the basis of two criteria, as a representation of "a masterpiece of human
creative genius" and as an "outstanding example of a type of building,
architectural or technological ensemble or landscape which illustrates (a)
significant stage(s) in human history".[83]

Interestingly, the rationale behind the granting of World Heritage status to Brasília closely corresponds to Kubitschek's initial call to add the
city to the heritage registry as a safety measure. This is apparent in ICO-
MOS's evaluation report to the World Heritage Committee, which recommended listing "the proposed cultural property":[84]

> In 1960, at the end of President Kubitschek's term of office, and espe-
> cially since 1964, when a new policy was adopted and the original
> team of architects was disbanded, the new capital of Brazil encoun-
> tered serious problems.[85]

Specifically, ICOMOS complained about the "absence of both a Master Plan and a code of urbanism"[86] to guide the later stages of Brasília's development. It argued that this absence had left the standards defined by Costa and Niemeyer "in the greatest disarray",[87] as the construction of "higher structures in certain sectors, construction in open spaces, modifications in the road network, and other transgressions have greatly altered a monumental landscape initially of great quality".[88] Thus, a mere 30 years after Kubitschek had commissioned Brasília's modern utopia, the new capital had come to be perceived as in urgent need of heritage preservation.

Certainly, by 1987 one could not deny the so-called Modern Movement in architecture and urban planning had come of age. Although modern architects and planners had always proclaimed to be at the forefront of progress and development, many of their designs had inevitably already become obsolete. Brasília had arguably also failed as a utopia of a better future: After many of its grand promises of economic development and social inclusion had been disappointed, it survived as a monumental remnant of an imagined future from the past. Though Brasília's listing as World Heritage was different from the *pro forma* declaration as cultural inheritance that Kubitschek had favored immediately on the city's construction, it did amount to a peculiar kind of instant heritage.[89]

The experts of the World Heritage Committee certainly courted controversy in their discussions about Brasília's addition to the World Heritage List, particularly struggling with the fact that the accrual of ever more recent relics made heritage ever harder to demarcate from the ongoing present.[90] After the granting of World Heritage status to Brasília, the World Heritage committee specifically altered its operational guidelines, which from 1988 onward, feature an extra paragraph:

> It is difficult to assess the quality of new towns of the twentieth century. History alone will tell which of them will best serve as examples of contemporary town planning. The examination of the files on these towns should be deferred, save under exceptional circumstances.[91]

Nonetheless, Brasília's protection as modern architectural heritage was not to remain an exception to the rule. In line with the World Heritage Committee's ambition to complete a global study of relevant categories of culture that would prove of "outstanding universal value", as well as meet the necessary "test of authenticity", inscriptions of instances of modern architecture and urban planning continued to be deemed important for a well-balanced World Heritage List.[92]

In 1988, the upcoming interest in modern architecture and urban planning as significant cultural heritage was further fueled by the founding of the International Working Party for the Documentation and Restoration of Early Modern Architecture in the Netherlands.[93] This NGO, which soon changed its name to the Working Party for the Documentation and Conservation of Buildings, Sites and Neighborhoods of the Modern Movement (DOCOMOMO), acknowledged a new historicity of modern architecture and urban planning and launched a campaign to raise awareness of its heritage value. In fact, just as early heritage preservationists had perceived remnants of important historical periods endangered by modern development projects, DOCOMOMO cautioned that instances of modern architecture and urban planning had come to face similar dangers.

DOCOMOMO counted among the predicaments of the Modern Movement the very success of heritage preservation as such: "During the 1970s modern architecture became the target of virulent criticism due to the enhanced aspirations of the public relating to the preservation of historic areas of their cities."[94] Moreover, DOCOMOMO contended that "in retrospect it is apparent that the seminal principles of the 'Modern Movement' have been compromised in part because those original objectives have been tempered due to economic pressures or technical exigencies".[95] Under these circumstances, DOCOMOMO lamented, the Modern Movement had "only slowly become aware of its cultural inheritance [and it had had] to wait until the 1980s before this conscience crystalized".[96]

In any case, DOCOMOMO was convinced of the uniqueness of the Modern Movement:[97]

> The 'Modern Movement' is probably the most significant product of architecture, urbanism and cultural landscape in the 20th century, and is distinguished by the value system established in its name. Without entirely abandoning local priorities, the international movement emphasized functional efficiency over appearance, representative value judgments resting on innovation and formal experimentation.[98]

Consequently, DOCOMOMO considered it "our urgent responsibility to preserve for future generations surviving works of the 'Modern Movement' which represent the rich heritage of the 20th century, an essential element in our cultural legacy which, for different reasons, are under imminent threat".[99]

Indeed, the NGO aimed to "come to the gathering of forces" in order to establish "an exchange of experiences and know how" and to draw the attention of the public to the significance of modern architecture and urban planning as cultural heritage.[100] For this purpose, DOCOMOMO quickly managed to establish an impressive array of national chapters or working parties, mainly in Europe, which lobbied for the formal acceptance of modern architecture and urban planning as cultural heritage in their home countries. Internationally, too, the NGO managed to establish itself as an authoritative body of expertise on the Modern Movement. In

1992, for example, DOCOMOMO received the status of an official consultative body to the UNESCO World Heritage Committee.[101] Moreover, ICOMOS commissioned DOCOMOMO's International Specialist Committee on Registers (ISC/R) to issue advice concerning the built heritage of the 20th century in a report on the heritage of the Modern Movement in relation to the World Heritage List first published in 1997.[102]

DOCOMOMO's establishment as a consultant to ICOMOS and the World Heritage Committee came after roughly a decade of intensifying debate about the representativeness of the World Heritage List. By the early 1990s, UNESCO was determined to formulate a global strategy in order to guarantee what it called the future credibility of the World Heritage Programme. To this end, ICOMOS and the World Heritage Committee in 1994 organized an Expert Meeting on the "Global Strategy" and Thematic Studies for a Representative World Heritage List. This meeting resulted in the advice to cease concentrating on single monuments in isolation, but rather to consider for inscription to the World Heritage List "cultural groupings that were complex and multi-dimensional, which demonstrated in spatial terms the social structures, ways of life, beliefs, systems of knowledge, and representations of different pasts and present cultures in the entire world".[103] Accordingly, the World Heritage Committee was urged "to set aside the idea of a rigid and restricted World Heritage List and instead to take into account all the possibilities for extending and enriching it by means of new types of property whose value might become apparent as knowledge and ideas developed".[104]

Significantly, one of these new types of property that was prominently singled out in 1994 was 20th-century architecture, which the proceedings of the expert meeting referred to as "a striking transformation of multiple meanings in the use of materials, technology, work, organization of space, and more generally, life in society".[105] A few of years later, DOCOMOMO essentially followed this line of reasoning in its final report on modern architectural heritage as World Heritage:

> Modernity that gives root to the 'Modern Movement' is a cultural mode, a form of civilization which permeated the world from the West, opposed to the idea of 'tradition', that is to say all earlier traditions, and is unswervingly dedicated to fundamental economic and social transformation.[106]

Ultimately, DOCOMOMO proposed its conception of modernity as the main standard for inscriptions of Modern Movement architecture and urban planning to the World Heritage List. Yet, the NGO's advice to ICOMOS and the World Heritage Committee also pointed to "principal problems,"[107] mainly concerning the necessary authenticity test.

According to the World Heritage Convention, one relevant measure for the inclusion of a particular property on the list is the "authenticity of the design, materials, workmanship and setting".[108] This, however, was exactly where DOCOMOMO saw a need for reinterpretation:

> Many modern buildings, intended to meet specialized or short-term needs, were designed to facilitate their replacement or adaptation to other uses, and were often constructed of experimental or short-lived materials and components[109]

Following DOCOMOMO, this "intentional transitoriness"[110] characteristic of modern architecture and urban planning made it difficult to apply conventional standards of material authenticity. When considering relevant buildings and sites of the "Modern Movement" for World Heritage status, the NGO instead suggested taking into account "criteria of technical, social and aesthetic innovation" as a "valuable qualitative test for modernity".[111]

ICOMOS requested DOCOMOMO's advice on "whether the current criteria for inscription to the World Heritage List are applicable to buildings and sites of the 'Modern Movement'".[112] DOCOMOMO's answer was no and, instead, suggested four alternative "aspects of authenticity" relevant to modern architectural heritage: authenticity of the idea and the design concept; authenticity of form, spatial organization and appearance; authenticity of construction and details; and, as one aspect among many, authenticity of materials.[113] DOCOMOMO justified its appeal to these alternative authenticities by referring to the fundamental transitoriness of Modern Movement architecture and urban planning, which it claimed "is now an important part of our cultural heritage and therefore deserves conservation".[114]

When the NGO referred to conservation in this context, it effectively meant that "some replacements of original materials and other alterations are acceptable as long as the original intentions of the architect's concept (idea) in the present form, space and appearance of a building or site are still recognizable".[115] Here, DOCOMOMO introduced a momentous—and only thinly disguised—revision of the deep rooted suspicion of stylistic restoration that had been dominant in the field of heritage preservation since Ruskin and Morris's conservationist mid-19th-century manifesto. In fact, DOCOMOMO's odd reference to transitoriness as the inheritance of the Modern Movement resulted in a blunt advocacy of conservation *as* stylistic restoration: In order to institutionalize modern architectural heritage, DOCOMOMO apparently felt it necessary to turn received dogmas of heritage preservation completely upside down.[116]

DOCOMOMO's sacrilege also becomes apparent when considering its advice regarding the safeguarding as heritage of modern 'new towns' such as Brasília:

> A new town is usually founded by a unitary authority set up for that specific purpose; once the town is built and running, its various

functions are allocated to the existing local authorities and it is just at that time that controls are relaxed and records are in danger of being lost. Although it is obvious that urban areas and cultural landscapes will change after their first layout, special care is needed for the guidance of these developments and to maintain respect for the essential intentions of the original concept. If there is no longer respect for the integrity of the planned ideas, this will affect also the future 'authenticity' of the setting or site.[117]

Here, DOCOMOMO highlights the complexity of modern architectural heritage. In spite of the fact that protecting modern architecture and urban planning as heritage was an attempt at saving an authentic past like any other, the NGO obviously dealt with a past that had promoted radical architectural innovation as the authentic expression of the future. Rather problematically then, DOCOMOMO's new concern was with a utopian past manifested in built form, a past that had been utterly unaccepting of the eventual possibility of its own historicity. As a matter of fact, the future of this particular past had always stood in a veritable opposition to heritage preservation *per se*. Consequently, when DOCOMOMO spoke of the necessity to protect the *future* authenticity of a given site of modern urbanism, it essentially reinterpreted heritage preservation in the name of the very ideology of radical architectural innovation against which the protection of heritage had always tried to be a counterweight.

As a result, the *mutadis mutandis* of heritage preservation for DOCO-MOMO was not that it needed to be reconciled with modern progress and development, as UNESCO suggested with its World Heritage Programme, at least not when it came to the heritage of the Modern Movement. Instead, DOCOMOMO accepted the very modernizing premises of modern architecture and urban planning as a kind of 'living heritage', claiming, for instance, that

> [a]s the "Modern Movement" is concerned, more than any other previous architectural school or movement with international interaction, its architectural and planning heritage exhibits a worldwide diffusion of the values of modernity, some of them still alive today. The most remarkable of them are evidence of attempts to improve the well-being of the population and to achieve a man-made environment in accordance with technological breakthroughs and universal democratic projects.

Thus, DOCOMOMO took what it referred to as "the Modern Movement's continuing and vital role in meeting social needs"[118] as a major legitimization of the institutionalization of modern architectural heritage.

Yet the very need for such an institutionalization of modern heritage pointed to a significant destabilization of the apparatus of modernization, of which the Modern Movement as such clearly was part and parcel. In 1997, DOCOMOMO's report to ICOMOS and the World Heritage Committee portrayed the legacy of the Modern Movement as "revolutionizing human aspirations and the expectations of society",[119] recommending that the inscription of selected buildings and sites of modern architecture and urban planning to the World Heritage List should be continued. Subsequently, in 2001, ICOMOS and UNESCO got together with DOCOMOMO to launch a "joint programme for the identification, documentation, and promotion of the built heritage of the 19th and 20th centuries—the Programme on Modern Heritage".[120] Still, when UNESCO first evaluated the protection of modern architecture and urban planning as World Heritage, it noted that "some governments and the civil society are not aware of the value of modern heritage, which is too often perceived as having no historical, aesthetic or anthropological value and therefore is not deemed worthy of preservation".[121] Seemingly paradoxically then, DOCOMOMO, ICOMOS and the World Heritage Committee had made it their task to convince the world of the Modern Movement's ongoing relevance as living heritage—in spite of a skeptical public with a "low appreciation"[122] of modern architecture and urban planning, let alone the historicity of their utopias of universal progress and development as traditions against themselves.[123]

Modern Architectural Heritage in Africa as an Anthropological Problem

In the 1970s, the unilinear narratives of progress and development informing the apparatus of modernization increasingly came to be criticized and widespread opposition began to arise against radical architectural innovation and urban reconstruction in Europe. By the 1980s, even mainstream histories of modern architecture proclaimed CIAM urbanism a failure, arguing it did not live up to its own, high expectations.[124] Architectural historians contended that realizations of the CIAM master plan for the modern city represented a "dismal picture of congestion, astronomical costs, air pollution, massive energy use, crime, and social malaise".[125] It is no coincidence, then, that this was when DOCOMOMO started its campaign to institutionalize modern architectural heritage. Its activism for the heritage preservation of modern architecture and urban planning demonstrated that the Modern Movement's basic ideologies often continued to be accepted as a given, despite an obvious dichotomy between "plan and reality".[126] If modern architecture and urban planning had been powerful tools of universal modernization to its practitioners, so they apparently remained for their heritage preservationists.

In the beginning, DOCOMOMO saw the evaluation of modern architecture and urban planning primarily as a matter of success or failure of masterful design, which the NGO measured according to the modern architects' and planners' own, presumably neutral, claims of functional performance. Accordingly, DOCOMOMO's first shortlist of potential nominations to the UNESCO World Heritage List exclusively consisted of iconic masterpieces of the Modern Movement. DOCOMOMO even suggested considering for inscription not only isolated buildings and sites, but whole oeuvres of prominent CIAM figureheads such as Le Corbusier, whose particular influence it praised as "so important to the Modern Movement and [possessive of] such a truly worldwide character".[127] By 1994, however, this reverent attitude had changed, as UNESCO's panel of experts on the global strategy recommended that

> 20th century architecture should not be considered solely from the point of view of 'great' architects and aesthetics, but rather as a striking transformation of multiple meanings in the use of materials, technology, work, organization of space, and, more generally, life in society. This new approach would naturally require something more than a "world prize" for architects[128]

Gradually then, instead of continuing to rely on the dominant historiography of modern architecture and urban planning that had long circled around a few male 'master architects' of European descent, DOCOMOMO adjusted its approach to match a more critical interpretation of the Modern Movement legacy.[129] In fact, the NGO began to consider the "darker sides"[130] of what it had first called the early-20th-century "heroic period" of modern architecture and urban planning; it shifted its focus away from the Modern Movement's alleged "maximum impact in Europe" and adopted a new awareness of modern architecture and urban planning as a markedly colonial heritage.[131]

DOCOMOMO's attention to other regions of the world,[132] as well as a certain distancing from its previously largely iconographic approach to modern architectural heritage was influenced by the NGO's participation in a host of initiatives to strengthen the credibility of the World Heritage List. Since 1994, the global strategy experts had criticized the World Heritage List for its overrepresentation of cultural heritage in Europe. The World Heritage Convention as such was furthermore criticized for its "almost exclusively 'monumental' concept of cultural heritage".[133] As a consequence, DOCOMOMO directed its attention more and more toward what was called "the heritage of the twentieth century, rather than the architecture alone", particularly in a context of colonialism.[134]

For the World Heritage Committee itself the pursuit of a representative and credible World Heritage List also resulted in a considerable change of perspective. Most important, the committee realized that in "the history of art and architecture, archeology, anthropology, and ethnology"[135] conceptions of culture and cultural heritage had broadened in "meaning, depth and extent".[136] Indeed, UNESCO's exclusive focus on culture as material artifacts of the past was particularly criticized for its neglect of "living cultures"; it was noted that "especially the traditional cultures, with their depth, their wealth, their complexity, and their diverse relationships figured very little on the list".[137] Yet when the World Heritage Committee decided—"in reference to the scientific community"[138]—to make a move to inscribe more "traditional living cultures"[139] on the list, this also meant a considerable reinterpretation of a defining feature of cultural heritage discourse thus far: The "pure" dichotomy of tradition and modernity and its dependency on unilinear understandings of history and progress.[140]

The World Heritage Committee's appeal to preserve traditional living cultures entailed that tradition was no longer limited to the distant past. And if tradition was to have a legitimate place in the present as living culture, modernity could likewise no longer simply and easily be focused on a better future. Hence, the committee's decision to protect traditional living cultures made for a dilemma that was reminiscent of the heterodoxy of the call to preserve Modern Movement legacy as living heritage. Indeed, under circumstances in which the old was declared coeval with the new, and the new was becoming the old, the notion of modern architectural heritage as living heritage reemerged as a veritable problematization of modernity.[141]

In the context of UNESCO's World Heritage Programme, this problematization of modernity basically took on the form of an assemblage of hetero-logoi concerning the concept of culture. As I have mentioned before, the World Heritage Convention initially endorsed a concept of culture restricted to material artifacts of "outstanding universal value to humanity". However, as UNESCO itself points out, over the course of the second half of the 20th century the organization's idea of culture changed.[142] When UNESCO launched the World Heritage Convention in 1972, its original aim had been to create "a link through common values" between cultural entities "separated by their own diversity".[143] Accordingly, the organization's intention was to achieve "social progress" by constructing "a new human unity".[144] In later years, however, UNESCO shed this notion of a "universal civilization", expanding its concept of culture to encompass that of identity itself.[145] By the end of the 20th century, UNESCO had essentially reversed its main emphasis on cultural heritage: Instead of focusing on the "uniformity"[146] of 'world culture', the organization proceeded to direct its efforts toward "maintaining the diversity of the world"—the singular, culture, had been altered into the plural, cultures.[147]

Still, UNESCO regarded its new occupation with cultural diversity adequately "rooted in an opposition between elements of a different kind—modernity and tradition".[148] It claimed that such an opposition continued to explain "the fear, which became more pronounced at the end of the twentieth century, of seeing ancient components of the cultural identity of each people disappear under pressure from an all encompassing and mass consumed global culture".[149] Although it was UNESCO's overriding worry that a globalizing process of modernization had "meant the loss of identity, sense of community and personal meaning", the organization did acknowledge that "most people wish to participate in 'modernity', but in terms of their own traditions".[150] Notably then, UNESCO had reinterpreted the opposition between tradition and modernity under the sign of "cultural diversity", which it affirmed as a "renewable treasure that must not be perceived as being unchanging heritage, but as a process guaranteeing the survival of humanity".[151]

In the early 21st century, such concern with cultural diversity fueled the persistent drive toward a global strategy for a representative and well-balanced World Heritage List. For instance, as I have hinted at before, one of ICOMOS's latest contributions to the global strategy is *The World Heritage List: Filling the Gaps—An Action Plan for the Future*, a report published in 2004. Its goal was to provide the World Heritage Committee with "a clear overview of the present situation, and likely trends in the short and medium term with a view to identifying under-represented categories".[152] ICOMOS was specifically reacting to previous expert advice on the World Heritage List that had considered representativeness to be necessary not only to "increase the number of types, regions, and periods of cultural property that are under-represented in the coming years, but also to take into account the new concepts of the idea of cultural heritage that had been developed over the past twenty years".[153]

After noting that "it goes without saying that in the decades since the World Heritage Convention was adopted, society's ideas of 'cultural heritage' have expanded considerably", ICOMOS asserted,

> To judge a different culture or a different period from one's own necessarily requires a learning process. In this respect, the World Heritage List is proving to be an international instrument of reference, which if properly interpreted and used could be seen as both a challenge and an opportunity to recognize the diversity and specificity of different cultures, past and present.[154]

In this light, the document was to contribute "to the development of a World Heritage List that may better reflect the cultural identity, significances and relevance of properties in defined regions of the world".[155]

A starting point for ICOMOS's analysis was a definition of "cultural regions" that it claimed needed to be a major factor in the global strategy for a balanced World Heritage List.[156] ICOMOS cautioned that these regions, which loosely followed the shape of the continents, did not necessarily correspond to political boundaries and that it was "therefore not possible to aim for a 'balance' at State Party or country level, nor even in relation to larger political entities".[157] The NGO found it "clear that as a result of the rise and fall of empires, cultural development in relation to a historic timeline varies from one cultural region to another, and cultural regions also vary from one era to another".[158] As a result, the *Filling the Gaps* report further expanded its notion of cultural regions, proposing a "holistic" approach based on three complementary frameworks: a typological framework based on categories, a thematic framework and a chronological-regional framework.[159]

Regarding the confusion about the notion of modern architectural heritage as "living heritage", the confines of ICOMOS's chronological-regional framework are particularly instructive. This framework is divided into several sections, referring to various regions of the world and to each region's relevant historical timeline.[160] The NGO makes two exceptions to this rule:

> [One] exception is the 'early evolution of humans', ranging from the Palaeolithic to the Bronze Age, which has been taken as a separate category that does not refer to any single region. This category does not have a specific timeframe either, reflecting the fact that evolution has been different from region to region. Another special category relates to the period of 'globalisation' since the First World War. This category has been called the 'modern world', and it also covers all regions.[161]

ICOMOS's chronological-regional framework is noteworthy given these exceptions alone. Similarly remarkable is the fact that the special modern world category did not exactly match its corresponding typological category in the *Filling the Gaps* report, which defined modern heritage as buildings, works of art, industrial properties, towns, urban or rural areas, as well as cultural landscapes dating from the late 19th century onward.[162] In the context of the global strategy, this incongruence between two different frameworks of modernity significantly complicated changing conceptions of culture and cultural diversity.

ICOMOS admitted in the *Filling the Gaps* report that each of its frameworks had strengths and weaknesses and each was "only one way of approaching the challenge of classification". The NGO even conceded that because cultural heritage was "fragmented and diverse" it was not really "predisposed to clear classification systems".[163] Nevertheless, ICOMOS did rely on its respective frameworks enough to identify gaps in the World Heritage List. Notwithstanding the difficulties conclusively classifying modern heritage, *Filling the Gaps* complained that in 2004 there was "only a single modern heritage property on the Tentative Lists of three of the five regions—Africa, the Arab States, and Asia Pacific".[164] ICOMOS thus advised that a special effort needed to be made to encourage states parties to the World Heritage Convention to nominate cultural properties underrepresented on the World Heritage List, such as modern heritage.[165]

ICOMOS's advice makes evident what I regard as two principal problems with both the dominant conceptions of culture and cultural diversity underlying the global strategy in general, as well as the structure of its own *Filling the Gaps* report. First of all, although the global strategy encouraged a transnational approach to identifying and rectifying the perceived imbalances, UNESCO obviously remains an *inter*national institution.[166] This means that despite all global strategy attempts to define culture at regional and global levels, nation-states effectively continue to function as unitary cultural entities within the World Heritage Programme.[167] Secondly, ICOMOS's chronological regional framework problematizes the temporality of the concept of cultural diversity. In fact, whereas ICOMOS noted in its report that it had "long been recognized that cultural values can vary from one culture to another, and also can evolve and change over time, even in the same culture",[168] the NGO's macro framework essentially presented the culture of the modern world as an epochal temporal whole.

The weight of these problems on the establishment of modern architectural heritage as world cultural heritage becomes apparent when considering what *Filling the Gaps* referred to as the underrepresentation on the World Heritage List of modern heritage, specifically in Africa. In 2004, UNESCO cooperated with ICOMOS and DOCOMOMO to counter this underrepresentation by bringing together representatives from a number of African countries, as well as other intergovernmental and NGOs at a regional *Meeting on Modern Heritage for Africa*. UNESCO's proceedings describe the event as follows:

> The *Meeting on Modern Heritage for Africa*, taking place in Asmara, Eritrea, formed part of a series of regional meetings initiated under the Programme on Modern Heritage as part of UNESCO's Global Strategy for a Credible, Balanced and Representative World Heritage List. The major objectives of the meeting were to:
>
> 1. address under-representation of Modern Heritage in the World Heritage List in the context of Africa;
> 2. discuss the above with a view to identifying properties for possible inclusion on national and even the World Heritage List;
> 3. debate what constitutes Modern Heritage in Africa.[169]

Indeed, the problem of "defining modern heritage in an African context" was recorded in the proceedings as a "major area of debate, with various opinions and positions presented".[170] Apparently, UNESCO first proposed "the timeframe of the 19th and 20th centuries with a focus on the built environment",[171] but some participants did not agree with limiting their conception of modern heritage on the African continent "exclusively to the architectural heritage of the past 200 years".[172] They took modern African heritage to mean "everything that is being used by humankind at the present time".[173]

Notably, the resultant lack of consensus on what constitutes modern heritage in an African context was also linked to the question whether modern heritage is exclusively colonial heritage.[174] As a matter of fact, such a latent equation of colonial heritage with modern heritage was nothing new. Already in 2001 ICOMOS had published a *Shared Colonial Heritage at Risk* report, which explained that

> [t]he nature of the Shared Colonial Heritage is represented by the architecture, urban planning and infrastructure introduced by various European Colonial regimes throughout the world [. . .] In essence, the significance and primary characteristics of the Shared Colonial Heritage are the responses made to the local situation and conditions that are reflected in the architectural and planning influences imported from the home country. In many cases, the architectural and planning themes across many different Colonies remain recognisably associated with the governing Colonial regime, but typically there is a degree of difference that expresses and responds to the individual local context. Colonial regimes typically erected buildings and other infrastructure that enabled them to control and manage the Indigenous populations and to exploit the resources of the Colony to the benefit of the homeland.[175]

Following ICOMOS, this shared colonial heritage was under threat due to a variety of reasons, including "emerging nationalism and the need to establish an independent identity", which had "often encouraged former Colonies to reach back to their Indigenous traditions at the expense of the remaining Colonial-period architecture and infrastructure".[176]

Ostensibly then, ICOMOS's concern for a shared colonial heritage at risk translated into one of the issues under debate during the *Meeting on Modern Heritage for Africa*. On this occasion it was debated whether the "interaction between vernacular and other forms of architecture" in an African context might not also constitute "an aspect of modern heritage" and whether modern heritage might not include "colonial as well as vernacular heritage".[177] Finally, the participants agreed that, in light of the respective differences of opinion, a compromise needed to be struck between the view introduced by the European colonial regimes that "modern heritage can be defined as a particular school of architectural thought"[178] and the imperative that "the onus should be on African State Parties, including African communities, to determine how they wished to define modern heritage in their own unique context".[179]

In the end, this struggle over exclusively classifying modern heritage in Africa as colonial illustrates how specific conceptions of culture and cultural diversity articulated in the wake of UNESCO's global strategy problematized modernity. The *Meeting on Modern Heritage for Africa* participants, for instance, unanimously acknowledged a need to accommodate colonial heritage in their approaches to modern African heritage. However, the Asmara event explicitly closed with the recommendation to establish national inventories and national lists of modern heritage in Africa, recalling the difficulty of establishing a transnational concept of culture such as the one informing the notion of a shared colonial heritage; this concept obviously could not gain solid ground.[180] After all, if the meeting's participants had subscribed to the notion of a shared culture of colonial modernity, this would also have implied sharing responsibilities for the inventory and protection of relevant modern heritage on the African continent between the national authorities representing former colonized and colonizers alike. Furthermore, the criticism directed against an understanding of modern heritage as only "represented by the architecture, urban planning and infrastructure introduced by various European Colonial regimes throughout the world" raised awareness of what UNESCO later referred to as the "cultures eclipsed, or even temporarily neglected by the colonial powers".[181] In other words, during the *Meeting on Modern Heritage for Africa* a pervasive equation of "modernity" with a "cultural mode permeating the world from the West"[182] conflicted with appeals to the fundamental cultural diversity of modern colonialism.

Effectively, all this resulted in a problematization of modernity as a coherent epochal and spatial whole or culture, thus pointing to a considerable destabilization of the apparatus of modernization. In fact, while fundamental assumptions of the apparatus of modernization remained influential during the *Meeting on Modern Heritage for Africa*—for example, participants agreed on the relevance of the preservation of cultural heritage for "sustainable development"[183]—the categorization of the modern world as a progressive temporality homogenously covering all regions of the globe came to be questioned. From a singular conception of modernity as a living culture, the heritage professionals gathered in Asmara shifted toward a more plural understanding of the modern, one that recognized the heterogeneity of historical manifestations and experiences of modernity in "non-Western and non-industrialized countries and regions", including "traditional living cultures".[184]

In 2011, similar skepticism of unilinear narratives of progress and development, or of a universal civilization defining modern heritage, came to the fore again at the Getty Conservation Institute in Los Angeles during the first meeting of ICOMOS's newly established *Scientific Committee on Twentieth Century Heritage*. Following the previous example of *Filling the Gaps*, this panel of experts aimed to develop a more specific "historic thematic framework to assess the significance of twentieth century heritage".[185] However, as the experts write in their notes, "the question of what constitutes 'modern' heritage was persistently troublesome".[186] Apparently, at a very basic level,

> [the] group grappled with the question of what constitutes twentieth-century heritage and whether it should be defined in a strictly temporal sense. It was agreed that some themes stretch back to earlier

periods, while others emerged or became more predominant during the twentieth century.[187]

As a consequence, the experts gathered in California agreed that "most periodizations are largely arbitrary", acknowledging that there are "multiple definitions of the beginning of modernity", and even thought it necessary to avoid "potentially culturally-loaded terms as 'progress' or 'improved' ".[188]

The *Scientific Committee on Twentieth Century Heritage* admitted that it experienced difficulties with its objective to establish a value-neutral framework that could "comfortably accommodate the identification of sites with troubled histories or the darker side of heritage".[189] Intriguingly, the problem seemed to boil down to the question of how to relate 20th century heritage to diversity:

> cultural heritage is a product of its time, place, and context. While there are specific phenomena that occurred almost universally during the twentieth century (such as mass migration or technological development), each was manifested in countless ways depending upon these factors. For the framework to be applicable both globally and locally, it must be flexible and adaptable enough to accommodate geographic, historical, and cultural diversity.[190]

As a result, the *Scientific Committee on Twentieth Century Heritage* continued the momentous shift away from a predominant understanding of modernity as an epochal culture that "engulfed the world after an initial period in Europe",[191] to a conception of modernity as expressly plural and culturally diverse. About a decade after DOCOMOMO's report on the Modern Movement in relation to the World Heritage List had first established modern architectural heritage as legitimate world cultural heritage, the committee's reference to geographic, historical and cultural diversity as an important factor in any framework of modern heritage presented a new theme complicating and latently transforming the apparatus of modernization: the theme of alternative modernities.

Already in 2005, architectural historian Maristella Casciato, then president of DOCOMOMO International, had introduced this theme in a foreword to a special edition of the NGO's journal focusing on modern architecture in Africa:

> Africans pursue an alternative project of modernity; its trajectories must follow autonomous paths, not implicitly intertwined with our categories of styles or our concepts of rationalism. Any positive change in evaluating the impact of modern heritage on human and social environment in Africa should be tempered with ethics, avoiding the destructive power of other western cultures; the way

European modernism has quite often [been] the protagonist. DOCO-MOMO wishes to suggest a non-linear approach to this issue, open to what is Africa today: tradition, modernization, racial conflicts, indigenous constructions, architectural design, town planning . . . and to give emphasis to African multifaceted phenomena.[192]

Arguably then, Casciato's recognition of a manifestly African project of modernity added a new dimension to criticism of a belief in the modern as a unified epoch and culture.

Casciato's observation of alternative modernities in Africa problematized the modern, just like the later appeal to modernity as a plurality of different times, places, and contexts issued by ICOMOS's *Scientific Committee on Twentieth Century Heritage* did.[193] Her statement marked the emergence of an unstable problem space in which—until today—modernity remains at stake as not only a temporality but also a locality; when Casciato considered modern architecture in Africa to be related as much to tradition as to modernization, at the same time and in the same place, this indicated the beginning of a momentous transformation of the dominant apparatus of modernization—from a powerfully stabilized logos into emergent assemblages of hetero-logoi revolving around contemporary cultural heritage practices. In essence, Casciato's invocation of alternative and specifically African modernities distinguished the issue of modern architectural heritage in Africa as a problematization of a conception of modernity as an ontological entity that ties diverse domains of practice and experience together into a coherent whole. And ultimately it is as such, as a fundamental and actual anthropological problem, that the issue of modern architectural heritage in Africa is worthy of further analysis.

Notes

1. In the original French, *dispositif.*
2. *Foucault quoted in* Rabinow, *Anthropos Today: Reflections on Modern Equipment.* 51.
3. Ibid.
4. Ibid., 53.
5. Pels, Meyer, and Geschiere, *Readings in Modernity in Africa.* 1.
6. Foucault, *The Archeology of Knowledge and the Discourse on Language;* "Anthropological Research on the Contemporary: bios-technika," www.bios-technika.net.
7. "Anthropological Research on the Contemporary: bios-technika".
8. "Wikipedia.org: Paul Rabinow," www.wikipedia.org.
9. "Anthropological Research on the Contemporary: bios-technika".
10. "Anthropological Research on the Contemporary: anthropos-lab," www.anthropos-lab.net.
11. Paul Rabinow and Gaymon Bennett, *Designing Human Practices: An Experiment with Synthetic Biology* (Chicago: Chicago University Press, 2012); "Anthropological Research on the Contemporary: bios-technika"; Rabinow, *Anthropos Today: Reflections on Modern Equipment.*

12. "SPAB: The Manifesto," http://www.spab.org.uk/what-is-spab-/the-manifesto/.
13. Ibid.
14. Quoted in Jukka Jokilehto, "Definition of Cultural Heritage: References to Documents in History, revised 15 January 2005," http://cif.icomos.org/pdf_docs/Documents%20on%20line/Heritage%20definitions.pdf.
15. ICOMOS, "The 1931 Athens Charter for the Restoration of Historic Monuments," http://www.icomos.org/en/charters-and-texts/179-articles-en-francais/ressources/charters-and-standards/167-the-athens-charter-for-the-restoration-of-historic-monument.
16. Ibid.
17. Compare Choay, *The Invention of the Historic Monument*; Francoise Choay and Denise Bratton, *The Rule and the Model: On the Theory of Architecture and Urbanism* (Cambridge, MA: MIT Press, 1997).
18. Quoted in Eric Mumford, *The CIAM Discourse on Urbanism, 1928–1960* (London: MIT Press, 2000).
19. Auke van der Woud, *CIAM: Volkshuisvesting, Stedebouw = CIAM: Housing, Town Planning*, Het Nieuwe Bouwen Internationaal (Delft: Delft University Press, 1983). Although highly praised and enormously formative in knowledgeable circles from the very beginning, the Athens Charter was initially left unpublished. Only in 1942 Le Corbusier, one of CIAM's self-acclaimed protagonists, reappropriated the document and—after having subjected it to heavy editing—issued and distributed it on a broad scale. The product of this, Le Corbusier's pamphlet "The Functional City", became the most famous manifesto of modern urban planning to be read and adopted by a whole generation of 20th-century architects and planners.
20. "The Getty Conservation Institute: 1933 Athens Charter", http://www.getty.edu/conservation/publications_resources/research_resources/charters/charter04.html.
21. Ibid.
22. Ibid.
23. Ibid.
24. Ibid.
25. ICOMOS, "The 1931 Athens Charter for the Restoration of Historic Monuments".
26. "The Getty Conservation Institute: 1933 Athens Charter".
27. Ibid.
28. Ibid.
29. Ibid.
30. Le Corbusier coined this phrase in reference to the modern house, but it also applies to his ideas about the modern city.
31. Holston, *The Modernist City: An Anthropological Critique of Brasilia*. 51.
32. Ibid., 56.
33. Ibid., 56; 60.
34. compare "The Getty Conservation Institute: 1933 Athens Charter".
35. Holston, *The Modernist City: An Anthropological Critique of Brasilia*. 39.
36. Ibid., 57.
37. Ibid., 53–58.
38. Ibid., 57.
39. ICOMOS, "The 1931 Athens Charter for the Restoration of Historic Monuments".
40. Zeynep Celik, *Urban Forms and Colonial Confrontations: Algiers under French Rule* (Berkeley : University of California Press, 1997); Mark Crinson, *Empire Building: Orientalism and Victorian Architecture* (London:

Routledge, 1996); Mark Crinson, *Modern Architecture and the End of Empire* (Aldershot: Ashgate, 2003); Anthony D. King, *Colonial Urban Development: Culture, Social Power and Environment* (London: Routledge & Kegan Paul, 1976);Anthony D. King, *Urbanism, Colonialism, and the World-Economy: Cultural and Spatial Foundations of the World Urban System*, Repr. in pbk. ed. (London: Routledge, 1991);Anthony D. King, *The Bungalow: The Production of a Global Culture* (Oxford: Oxford University Press, 1995).

41. Jane Drew and Maxwell Fry, *Tropical Architecture in the Dry and Humid Zones* (Malabar, FL: Robert E. Krieger Publishing Company, 1982); Crinson, *Modern Architecture and the End of Empire*.

42. Holston, *The Modernist City: An Anthropological Critique of Brasilia.* 77.

43. Ibid., 78; 84.

44. Ibid. 78.

45. Compare for instance: Crinson, *Modern Architecture and the End of Empire.* 136; Jane C. Loeffler, *The Architecture of Diplomacy: Building America's Embassies* (New York: Princeton Architectural Press, 1998); Annabel Jane Wharton, *Building the Cold War: Hilton International Hotels and Modern Architecture* (Chicago, IL: University of Chicago Press, 2001).

46. Compare Choay, *The Invention of the Historic Monument.*

47. ICOMOS, "Venice Charter," http://www.icomos.org/charters/venice_e.pdf.

48. ICOMOS, "History of the Venice Charter," http://www.icomos.org/venice charter2004/history.pdf.

49. Ibid.

50. ICOMOS, "Venice Charter".

51. Ibid.

52. Ibid.

53. Ibid.

54. Ibid.

55. Malraux quoted in Pol-Droit, *Humanity in the Making: The Intellectual History of UNESCO.* 134.

56. UNESCO, "1972 Convention Concerning the Protection of the World Cultural and Natural Heritage".

57. ICOMOS, "Venice Charter".

58. Pol-Droit, *Humanity in the Making: The Intellectual History of UNESCO.* 134.

59. UNESCO, "1972 Convention Concerning the Protection of the World Cultural and Natural Heritage".

60. Lowenthal, *The Heritage Crusade and the Spoils of History.*

61. UNESCO, "1972 Convention Concerning the Protection of the World Cultural and Natural Heritage".

62. Ibid.

63. UNESCO, "World Heritage Committe: Operational Guidelines 2001," http://whc.unesco.org/archive/opguide11-en.pdf.

64. UNESCO, "1972 Convention Concerning the Protection of the World Cultural and Natural Heritage".

65. Ibid.

66. Edward W. Said, *Culture & Imperialism*, Reprinted ed. (London: Vintage, 1994).

67. UNESCO, "1972 Convention Concerning the Protection of the World Cultural and Natural Heritage".

68. ICOMOS, "Venice Charter".

69. UNESCO, "1972 Convention Concerning the Protection of the World Cultural and Natural Heritage".

70. UNESCO, *Report of the Working Group Set up at the 11th Session of the World Heritage Committee, 1988, SC-88/CONF.001/02.* 4.
71. Ibid., 4.
72. Ibid., 6.
73. Ibid., 14.
74. Ibid., 9.
75. Ibid., 5.
76. Ibid., 5.
77. Also see Pels, Meyer, and Geschiere, *Readings in Modernity in Africa.* 3.
78. Holston, *The Modernist City: An Anthropological Critique of Brasilia.* 84.
79. Ibid., 201.
80. Kubitschek, on 15.6.1960 two months after *the city's* inauguration. Quoted by El-Dahdah in *DOCOMOMO Journal on Brasilia,* 43–2010/2.
81. UNESCO, "World Heritage List Entry: Brasilia," http://whc.unesco.org/en/list/445.
82. Ibid.
83. Ibid.
84. ICOMOS, "World Heritage List, Advisory Body Evaluation No. 445," http://whc.unesco.org/archive/advisory_body_evaluation/445.pdf.
85. Ibid.
86. Ibid.
87. Ibid.
88. Ibid.
89. Lowenthal, *The Heritage Crusade and the Spoils of History.*
90. Ibid.
91. UNESCO, *Report of the Working Group Set up at the 11th Session of the World Heritage Committee, 1988, SC-88/CONF.001/02.* 7.
92. UNESCO, "Global Strategy for a Representative and Balance World Heritage List".
93. "International Working-Party for Documentation and Restauration of Early Modern Architecture: First Newsletter," (1989).
94. DOCOMOMO ISC/Registers, "The Modern Movement and the World Heritage List: Advisory Report to ICOMOS," *DOCOMOMO Journal* 18 (1998). 47.
95. Ibid.
96. Ibid.
97. Ibid., 42.
98. Ibid.
99. Ibid., 48.
100. "International Working-Party for Documentation and Restauration of Early Modern Architecture: First Newsletter."
101. UNESCO, "1972 Convention Concerning the Protection of the World Cultural and Natural Heritage".
102. First published in 1997, ISC/Registers, "The Modern Movement and the World Heritage List: Advisory Report to ICOMOS." 41.
103. UNESCO, "Expert Meeting on the "Global Strategy" and thematic studies for a representative World Heritage List," http://whc.unesco.org/archive/global94.htm#debut
104. Ibid.
105. Ibid.
106. ISC/Registers, "The Modern Movement and the World Heritage List: Advisory Report to ICOMOS." 42.
107. Ibid., 48.
108. Ibid.

109. Ibid., 50.
110. Ibid.
111. Ibid., 41.
112. Ibid.
113. Ibid., 49; also compare Marieke C. Kuipers, "Authenticiteit versus attrappenkult?," in *Reco.Mo.Mo: Hoe Echt Is Namaak, Hoe Dierbaar Het Origineel?* ed. Sara Stroux, et al. (Delft: DOCOMOMO, 2011).
114. ISC/Registers, "The Modern Movement and the World Heritage List: Advisory Report to ICOMOS." 50.
115. Ibid.
116. Ibid.
117. Ibid.
118. Ibid., 48.
119. Ibid., 42.
120. Ron van Oers, ed. *World Heritage Papers 5: Identification and Documentation of Modern Heritage* (Paris: UNESCO). 8.
121. UNESCO, "World Heritage: Challenges for the Millennium." http://whc. unesco.org/documents/publi_millennium_en.pdf. 108.
122. van Oers, *World Heritage Papers 5: Identification and Documentation of Modern Heritage.* 8.
123. Paz, *Children of the Mire: Modern Poetry from Romanticism to the Avant-Garde.*
124. Frampton, *Modern Architecture: A Critical History.* 230; Peter Blake, *Form follows Fiasco: Why Modern Architecture Hasn't Worked*, Atlantic Monthly Press book (Boston: Atlantic Monthly Press, 1977).
125. Anthony D. King, *Spaces of Global Cultures: Architecture, Urbanism, Identity* (London: Routledge, 2004). 74.
126. Holston, *The Modernist City: An Anthropological Critique of Brasilia.*
127. Ibid., 48.
128. UNESCO, "Expert Meeting on the 'Global Strategy' and thematic studies for a representative World Heritage List".
129. Hubert-Jan Henket and Hilde Heynen, *Back from Utopia: The Challenge of the Modern Movement* (Rotterdam: 010 Publishers, 2002); Panayotis Tournikiotis, *The Historiography of Modern Architecture* (Cambridge: MIT Press, 1999), 5–8;Panayotis Tournikiotis, "Modernism and the Issue of Otherness," *DOCOMOMO Journal* 36, no. Other Modernisms: A Selection from the DOCOMOMO Registers (2007).
130. ICOMOS, "Experts Meeting Report: Developing an Historic Thematic Framework to Assess the Significance of Twentieth Century Cultural Heritage: An Initiative of the ICOMOS International Scientific Committee on Twentieth Century Cultural Heritage," http://www.getty.edu/conservation/ publications_resources/pdf_publications/pdf/mod_arch_bib_aug11.pdf. 6.
131. ISC/Registers, "The Modern Movement and the World Heritage List: Advisory Report to ICOMOS." 42.
132. van Oers, *World Heritage Papers 5: Identification and Documentation of Modern Heritage.* 8.
133. UNESCO, "Expert Meeting on the "Global Strategy" and thematic studies for a representative World Heritage List".
134. van Oers, *World Heritage Papers 5: Identification and Documentation of Modern Heritage.* 11.
135. UNESCO, "Expert Meeting on the "Global Strategy" and thematic studies for a representative World Heritage List". 2.
136. Ibid.
137. Ibid.

138. Ibid.
139. UNESCO, "Expert Meeting on the "Global Strategy" and thematic studies for a representative World Heritage List".
140. Pels, Meyer, and Geschiere, *Readings in Modernity in Africa*. 3.
141. Helga Nowotny, *Insatiable Curiosity: Innovation in a Fragile Culture* (Boston: MIT Press, 2010).
142. Pol-Droit, *Humanity in the Making: The Intellectual History of UNESCO*. 170.
143. Ibid., 172.
144. Wiktor Stoczkowski, "Claude Lévi-Strauss and UNESCO," *UNESCO Courier*, 2008. 7–8.
145. Pol-Droit, *Humanity in the Making: The Intellectual History of UNESCO*. 170.
146. Ibid.
147. Ibid., 169.
148. Ibid., 176.
149. Ibid.
150. Ibid.
151. UNESCO, "Universal Declaration on Cultural Diversity," http://unesdoc.unesco.org/images/0012/001246/124687e.pdf#page=67.
152. Jokilehto, *The World Heritage List: Filling the Gaps—An Action Plan for the Future*. 2.
153. Ibid., 10.
154. Ibid., 8.
155. Ibid., 3.
156. Ibid., 8.
157. Ibid.
158. Ibid., 23.
159. Ibid., 10.
160. Ibid., 23.
161. Ibid.
162. Ibid.
163. Ibid., 3.
164. Ibid., 42.
165. Ibid.
166. Ibid., 5.
167. Pol-Droit, *Humanity in the Making: The Intellectual History of UNESCO*. 170.
168. Jokilehto, *The World Heritage List: Filling the Gaps—An Action Plan for the Future*. 8.
169. Ron van Oers, *Meeting on Modern Heritage for Africa: Asmara, Eritrea, 4–7 March 2004* (Paris: UNESCO, 2004). 1.
170. Ibid., 3.
171. Ibid.
172. Ibid.
173. Ibid.
174. Ibid.
175. ICOMOS, "Heritage at Risk 2001–2002: Shared Colonial Heritage," http://www.international.icomos.org/risk/2001/colonial2001.htm.
176. Ibid.
177. van Oers, *Meeting on Modern Heritage for Africa: Asmara, Eritrea, 4–7 March 2004*. 3.
178. Ibid.
179. Ibid.

180. Ibid., 4.
181. Pol-Droit, *Humanity in the Making: The Intellectual History of UNESCO.* 169.
182. ISC/Registers, "The Modern Movement and the World Heritage List: Advisory Report to ICOMOS."42.
183. van Oers, *Meeting on Modern Heritage for Africa: Asmara, Eritrea, 4–7 March 2004.*
184. ICOMOS, "Experts Meeting Report: Developing an Historic Thematic Framework to Assess the Significance of Twentieth Century Cultural Heritage: An Initiative of the ICOMOS International Scientific Committee on Twentieth Century Cultural Heritage." 6.
185. Ibid., 1.
186. Ibid., 6.
187. Ibid., 3.
188. Ibid., 6.
189. Ibid.
190. Ibid., 3.
191. van Oers, *World Heritage Papers 5: Identification and Documentation of Modern Heritage.* 10.
192. Maristella Casciato, "Editorial: Modern Architecture in Africa," *DOCOMOMO Journal Special Edition* (2005). 1.
193. Paul Rabinow, *Reflections on Fieldwork in Morocco (30th Anniversary Edition)* (Berkeley: University of Berkeley Press, 2007). xxii.

4 Analysis
Global Heritage Assemblages and Modern Architecture in Africa

The pathway presented earlier illustrates how appeals to modern heritage in Africa now amount to a significant anthropological problem. Starting from a diagnosis of how the issue of modern architectural heritage originally emerged as a problematized domain in the middle of the 19th century, I went on to show how, throughout the 20th century, modern architecture and heritage preservation simultaneously formed integral parts of a dominant apparatus of modernization until, by the beginning of the 21st century, the institutionalization of modern architectural heritage on the African continent came to reproblematize progressive modernity both as an epoch and as a culture within this apparatus. The actual urgency of this particular problematization of the modern becomes clearer reflecting back on the construction, deconstruction and subsequent reconstruction of the Crystal Palace as a constitutive event.

The Crystal Palace was emblematic of an initial understanding of modern progress as singular and epochal. Utilized as an exhibition hall for the first World's Fair in 1851, the structure represented the belief that cultural change was inevitably unidirectional and that progress would eventually do away with all 'backward' tradition and lead to the development of a universal modern civilization. The preservation of the Crystal Palace as modern architectural heritage, however, signified an immediate need to remember such utopias of progress and development as the site and source of cultural disquiet.[1] In fact, the construction, deconstruction and reconstruction of the Crystal Palace pointed to the emergence of a crisis of diachronicity at the turn of the 19th century: the building's preservation, which went against its planned transitoriness, as part of a paradoxical 'tradition of the new' indicated that tradition and modernity were no longer so opposed, but rather paired. Through the Crystal Palace, the issue of modern architectural heritage became simultaneously articulated as problem and solution, thus emerging as a veritable problematization of modernity.[2]

At first sight, the most recent manifestation of this problematization of progressive modernity in terms of a crisis of diachronicity appears to be the invocation of an African modern heritage. When UNESCO shifted away from a singular conception of modernity as a living culture toward a more plural understanding of the modern which explicitly included traditional living cultures in Africa as alternative modernities, it still saw this new approach rooted in what it referred to as an "opposition between elements of a different kind—modernity and tradition".[3] On closer inspection, however, what the institutionalization of modern architectural heritage on the African continent puts at stake is not so much the opposition between modernity and tradition (nor therefore a residual crisis of diachronicity) but, instead, what I would like to call an emergent crisis of coevalness: a crisis that problematizes the *pairing* of modernity and tradition rather than their opposition and that directly results from changes in the dominant conceptions of 'the cultural'.

My pathway described how the issue of modern architectural heritage on the African continent led to a breakdown of faith in progressive modernity as a singular ontological entity or culture. I have shown how, at the turn of the 20th century, the need to reckon with cultural diversity under conditions of globalization posed a problem for heritage practices that had come to function within a dominant apparatus of modernization. One consequence was the formulation of a plural conception of modernity as different modern cultures. When approaches to the preservation of modern heritage gradually diverged from a reliance on the idea of 'modernity-as-culture' toward ideas of 'alternative-cultural-modernities', however, this gave rise to a problematic assemblage of heterologoi concerning conceptions of culture and cultural diversity. It is in this context that the issue of African modern heritage denotes a crisis of coevalness. Today, the notion of alternative modernities—existing at the same time and in the same place—produces a new sense of cultural disquiet: it assembles different stylized configurations of the modern together in a contingent problem space.

This problem space around classifications, practices and things modern is the object of my analysis here. If one no longer assumes that the modern is dominant and that the traditional is somehow residual—which is exactly what my pathway indicates is presently happening in the realm of cultural heritage practices—then the question of how these elements (traditional and modern, old and new) simultaneously take shape and work together, either well or poorly, becomes an important site of inquiry.[4] It is this site of inquiry, constituted by different heterodoxies and going against received understandings of the modern, that I aim to explore further.

A Crisis of Coevalness

The relevant site of inquiry for my analysis of the emergence of modern architectural heritage on the African continent is characterized by a crisis of coevalness, a situation Paul Rabinow captures very well with his conception of 'the contemporary'. In his *Marking Time: On the Anthropology of the Contemporary*, he first explains this by citing the *Oxford English Dictionary*, according to which the ordinary meaning of the word is "existing or occurring at, or dating from the same period of time as something or somebody else". The second meaning of the word, however, is "distinctively modern in style". The difference between the two is that the first does not carry a historical connotation, only a temporal one, whereas the second meaning does carry a historical connotation. Rabinow finds this curious because it can be used to both equate the contemporary with, and differentiate it from the modern.[5] It is against this backdrop that Rabinow sketches the contemporary as an important site of inquiry predicated on a crisis of coevalness. His definition of the contemporary is "the moving ratio of modernity, moving through the recent past and the near future in a (non-linear) space that gauges modernity as an ethos already becoming historical".[6]

It follows that Rabinow's contemporary is an experimental and experiential site in the present where one can observe "the emergence of forms within which old and new elements take on meanings and functions".[7] Essentially, Rabinow conceives of the contemporary as a state of emergence in which "multiple elements combine to produce an assemblage whose significance cannot be reduced to prior elements and relations".[8] In this respect, the contemporary stands in an important opposition to the modern:

> [It] is not especially concerned with 'the new' or with distinguishing itself from tradition. Rather, its practitioners draw attention to the distinction modern/contemporary as the clustered elements and configurations of the modern are observed in the process of declusterings and reconfigurations.[9]

Thus, Rabinow defines the contemporary as grounded in a certain crisis of coevalness. According to him, the "contemporary" indicates "a mode of historicity whose scale is relatively modest and whose scope is relatively short in range", and he claims that "within that mode and observed from the actual, many types of objects are made available for analysis".[10]

However, when Rabinow imagines the contemporary as "an actual object domain in the present whose recent past, near future, and emergent forms can be observed",[11] he does not only forge it as a relevant *site* of inquiry. Rather, in his line of reasoning the contemporary also prescribes a distinct *mode* of inquiry. Actually, Rabinow argues that the contemporary not only forces its practitioners, but also their observers to reckon with emergent phenomena that can only be partially explained or comprehended by previous practices and/or modes of analysis.[12] According to Rabinow, practitioners and observers of the contemporary *alike* need to ask, "[W]hat difference does today make with respect to yesterday—and to tomorrow?"[13]

So far, my pathway has obviously only asked this question of the emergent practices that inform the institutionalization of modern architectural heritage on the African continent. In Rabinow's definition, these heritage practices are contemporary because their emergence illustrates how the previously prevalent faith and belief in progressive modernity as an epoch and as a culture are currently being challenged. That is, if the notion of modern heritage reinterprets modernity as a hybrid temporality within which old and new elements can coexist in multiple variations, then this points to the contingencies as well as the inconsistencies inherent to received understandings of the modern.[14] The issue of modern heritage in Africa thus amounts to a distinctly contemporary anthropological problem.

When the emergence of an African modern heritage questions modernity as a temporality and as a locality, however, this not only complicates cultural heritage practices. In terms of their assemblage as hetero-logoi of the modern, those practices also pose a real problem for their observers and analysts, including myself. In fact, Rabinow's question—what difference does today make with respect to yesterday and to tomorrow?[15]—demands that any observer of the contemporary move beyond the dominant logos of the modern as an object of study. Observers of the contemporary who accept Rabinow's imperative thus need to develop appropriate means of analyzing how various logoi are currently assembled into contingent forms.[16]

In my particular case, an appropriate mode of inquiry into current heritage practices must be able to account for the institutionalization of modern architectural heritage on the African continent as a contemporary anthropological problem. But for me as an incipient *anthropologist* of the contemporary, the notion of an African modern heritage not only poses an urgent anthropological problem because it assembles specific heritage practices into hetero-logoi of modernity. I also find myself amidst anthropology's own problems with the modern—a situation that considerably complicates my task of finding a suitable mode of analysis.

Similar to cultural heritage practices, the discipline of anthropology, founded in the 19th century, was based on a singular and epochal concept of culture defined as "either the unified way of life of a people or the dominant sensibility of its elite, or its oppressed".[17] Long into the 20th century, anthropologists chose to research 'backward' or 'primitive' culture, which they invariably found far away and went on to describe as a bounded whole. As Johannes Fabian reveals in his classic *Time and the Other: How Anthropology Makes its Object*, from the perspective of the modern anthropologist of the 19th and early to mid-20th centuries, who more or less took for granted the inevitability of modern progress toward a universal civilization, the cultural "other" had to be constructed "out of time" and "out of place".[18]

Fabian's argument begins with the claim that, in the 19th century, the discipline of anthropology "sanctioned an ideological process by which relations between the West and its Other, between anthropology and its object, were conceived not only as difference, but as *distance* in space and time".[19] He illustrates how 20th-century anthropology continued to deny its object of study coevalness, despite a gradual but effective institutionalization of ethnographic fieldwork carried out in direct personal encounter with the other. In fact, Fabian contends that anthropology— once established within a powerful apparatus of modernization— *strategically* denied coevalness to the people, practices and things it studied, even though anthropologists exclusively came to rely on the method of fieldwork for their legitimacy and thus literally met their objects of study in the here and now.[20]

According to Fabian, anthropology's strategy of denial was twofold: On one hand, anthropologists circumvented the question of coevalness through cultural relativity, and on the other hand, they preempted that question with the help of a radical taxonomic approach.[21] Cultural relativism allowed anthropologists to encapsulate time as the other's time, that is, epochally different from but likely aspiring to the anthropologists' own, more modern time. Taxonomic approaches enabled anthropologists to reject any notion of a shared time in favor of a "glorification" of spatial distribution as the marker of an orderly differentiation between "cultural isolates".[22] In the end, Fabian asserts that anthropology's strategic denial of coevalness is expressive of how, by and large, a myth of modernization established a total grip on the discipline.[23]

It was not until the late 20th century that anthropologists began to break with the concept of progressive modernity as their disciplinary legacy, at which point Fabian's critique took center stage. At the beginning of the 21st century, however, anthropology's struggle with coevalness finally moved the discipline away from its traditional emphasis on the far away and timeless into new terrains.[24] For example, while anthropology today acknowledges its tradition of studying 'local culture' and dealing ethnographically with problems of an entirely different level of scale and abstraction than the global, critical anthropologists now also innovatively work on phenomena such as globalization, which they describe as characteristic of, and giving shape to, the here and now.[25] But, whereas anthropology tries to do away with the idea of a bounded culture that is singular and epochal, the discipline remains interested in the cultural, specifically in cultural difference and diversity.[26] Arguably then, Fabian's question of coevalness lingers as one of anthropology's most fundamental problems. Though many anthropologists no longer attribute analytic acuity to the concept of modernity-as-culture, this leaves open the question of how best to describe the cultural in time and space today; certainly when, as Fabian has put it, mere affirmations of coevalness will not compensate for long-standing and systematic denials of coevalness.[27]

With regards to the temporal as well as the spatial dimensions and dynamics of the cultural, anthropologists currently find themselves in critical dialogue with other social sciences. While anthropology is today fueled by multiple intellectual agendas, there is no doubt that it can be situated in a transdisciplinary arena that hosts a variety of attempts to substitute received conceptions of modernity-as-culture with plural conceptions of the modern in terms of cultural diversity, such as globalization and alternative modernities.[28] Nevertheless, as a consequence of this late break with teleological theories of modernization and because suggestions for alternatives abound, anthropology presently finds itself in a real crisis of coevalness, quite similar to the one informing the issue of modern architectural heritage; by now, the discipline of anthropology itself has effectively become part and parcel of a problematic assemblage of hetero-logoi of the modern.

Site of Inquiry/Mode of Inquiry

At this point, it is necessary to refer back to Paul Rabinow's notion of the contemporary. Conceived as an assemblage of hetero-logoi of the modern, the contemporary explains how the issue of modern architectural heritage on the African continent as an actual and emergent anthropological problem is *con*temporary with a comparable anthropological problem resultant from anthropology's struggle with its very own 'modern heritage'. Clearly both problems constitute elements of a larger problematization of progressive modernity. And this is how—and why—their simultaneous emergence and assemblage into contingent forms really circumscribes their urgency, turning it into a joint conjecture of the contemporary that is destabilizing and gradually transforming a dominant apparatus of modernization.[29]

For my inquiry into cultural heritage practices under current conditions of globalization, this conflation of two anthropological problems poses intricate questions of where and how best to observe and analyze their subsidiary couplings.[30] Since I want to contribute to an anthropology of the contemporary, it is my task with this study to engage in work that helps develop modes of inquiry into underdetermined, emergent and discordant human relations today.[31] To paraphrase Rabinow, I need to develop and/or apply methods, practices and forms of narration coherent and cooperable with understandings of the different modes currently taken by anthropos as a figure and an assemblage.[32] This is why I have decided to research specific global heritage assemblages and their relations to modern architecture and urban planning in Africa, on and within which I have conducted multisited anthropological fieldwork. However, before I elaborate my decisions regarding the form of inquiry most suitable for achieving my aims with this book, let me first justify my broader analytical focus on Africa and then my choice of global heritage assemblages as the specific empirical points of reference for my analysis.

In this book, I look at Africa as a category through which both cultural heritage practices and the discipline of anthropology are meaningfully structured. My pathway already concluded with the emergence of modern architectural heritage in Africa as a contemporary anthropological problem. Yet not only heritage practices have always been "haunted in subtle and not so subtle ways by the imagined teleologies of the modern" and their relations to Africa, the discipline of anthropology is also historically implicated in constructions of Africa as a temporally and spatially distant 'place in the world'.[33]

Indeed, as James Ferguson has recently stated in his *Global Shadows: Africa in the Neoliberal World Order*—and he really deserves to be quoted extensively:

> Africa has always seemed to come to the question of modernity from without. Generations of Western scholars have regarded Africa as either beyond the pale of modernity (the savage heart of darkness that lurks beyond the edges of the civilized world) or before it (the 'primitive', 'traditional' place that is always not yet in the time of the up-to date present). Today, scholars who are critical of evolutionist timelines and static essentialisms of older modernization paradigms struggle to redescribe Africa as within the modern and to sever its automatic connection with the West, they prefer to locate contemporary African social realities within a broader, pluralized idea of the modern as constituting an 'alternative' modernity.[34]

Nevertheless, Ferguson questions whether this idea of alternative cultural-modernities is a useful critique of anthropology's modernization myth and its effects on the African continent.

Certainly, Ferguson notes that "anthropologists today are eager to say how modern Africa is", but he continues by saying,

> Many ordinary Africans might scratch their head at such a claim. As they examine the decaying infrastructure, non-functioning institutions and horrific poverty that surround them, they may be more likely to find their situation deplorably *non*-modern, and to say: [. . .] 'This place is not up to date!' Of course the two claims have different referents. The anthropologists refer to cultural practices and their previously unappreciated historicity; hence Africa is modern, not 'traditional'. But Africans who lament that their life circumstances are not modern enough are not talking about cultural practices. They are speaking instead about what they view as shamefully inadequate socioeconomic conditions and their low global rank in relation to other places. These questions of status and standard of living were

squarely avoided by the development timeline narratives, if only in the form of a promise; 'If you are dissatisfied with your conditions, just wait; your society is moving forward and moving upward'. Today, they are more often evaded—by culturally minded anthropology and neoliberal economics alike.[35]

Ultimately then, Ferguson believes that it is necessary to ask: Why are anthropologists so out of step with the locals on the meaning of modernity? Or, to frame the question differently: What actually *happens* if the modernization myth is "turned upside down, shaken and shattered?"[36]

Of course, Ferguson grants that when teleological theories of modernization were abandoned, there was apt to be disillusionment with the "taken-for-granted faith" in modern development as a "universal prescription" for poverty and inequality on the African continent.[37] However, he notes,

> Once modernity ceases to be understood as telos, the question of rank is de-developmentalized and the stark status differentiations of the global social system sit raw and naked, no longer softened by the promises of the 'not yet'. The developmentalist reassurance that history would, by its nature, transform status and that Third World people needed only to wait and to have patience and their turn would come ceases to convince.[38]

Consequently, according to Ferguson, it does not work to simply say that the end of development has come, as that would just continue the teleology. For him, it is one thing to acknowledge the "modern metanarrative" of development as "a dubious theoretical model" but quite another to recognize it as the outcome of ongoing practices that yield real inequalities and human suffering.[39]

Ferguson asserts that if the belief in progressive modernity is waning, it needs to be asked what can substitute for it and render legible the stark economic, political and social differences that are perhaps most visible in Africa today. He too refers back to Fabian's understanding of cultural differences as coeval—no longer thought of as backward versus developed/traditional versus modern—emphasizing that "the telos is gone".[40] Nonetheless, the very acknowledgment of modernity as something plural and of history as contingent, thereby fueling popular notions of 'alternative-cultural-modernities', stems directly from such an understanding. Ferguson convincingly argues that insofar as these notions imply a detemporalization of global inequalities and status, they are inadequate accounts of present-day cultural dynamics.

Indeed, in his *Expectations of Modernity: Myth and Meaning of Urban Life on the Zambian Copperbelt*, Ferguson shows how, in contrast to the belief in progressive change over time, nonprogressive temporalizations (such as notions of degeneration) have come to dominate the stories told by his Zambian interlocutors. Adding to such divergent temporal ways of establishing meaning and differentiating between social relations, Ferguson notes a new reliance on spatial mobility through migration. For example, the question his contacts in Zambia invariably seem to ask is, "How is one to escape the low global status of being 'a poor African'?"[41] Hence, Ferguson's account reveals how on the African continent the 'new world order' of relations between history and hierarchy is often reconfigured from progress to decline, exclusion and abjection.[42] He maintains that, as a result, in order to come to terms with the modernization myth falling apart, instead of telling a "happy story about plurality and non-ranked cultural difference", anthropologists need "to force the question of Africa's political economic crisis to the center of the contemporary discussion of modernity".[43]

This is exactly what I set out to do in this book. With James Ferguson I propose to study Africa as a category through which the world is structured, that is, as a category that

> (like all categories) is historically and socially constructed (indeed, in some sense arbitrary), but also as a category that is 'real', that is imposed with force, that has mandatory quality; a category within which, and according to which, people must live.[44]

In this sense, and because Africa can no longer be taken as a radical other for anthropology's own constructions of modern progress and development, I take it to be a particularly well-suited place in the world for my anthropological inquiry into an emergent problematization of modernity. My analytical focus on global heritage assemblages around modern heritage in Africa allows me to describe the contemporary as a site as well as a mode of inquiry.[45]

However, even though my genealogies of cultural heritage practices and the discipline of anthropology in their respective relations to Africa so far have met an initial challenge in demarcating a specific relational field from an underdetermined problem space around conceptions of modernity as a temporality and as a locality, it remains a challenge to select specific objects of study that can account for particular changes within this problem space today.[46] In other words, to describe the actual shaping of the contemporary as a "(re)-assemblage of old and new elements and their interactions and interfaces",[47] I must analyze concrete examples of hetero-logoi of the modern and their present global forms.

This is why I have chosen to focus on global heritage assemblages around instances of modern architecture in Africa. My argument so far has been that the institutionalization of modern architectural heritage on the African continent indicates an emergent, considerably unstable problem space around hetero-logoi of the modern. As a consequence, I have to concentrate my further analysis on those nascent organizational forms that signal the insufficiency and discord of a previous apparatus of modernization and that attempt to identify and associate diverse elements in response to specific events and in relation to emergent problems. It will be necessary for me to study global heritage assemblages as sites for the formation and reformation of problematizations of modernity.[48]

As previously mentioned, I agree with Aihwa Ong and Stephen Collier that global heritage assemblages are "domains in which the forms and values of individual and collective existence are problematized or at stake, in the sense that they are subject to technological, political and ethical reflection and intervention".[49] Here, I take as 'the political' forms and scopes of jurido-legal institutions to resolve problems of collective life, as 'the technological' means for achieving organizational or administrative ends or goals, and as 'the ethical' questions of value and morality and of how one should live—this latter category is obviously wrapped up with political and technological problems.[50] In order to find out more about how the historically forged domains of the modern change when brought into the encompassing frame of African modern heritage, I circumscribe as exemplary objects of study for detailed analysis in Part II of this book three specific global heritage assemblages that revolve around instances of modern architecture and urban planning in Africa and that should allow me to investigate how politics, technologies and ethics change when they can no longer exclusively rely on a dominant apparatus of modernization.[51]

I have chosen to observe heritage practices networked on a scale that goes beyond the nation-state, thus involving new transnational entities such as intergovernmental and nongovernmental organizations, as well as corporate and private actors. My first example concerns Asmara, the capital of Eritrea, situated on the horn of Africa. Its modern architecture and urban planning were largely built under the Italian colonial regime in the early 20th century. Today, the preservation of Asmara's so-called historic perimeter is the center of attention of the Eritrean government, which instrumentalizes it in its pursuit of violent nationalism as well as its radical policy of self-reliance. Transnational organizations such as the World Bank and the European Union delegation also argue for a valorization of the city's modern heritage, mainly for the purposes of what the World Bank calls postconflict resolution, nation building, economic development, and poverty reduction.[52] This forces me to ask how a global heritage assemblage around Asmara's urban built environment asserts politics of sovereignty and security as problematic modern practices.

My second example is the rediscovery, translocation, commoditization and display of three so-called *Maisons Tropicales*. These Maisons Tropicales are prototypes of prefabricated modern architecture conceived in the mid-20th century for use in the former French colonies of West Africa by the industrial designer Jean Prouvé. In 2001, the houses were removed from their original sites in Brazzaville, the capital of the Republic of the Congo, and Niamey, the capital of Niger. Subsequently the prototypes were brought to Europe for restoration—notably going against requests from the French Ministry of Culture and the UNESCO World Heritage Center to preserve them *in situ*. Since 2005, one of the Maisons Tropicales is on permanent loan to the Centre Pompidou in Paris. Moreover, Christie's New York sold a second Maison to a private buyer for several million US dollars in 2007. The third Maison Tropicale remains in the collection of a French art gallery. All this brings me to ask how a global heritage assemblage around the Maisons Tropicales contests technologies of authenticity and value that are problematizing of things modern.

My third and last example deals with the non-governmental organization ArchiAfrika. In 2001, a group of five Dutch architects founded ArchiAfrika as a Dutch charitable organization with the aim "to put (modern) African architectural culture on the world map".[53] Originally inspired by the work of the architect Anthony B. Almeida, who built for the colonial regime of the British East Africa Protectorate, as well as for the subsequent postcolonial national governments of Tanganyika and Tanzania, ArchiAfrika organized a student workshop and academic conference under the title *Modern Architecture in East Africa around Independence*, which took place in Dar es Salaam in 2005. During this event, the NGO's interest in the colonial and postcolonial legacy of Almeida's oeuvre led participants to a discussion about assumptions of a distinctly East African identity of modern architecture, as well as about the notion of modern architectural heritage in Africa. For ArchiAfrika, this debate resulted in considerable normative uncertainty concerning its nascent aims and structure, which ultimately led to the NGO's reorganization and its engagement in a social experiment with contemporary norms and forms of collaboration in the production of scientific knowledge and expertise. Correspondingly, my interest is in how a global heritage assemblage around the notion of a distinctly East African modern architecture negotiates ethics of legitimacy and responsibility regarding problematic classifications of the modern.

Form of Inquiry

As my respective attention to politics of sovereignty and security, technologies of authenticity and value, and ethics of legitimacy and responsibility indicates, my choice of exemplary global heritage assemblages has followed Paul Rabinow's imperative that an anthropology of the contemporary has to take up

> recent changes in the logoi of life, labor, and language not as indicating an epochal shift with a totalizing coherence [. . .] but, rather, as fragmented and sectorial changes that pose problems, both

in-and-of-themselves as well as for attempts to make sense of what form(s) anthropos is currently being given.[54]

In order to capture such relevant sectorial changes, to describe their fragmented character and to distinguish the resultant problems, I have attempted to gear my anthropological inquiry to renewed problematizations of practices, classifications and things modern as they emerge in specific global heritage assemblages today.

A major difficulty in my research of global heritage assemblages was to find a suitable form of anthropological inquiry that would allow me to observe how particular networks of heritage practices shape such renewed problematizations of modernity in and as the contemporary. This was primarily difficult because an appropriate form of inquiry had to acknowledge that with my disciplinary baggage as an anthropologist, I am myself an integral part of those very problematizations. To speak in Rabinow's terms, I had to ask myself, "What is distinctly anthropological when anthropologists no longer study ethnos, culture, or society, when what is being studied instead are contemporary events and processes?"[55]

Of course, this question is not new at all. It has been asked many times, at least since anthropology's so-called reflexive turn in the 1980s.[56] Again, Johannes Fabian's *Time and the Other* was one of the publications that initiated profound disciplinary self-reflection. In 1983, Fabian contended that anthropology suffered from a "concrete practical contradiction" between coeval research and 'allochronic' interpretations of culture:[57]

> In order to claim that primitive societies (or whatever replaces them now as the object of anthropology) are the reality and our conceptualizations the theory, one must keep anthropology standing on its head. If we can show that our theories of their societies are *our praxis*—the way in which we produce and reproduce knowledge of the Other for our societies—we may (paraphrasing Marx and Hegel) put anthropology back on its feet.[58]

At the time, Fabian concluded that a critical review of the practice of ethnographic fieldwork, which had become a defining methodological feature of his discipline, constituted "the crux of anthropology, the crossroads, as it were, from which critique must take off and to which it must return".[59] And take off it did.

Another major critique of ethnographic fieldwork as one of the foundations of anthropology was *Writing Culture: The Poetics and Politics of Ethnography*, edited by James Clifford and George E. Marcus and first published in 1984. According to Marcus—speaking in 2008—*Writing Culture* had two important effects:

> To make explicit the inadequacy of standard forms of ethnographic writing in dealing with the realities of fieldwork and, therefore, to

encourage critique of the actual process of research itself, of field-work. The former effect occurred, in excess, from the 1980s on; the latter has hardly occurred at all. But the process of research is now very much in question because of the ways the world has changed and how these changes press on the conditions for conceptualizing and doing fieldwork.[60]

Indeed, to cite another contribution to anthropology's reflexive turn—this time from the late 1990s—Akhil Gupta and James Ferguson's edited volume *Anthropological Locations: Boundaries and Grounds of a Field Science*: "The practice of fieldwork and its associated genre, ethnography, has perhaps never been as central to the discipline of anthropology as it is today, in terms of both intellectual principles and professional practices."[61]

In 1997, Gupta and Ferguson claimed that ethnographic fieldwork served as "the single most important factor determining whether a piece of research will be accepted as (that magical word) 'anthropological'."[62] Experience in the field—intensive participant observation of a long duration and away from home—seemed to be quintessential for aspiring anthropologists to prove their merits. Since the 1980s, however, confusion abounds as to what constitutes the field of anthropology. If a consensus emerged within the discipline that the world is not made up of discrete, originally separate cultures to be found in exotic locations far away from the anthropologist's everyday place of residence and work, and thus requiring long-distance traveling to do fieldwork there, where *is* the field of anthropology? And how could and should one access it to do what precisely?

There is widespread agreement today that the field is not simply out there for anthropologists to find and to immerse themselves in. Rather, as Gupta and Ferguson put it, "the field is a clearing whose deceptive transparency obscures the complex processes that go into constructing it".[63] Vered Amit, editor of the book *Constructing the Field: Ethnographic Fieldwork in the Contemporary World*, draws on Gupta and Ferguson when she maintains in 2000:

> The notion of immersion implies that the 'field' which ethnographers enter exists as an independently bounded set of relationships and activities which is autonomous of the fieldwork through which it is discovered. Yet in a world of infinite interconnections and overlapping contexts, the ethnographic field cannot simply exist, awaiting discovery. It has to be laboriously constructed, prised apart from all the other possibilities for contextualization to which its constituent relationships and connections could also be referred. This process of construction is inescapably shaped by the conceptual, professional, financial and relational opportunities and resources accessible to the ethnographer.[64]

To come back to Gupta and Ferguson, "if fieldwork thus helps define anthropology as a discipline in both senses of the word, constructing a space of possibilities while at the same time drawing the lines that confine that space", it needs to be asked how one can—given one's position as an anthropologist within the academy—construct and work the field, today.[65]

I want to stress that though there obviously are many possible potentially satisfying answers to these questions, I offer as one conceivable solution to the problem of constructing and working the field of anthropology today my account of the institutionalization of modern architectural heritage on the African continent as an urgent anthropological problem.[66] My diagnostic and genealogical work on events and problematizations functions as an orientation of my anthropological inquiry into the contemporary, which in turn allows me to construct an experiential field of experimentation in the form of global heritage assemblages. Significantly then, I conceive of global heritage assemblages as problematizations of modernity that exist both as empirical points of reference in the field of cultural heritage practices *and* as field sites for the reconstruction of anthropological research practices.

In this respect, I stay close to Foucault's conception of a problematization as "simultaneously the object, the site and ultimately the substance, of thinking".[67] As Paul Rabinow explains Foucault's line of reasoning,

> [i]n contrast to earlier positions that he held, Foucault's thinker is by definition neither entirely outside of the situation in question nor entirely enmeshed within it without recourse or options. The defining trait of problematization does not turn on the coupling of opposites (outside or inside, free or constrained) but rather on the type of relationship forged between observer and problematized situation. The specificity of that relationship entails taking up the situation simultaneously as problematic and as something about which one is required to think.[68]

Accordingly, my diagnosis of the emergence of modern architectural heritage as a problematization of the modern, together with my pathway toward the institutionalization of an African modern heritage as a distinctly contemporary anthropological problem circumscribe a situation that calls for a new form of inquiry that would allow me to engage in new kinds of relations with the objects of my research.

Toward a New Form of Inquiry

Indeed, Rabinow suggests that such a new form of inquiry is a hard requirement for an anthropology of the contemporary. For him, an anthropologist of the contemporary has to identify emergent assemblages

and set them in an environment that is "partially composed of apparatuses and partially of a variety of other elements (such as institutions,
symbols and the like)", all the while staying close to practices and specific
problems.[69] An anthropologist of the contemporary has to work "with
problems, diagnoses and exemplars rather than theories, hypotheses and
data sets" as a method of grasping the significance of human practices
from within.[70]

Ultimately, however, this still implies a form of fieldwork-based inquiry,
as Rabinow notes,[71]

> [o]ne of the defining traits of fieldwork is its existential and experien-
> tial character. One encounters directly, and frequently not at the time
> and place of one's choosing, a range of problems that a text-based
> discipline might miss or at least would have the luxury of choosing
> how and when such issues should be addressed.[72]

Yet, if I have appropriately constructed as my anthropological field of
inquiry three global heritage assemblages around specific instances of
modern architecture and urban planning that are—figuratively speaking—
scattered all over the African continent, then my fieldwork could per
definition not maintain even as a "serviceable fiction"[73] a method of
long and intensive participant observation in one particular place away
from home. Nor could the result be a publication written in the form of
a classical ethnography, as I, too, would have to admit a "now widely
expressed doubt about the adequacy of traditional ethnographic methods
and concepts to the intellectual and political challenges of the contemporary postcolonial world".[74] As the title of a recent publication on anthropological method has it, my study attests to the fact that anthropological
fieldwork "is not what it used to be",[75] at least in two fundamental
ways: (1) fieldwork is now likely to be multisited and (2) as a necessary
consequence—but also because of mutable vocational requirements of
the discipline of anthropology—forms of writing about experiences in
the field are currently changing.

First then, my conception of global heritage assemblages entails that
my field is constructed on a transnational scale and as a result has to
be accessed as a network of multiple sites. This is why my fieldwork is
inspired by much of George Marcus's recent thought about what he calls
"multi-sited ethnography" as a means to "discover new paths of connection and association by which traditional ethnographic concerns with
agency, symbols, and everyday practices can continue to be expressed
on a differently configured spatial canvas".[76] For Marcus, the traditional
anthropological field "is no longer" but doing multisited fieldwork means
networking oneself into "a concept of the field" through research relations all the way along. It follows that connections with interlocutors are
"of equal importance to the fact that the fieldworker may find herself in

Poland, Nigeria, or India, for example, at the beginning, middle or end of a course of research".[77] Accordingly, the multisited field of anthropology has to be understood as emerging from the strategic collaborations with which anthropological fieldwork begins.[78]

In my particular case, I started making connections close to home by meeting with heritage practitioners across the European Union. Gradually they introduced me to their own contacts, some living and working on the European or African continents, whom I would visit; others based on the North American or Asian continents, whom I would call or e-mail. Initially then, I traveled exclusively within Europe for short stints of interviews conducted at people's homes or offices, for example, at various governmental, intergovernmental and nongovernmental organizations, or even in cafés and bars. I also traveled across Europe to visit exhibitions and their respective openings, as well as to observe professional conferences and events. In a second phase of my fieldwork I flew to Asmara, Eritrea, and on to Dar es Salaam, Tanzania, for a more extended, but relatively short period of participant observation that included another series of interviews (the exact dates and details are listed in the Appendix).

In a sense my multisited anthropological fieldwork has thus been characterized by my absences from the traditional field as much as by my presences in it. I have also somehow followed what Marcus called a "norm of incompleteness", by which he means that multisited fieldwork cannot possibly be comprehensive simply because inventorying and mapping the complexity of relations that it involves is such an enormous task.[79] Consequently, besides traveling in and out of the field for participant observation and interviews, my fieldwork also consisted of a variety of corresponding methods, which I employed from my office at Maastricht University in the Netherlands, and even from my home office in the countryside outside of Maastricht. These methods included doing interviews on the telephone and via the Internet, consulting online archives, reading policy documents, professional publications, newspaper articles and blogs, or even watching documentaries. Then again, when I did travel abroad, it was not always for conventional fieldwork purposes but also to visit buildings and urban sites or physical archives, as well as to meet colleagues at academic conferences and seminars or just to informally exchange experiences. Last but not least, I was a visiting researcher at the University of California in Berkeley.

This brief description of my unorthodox engagement in multisited anthropological fieldwork brings me to the second way my research reflects—and reacts to—changes within the discipline of anthropology. There is a reason I speak of multisited *anthropological fieldwork* instead of Marcus's much-cited multisited ethnography, which is that to me the definition of *ethno*graphy on which anthropology has so long relied no longer holds. Although I write about my field—global heritage assemblages—and I reflect in written form about my fieldwork, which, for better or for worse appears as multisited, my concept work suggests that it is necessary to move beyond the critique found in Clifford and Marcus's *Writing Culture*—not just in the sense of further developing its criticism of anthropological writing as about culture or *ethnos* but also in the sense of a need to cease conceiving of it as merely writing culture.

On the Frontlines

I expressly do not write about culture or ethnos, and my work almost certainly does not *only* qualify as 'writing culture'—I have not produced ethnography. Rather, in writing about problematizations of 'modernity-as-culture' in global heritage assemblages, my aim is to circumscribe the cultural within the contemporary. At the same time, I acknowledge that as an anthropologist I have significant stakes in the particular forms of 'the cultural' I describe and analyze, as well as in the contemporary—stakes I, of course, am obliged to write about as well. This obligation manifests itself on two fronts of my research: it influences the practical nature of my field relations, and it concerns my attempts to meet the vocational require-ments for a professional career in anthropology within the academy.

Regarding the first front, George Marcus claims that nowadays "rela-tionships with experts or counterparts (and not just colleagues or consult-ants) very often provide the intellectual capital for conceptually defining the bounds of fieldwork".[80] And, indeed, with my pathway toward the institutionalization of modern architectural heritage on the African con-tinent I have already indicated how the constituencies of cultural heritage practices and anthropology are intertwined. One side of the coin is that ICOMOS's *Filling the Gaps* report proclaimed a move "away from a purely architectural view of the cultural heritage of humanity towards one which was much more *anthropological* [my emphasis], multi-functional, and universal",[81] toward a consideration of world cultural heritage "in its "broad *anthropological* [emphasis mine] context over time".[82] The other side of the coin is that I can only adequately further carve out the issue of African modern heritage as a fundamental anthro-pological problem in close collaboration with what Marcus calls 'epis-temic partners' from my field of inquiry.

As I have shown, the discipline of anthropology faces the same or at least similar problems with the notion of African modern heritage as my field of cultural heritage practices. To invoke Marcus again, one could say that the heritage practices I study significantly overlap with my own intellectual apparatus and terms of analysis as an anthropologist. Yet the movement of my research project's "intellectual center of gravity" into the bounds of my fieldwork cannot be helped, nor could attempts at keeping this operation normatively invisible possibly do so.[83] I can only hope that my concept of global heritage assemblages accounts for this

latter-day "threat of 'going native' ".[84] After all, as an aspiring anthropologist of the contemporary, I have to be close to things when they happen,
all the while also wanting to, by virtue of my analytical aims, "preserve a
certain critical distance, an adjacency, untimeliness".[85]

This ambition to combine participatory fieldwork with 'critique' brings
me to the second front, which happened to be that of academic dissertation writing and publishing. If my diagnostic and genealogical concept
work reveals how the contemporary links the recent past and near future
in global heritage assemblages, and if these in turn form multisited and
experiential fields of experimentation for a reconstruction of anthropological inquiry, then my dissertation, which I defended in 2013 and on
which the present book is based, constituted a "strategic site" for what
Marcus refers to as "muddling through" the changing current vocational
requirements of the discipline of anthropology.[86] After all, if doing fieldwork remains an important initiation rite into the 'cult' of anthropology
today, thesis writing remains so too. And an anthropological dissertation
is still supposed to be *critical*. Ever since the field of anthropology and of
anthropological fieldwork was first contested, any dissertation must as a
rule, in order to be accepted by the academy, include meditations on its
very own conditions of production. Consequently, aside from needing
to be critical of its objects of study—global heritage assemblages—my
thesis at the same time also needed to be able to critically account for the
processes of research and writing that have originally shaped it.

Marcus has noted that accounts for fieldwork within anthropological
publications have lately come to constitute "a primary form of evidence
for arguments, and often *are* the primary form of argument".[87] Here,
however, I do not necessarily want to join this practice of dissecting with
which backing and under what conditions I have done my research and
writing. Instead, I elaborate some of the circumstances of producing this
book in the Acknowledgments and provide more detailed information
on my fieldwork in the Appendix, which should—in combination with
my treatise of anthropological method so far—contribute enough to the
imperative for self-reflection. I believe it is infinitely more interesting and
relevant for me to reflect on how recent changes in the vocational infrastructure of the 21st-century discipline of anthropology have influenced
my choice of a particular *form* of presenting the results of my inquiry.

Traditionally, an anthropological PhD thesis was based on fieldwork
and would, eventually, result in a monograph fit for publication as a
book. Those used to be the basic gatekeepers maintained by anthropology departments hiring junior faculty. However, over the course of
a neoliberalization of the modern research university, there is increasing pressure to publish in peer-reviewed academic journals. A single
monograph—however well placed with a renowned academic publisher—
no longer secures scarce postdoctoral funding, let alone guarantees a rare
tenure offer. In this respect, when George Marcus claims that "at the

level of graduate pedagogy, the dissertation should not be a rough draft of an eventual book but some sort of middle-range production of texts that engage intensively with the kinds of materials that it produces", he is right.[88] I believe he thus means to lessen the weight on his graduate student's shoulders by insinuating that a number of working papers would work just fine as a thesis, and they should. Only, while what really seems to be necessary in order to make a career in anthropology these days is to produce a middle-range of papers fit for journal submission *aside from* that monograph style dissertation.

This suspicion has influenced me in shaping the present book. In Part II, I present three chapters in which I analyze my examples of global heritage assemblages. As these three chapters could stand on their own, I hope my multisited approach to fieldwork has enabled me to produce Marcus's middle range of writing. Combined with the diagnostic and genealogical chapters that make up Part I of my book, then, as well as wrapped up by my synthesis in Part III, I should also have found a way of giving this analytical middle range a place in the present monograph.

In conclusion, what I attempt to do with this book is to move beyond modernity as an object of study: I want to contribute to rescuing modernity from its conception as an all-encompassing culture. In the process, I present my analysis of global heritage assemblages as a form of critical global knowledge in and of the contemporary.[89] Speaking with Rabinow and Marcus, I have tried to bring together in one research project the residual, the emergent and the dominant, intending to show that multisited anthropological fieldwork can study the three in play with each other.[90] As Gupta and Ferguson have argued, a good anthropological field site is 'made' by the vocational requirements of the discipline, as well as by its "suitability for addressing issues and debates that matter to that very discipline".[91] With any luck then, my analysis of global heritage assemblages around the issue of modern architectural heritage on the African continent attests to this by circumscribing "a space of concrete dangers and hopes that is actual, emergent, and virtual".[92]

Notes

1. Terdiman, *Present Past: Modernity and the Memory Crisis.* 52.
2. Pol-Droit, *Humanity in the Making: The Intellectual History of UNESCO.* 20.
3. Rabinow, *Anthropos Today: Reflections on Modern Equipment.* 176.
4. Rabinow, *Reflections on Fieldwork in Morocco (30th Anniversary Edition).* xxii.
5. Rabinow, *Marking Time: On the Anthropology of the Contemporary.* 2.
6. Ibid.
7. Ibid., 24; Paul Rabinow et al., eds., *Designs for an Anthropology of the Contemporary* (London: Duke University Press, 2008). 87.
8. "Wikipedia.org: Paul Rabinow," www.wikipedia.org.
9. Rabinow et al., *Designs for an Anthropology of the Contemporary.* 58.

10. Ibid.
11. Rabinow, *Marking Time: On the Anthropology of the Contemporary.* 5.
12. Ibid., 4.
13. Ibid., 13.
14. Rabinow, *Reflections on Fieldwork in Morocco (30th Anniversary Edition).* xxii.
15. Rabinow, *Marking Time: On the Anthropology of the Contemporary.* 13.
16. Rabinow, *Anthropos Today: Reflections on Modern Equipment.* 15.
17. Rabinow, *Marking Time: On the Anthropology of the Contemporary.* 78.
18. Johannes Fabian, *Time and the Other: How Anthropology Makes Its Object* (New York: Columbia University Press, 1983).
19. Ibid., 147.
20. Ibid., 148.
21. Ibid., 38.
22. Ibid., 38; 65; 55.
23. Ibid., 152.
24. Rabinow et al., *Designs for an Anthropology of the Contemporary.* 13; Rees in ibid., 7; also compare George E. Marcus, ed. *Critical Anthropology Now: Unexpected Contexts, Shifting Constitutencies, Changing Agendas* (Santa Fe: School of American Research Press, 1999).
25. Ferguson, *Global Shadows: Africa in the Neoliberal World Order.* viii.
26. Faubion in Rabinow et al., *Designs for an Anthropology of the Contemporary*; Appadurai, *Modernity at Large: Cultural Dimensions of Globalization.* 16.
27. Fabian, *Time and the Other: How Anthropology Makes its Object.* 37; 156.
28. For instance, these catchphrases have recently served as the emblematic titles of two influential collections of anthropological research edited by Arjun Apadurai and Dilip Gaonkar, respectively: Arjun Appadurai, ed. *Globalization, Millenium Quartet* (London: Duke University Press, 2001); Dilip Gaonkar Parameshwar, *Alternative Modernities* (Durham: Duke University Press, 2001).
29. Rabinow, *Anthropos Today: Reflections on Modern Equipment.* 114.
30. Ibid.
31. "Wikipedia.org: Paul Rabinow," www.wikipedia.org.
32. Ibid.
33. Ferguson, *Global Shadows: Africa in the Neoliberal World Order.* 16; 2.
34. Ibid., 176.
35. Ibid., 186.
36. Ibid., 13.
37. James Ferguson, *Expectations of Modernity: Myths and Meanings of Urban Life on the Zambian Copperbelt* (Berkeley: University of California Press, 1999). 247.
38. Ferguson, *Global Shadows: Africa in the Neoliberal World Order.* 186.
39. Ibid., 16.
40. Ibid.
41. Ibid., 191.
42. Ferguson, *Global Shadows: Africa in the Neoliberal World Order.* 191; Ferguson, *Expectations of Modernity: Myths and Meanings of Urban Life on the Zambian Copperbelt.* 236.
43. Ferguson, *Global Shadows: Africa in the Neoliberal World Order.* 192.
44. Ibid., 5.
45. Ibid.
46. "Anthropological Research on the Contemporary: bios-technika".
47. "Wikipedia.org: Paul Rabinow".

48. "Anthropological Research on the Contemporary: bios-technika".
49. Ong and Collier, *Global Assemblages: Technology, Politics, and Ethics as Anthropological Problems*. 4.
50. Ibid., 4; 8.
51. Rabinow, *Anthropos Today: Reflections on Modern Equipment*. 114.
52. Worldbank, "Implementation Completion and Results Report on a Learning and Innovation Loan to the State of Eritrea in the Amount of SDR 4.0 Million (US$ 5 Million Equivalent) for a Cultural Assets Rehabilitation Project," ed. Conflict and Social Development Unit (AFTCS) Fragile States, Eritrea Country Department, Washington, DC, 2008.
53. ArchiAfrika policy plan 2009, 7–8.
54. Rabinow in Ong and Collier, *Global Assemblages: Technology, Politics, and Ethics as Anthropological Problems*. 41.
55. Rabinow et al., *Designs for an Anthropology of the Contemporary*. 55.
56. James Faubion and George E. Marcus, eds., *Field Work Is Not What It Used to Be* (Ithaca: Cornell University Press, 2009).
57. Fabian, *Time and the Other: How Anthropology Makes Its Object*. 159.
58. Ibid., 165.
59. Ibid., 159.
60. Rabinow et al., *Designs for an Anthropology of the Contemporary*. 25.
61. Akhil Gupta and James Ferguson, eds., *Anthropological Locations: Boundaries and Grounds of a Field Science* (Berkeley: University of California Press, 1997). 1.
62. Ibid.
63. Ibid., 5.
64. Vered Amit, ed. *Constructing the Field: Ethnographic Fieldwork in the Contemporary World* (London: Routledge, 2000). 6.
65. Ibid., 2.
66. Mark-Anthony Falzon, ed. *Multi-Sited Ethnography* (Farnham: Ashgate, 2009); Valentina Mazzucato, "Bridging Boundaries with a Transnational Approach," in *Multi-Sited Ethnography*, ed. Mark-Anthony Falzon (Farnham: Ashgate, 2009).
67. Rabinow on Foucault in Ong and Collier, *Global Assemblages: Technology, Politics, and Ethics as Anthropological Problems*. 44.
68. Rabinow in Ibid., 45.
69. Rabinow, *Anthropos Today: Reflections on Modern Equipment*. 56; Ong and Collier, *Global Assemblages: Technology, Politics, and Ethics as Anthropological Problems*. 17.
70. Rabinow, *Anthropos Today: Reflections on Modern Equipment*. 130; Hubert L. Dreyfus and Paul Rabinow, *Michel Foucault: Beyond Structuralism and Hermeneutics* (Chicago: University of Chicago Press, 1983). 103.
71. Rabinow et al., *Designs for an Anthropology of the Contemporary*. 93.
72. Rabinow, *The Accompaniment*. 179.
73. Amit, *Constructing the Field: Ethnographic Fieldwork in the Contemporary World*. 2.
74. Gupta and Ferguson, *Anthropological Locations: Boundaries and Grounds of a Field Science*. 3.
75. Faubion and Marcus, *Field Work Is Not What It Used to Be*.
76. George E. Marcus, "Ethnography in/of the World System: The Emergence of Multi Sited Ethnography," *Annual Review of Anthropology* 24, (1995). 98.
77. George E. Marcus, "Multi-Sited Ethnography: Five or Six Things I Know About It Now," in *Multi-Sited Ethnography: Problems and Possibilities in the Translocation of Research Methods*, ed. Simon Colemann and Pauline Hellerman (London: Routledge, 2011). 28.

78. Ibid., 23.
79. Amit, *Constructing the Field: Ethnographic Fieldwork in the Contemporary World*. 12.
80. Faubion and Marcus, *Field Work Is Not What It Used to Be*. 30.
81. UNESCO, "Expert Meeting on the "Global Strategy" and thematic studies for a representative World Heritage List".
82. Jokilehto, *The World Heritage List: Filling the Gaps—An Action Plan for the Future*. 10.
83. Faubion and Marcus, *Field Work Is Not What It Used to Be*. 30.
84. Ibid.
85. Rabinow et al., *Designs for an Anthropology of the Contemporary*. 58.
86. Marcus, "Multi-Sited Ethnography: Five or Six Things I Know About It Now." 17.
87. Rabinow et al., *Designs for an Anthropology of the Contemporary*. 18.
88. Marcus, "Multi-Sited Ethnography: Five or Six Things I Know About It Now." 29.
89. Collier, "Global Assemblages."
90. Rabinow et al., *Designs for an Anthropology of the Contemporary*. 99; 94–95.
91. Gupta and Ferguson, *Anthropological Locations: Boundaries and Grounds of a Field Science*.
92. *Rabinow in* Ong and Collier, *Global Assemblages: Technology, Politics, and Ethics as Anthropological Problems*. 50.

Part II

5 Modern Nostalgia
Asserting Politics of Sovereignty and Security in Asmara, Washington and Brussels

In the late 1980s, the World Bank announced a "holistic approach"[1] to development and subsequently turned its attention to cultural heritage as a tool in what it called postconflict reconstruction, nation building, economic development and poverty reduction. The bank considered Eritrea a "natural experiment"[2] to test this new approach. In 1993, Eritrea had declared its independence from Ethiopia after decades of violent conflict, making it one of the youngest nation-states on the African continent. A symbol of Eritrea's newly won sovereignty is its capital, Asmara. Asmara remained virtually undamaged throughout Eritrea's long struggle for national independence, as well as during another war between Eritrea and Ethiopia in 1998. Largely built under Italian colonialism, the city survives as an ensemble of early-20th-century modern architecture and urban planning.

In 2002, the Eritrean government started the Cultural Assets Rehabilitation Project (CARP), which the World Bank financed with a US$5 million development loan. Focused on the preservation of Asmara's modern architectural heritage, CARP generated much attention, as well as support, particularly after the addition of Asmara's so-called historic perimeter to UNESCO's tentative World Heritage List. After the World Bank in Washington in 2007 terminated its loan to CARP, the European Union in Brussels launched a follow-up 'national heritage programme', through which €5 million in development aid was invested exclusively in the restoration of Asmara's modern architecture. All this while Eritrea remains one of the poorest countries in the world and a dictatorial Eritrean government under President Isaias Afwerki and his Maoist People's Front for Democracy and Justice sustains ongoing conflict over its border with Ethiopia in defiance of foreign intervention. Afwerki endorses a radical policy of self-reliance, which, as the European Union delegation to Eritrea complains, endangers food security and causes massive emigration.

In this chapter, I examine the heritage valorization of Asmara's modern architecture. Based on multisited anthropological fieldwork, I describe the practices of relevant state and nonstate actors that, I argue, raise a number of significant questions concerning norms and forms of government today. Changing forms of government under conditions of globalization are at the center of attention of recent anthropological and interdisciplinary social-scientific scholarship, much of which reflects on how the nation-state's abilities to claim powerful encompassment and legitimacy are increasingly challenged by transnationally networked and globally imagined organizations and movements.[3] In this respect, I am specifically interested in the emergence of a global heritage assemblage around the modern architecture of Asmara. I ask how the modern architectural heritage of Asmara is instrumental both to the national Eritrean government and to transnational organizations. In particular, I would like to know what happens when a young nation-state on the African continent is forced to operate in the same global space as an emergent transnational apparatus of governance represented by the World Bank and the European Union.

My analysis indicates how the Eritrean government crucially depends on the appropriation of the modern architecture of Asmara as national heritage to ensure a reterritorialization of its sovereignty along the lines of its former Italian colonial borders with Ethiopia. The Eritrean government's dominant concern with political and economic sovereignty, however, is compromised by its dependency on the sizable World Bank loan and on the transnational recognition of and support for Asmara's modern heritage. In turn, the Eritrean quest for self-reliance at all costs, including serious human rights violations, disappoints the World Bank's high hopes of postconflict reconstruction, nation building, economic development and poverty reduction through cultural heritage preservation. Surprisingly, though, the project's 'failure' seems to be irrelevant to a positive assessment as well as the further promotion of culture-bound development aid to Eritrea. In fact, the European Union delegation continues to refer to the modern heritage of Asmara as a resource for the European Union's overall development program to improve food security and to contain emigration on the Horn of Africa.

In this context, I argue that the relevant cultural representations of national and transnational authorities are essentially dependent on Asmara's colonial built heritage. In fact, considering the popular resonance of Asmara's image as "Africa's secret modernist city"[4] and a "City of Dreams",[5] I contend that a form of modern nostalgia plays a role in determining the policies of transnational development organizations such as the World Bank and the EU delegation, as well as those of the Eritrean national government. I claim that different notions of nostalgia for colonial modernities revolving around Asmara's modern architectural heritage problematize norms and forms of government in terms of the politics of sovereignty and security.

Politics of Sovereignty and Security

My understanding of politics hinges on the work of Michel Foucault. With Foucault, I consider politics to be the situated practices through which existing governmental rationalities are reflected on and transformed.[6] Accordingly, the purpose of government is to articulate the nature of problems of authority, as well as to propose solutions to these problems.[7] At the core of Foucault's genealogy of the modern nation-state, for instance, are the problematic relations between the governmental rationalities of sovereignty and security.[8] Foucault shows how, throughout the 18th and 19th centuries, the problem of security, which relates to the protection of a population's collective welfare, gradually complicates the initial problem of sovereign rule over a territory.[9] He argues that in order to preserve and legitimize the comprehensive encompassment of a given space of sovereignty, the modern state constitutes itself based on the notion of civil society. For Foucault, civil society (or, simply, society) makes it possible to align relationships of state authority with social bonds that go beyond purely economic and juridical bonds.[10] The nation, then, is nothing more than the articulation of history on such social bonds.[11] Foucault claims that civil society is most effectively regulated through a self-limitation of government. He argues that the power of the modern nation-state is based on a liberalism that facilitates government in a general and omnipresent form.[12] The result is a political shift from a dominant pursuit of sovereign power over a territory to a modern art of government concerned with the security of a population in a given environment.[13]

Foucault famously situates his account of the transformation of modern governmental reason in the social environment of the town.[14] Paul Rabinow, drawing on and adding to Foucault's analysis, has also shown how the modern art of government is intricately intertwined with innovative technologies of social regulation through urban planning and modern architecture.[15] Rabinow extends Foucault's somewhat Eurocentric scope by zooming in on urbanization in France's North African colonies at the turn of the 19th century. He argues that the French colonies "constituted a laboratory of experimentation for new arts of government capable of bringing a modern and healthy society into being".[16] As part of the military project to guarantee France's sovereign rule of an expanded territory, the colonial built environment was developed to effectively rule over a population. Based on ideologies of progress and development and precisely through the organization of urban space in its territories abroad, the French state developed the norms and forms of its social modernity.

Rabinow's analysis of colonial politics as a productive tension between governmental rationalities of sovereignty and security that is manifested in the modern built environment is confirmed by a number of other scholars.[17] Mia Fuller notably applies Rabinow's findings in her study of Italian colonialism, indicating how the Italian colonial government fundamentally relied on theories and practices of modern architecture and urban planning, particularly under Mussolini's fascist rule. Among other examples, she analyzes the urban development of Asmara between 1898 and 1941, the period when it was the capital of the Italian colony of Eritrea.[18]

Initially, Asmara consisted of little more than a number of Italian military installations, with a colonial settlement growing into a small town by the 1920s. In the 1930s, though, Asmara experienced a building boom as Italy invested heavily in its Eritrean infrastructure. This boom was linked to Mussolini's preparations to invade neighboring Ethiopia, which after a massive European "scramble for Africa",[19] remained the only independent kingdom on the continent. Then regarded an imperial model, Asmara's subsequent urban growth was regulated according to a fascist master plan meant to control "all that concerns the organiza-tion of a population's life".[20] This master plan decreed the separation of living areas for colonizers and colonized, who were thought to form distinctly separate civilizations.[21] In fact, while the architects and plan-ners of Asmara believed that "the native must join his new nation",[22] he or she was explicitly not considered part of Italian civil society. Rather, the subjection of 'the natives' to the colonizers' sovereign power was taken for granted; in the colony they were considered "a guest rather than a former master".[23] The disciplinary design of Asmara's urban grid according to strict principles of racial, ethnic and religious segregation thus confirms a particular tension between governmental rationalities of sovereignty and security, especially against the backdrop of Mussolini's colonial policy of territorial expansion. As Fuller and Makki argue, the Italians appeared to want to "have their cake and eat it too". While con-trolling the colonized, they imagined themselves as both beneficent and beloved at the same time".[24]

These days, the Eritreans have inherited Asmara's modern architecture, and many Asmarinos live and work in their former colonizers' houses and offices or, alternatively, in the slums of the former indigenous zones. No changes to the urban makeup of Asmara were made when Eritrea became a British protectorate following the 1941 defeat of the Italians in World War II. After the United Nations had decided on a contested federation between Eritrea and Ethiopia in 1950, the Eritrean war of independence prohibited any major urban development of Asmara. The only visible alterations to Asmara's street view concern the walls around properties, which many owners raised for reasons of privacy and safety under the Ethiopian occupation. For a large part, the modern architec-tural heritage of Asmara thus continues to represent early-20th-century Italian colonial urbanism. But what happens when, as is the case with the heritage valorization of the modern architecture of Asmara, political practices are tested over the built environment of a colonial past?

A Global Heritage Assemblage around the Modern Architecture of Asmara

As I already noted, development organizations in the late 1980s and throughout the 1990s moved toward what was called a holistic approach to development. In this policy, shift 'culture' was deemed essential. UNE-SCO even declared 1988 to 1997 the "World Decade for Cultural Development", asserting that "from now on, culture should be regarded as a direct source of inspiration for development, and in return, development should assign to culture a central role as social regulator".[25] The World Bank endorsed a similar view when James D. Wolfensohn was appointed its president in 1995. Wolfensohn reflected on the role of the World Bank by stating that "[we need to do] development differently"[26] and that "we must not lose sight of culture and cultural heritage".[27] He commissioned a Framework for Action on culture and sustainable development, personally chairing a working group with what Arlene Fleming, a senior heritage consultant to the World Bank, calls the qualities of an encouraging believer.[28] Wolfensohn's policy objective was "to mainstream culture into Bank operations".[29]

Seeking partnerships with cultural heritage organizations such as UNESCO, the Bank started lending "specifically for culture"[30] in the late 1990s. This was facilitated mainly through so-called Learning and Innovation Loans (LILs), which were meant to "afford opportunities to test new approaches, pilot efforts for later expansion, and develop programmatic strategies".[31] Wolfensohn maintained that investment in culture "makes sound business sense. From tourism to restoration, investments in cultural heritage and related industries promote labor intensive economic activities that generate wealth and income."[32] He regarded it as imperative that "when the World Bank supports conservation of monuments and heritage sites it is to achieve economic and social objectives".[33]

At the same time as the World Bank included culture in its development policy, it also claimed it was stepping up its "work on post-conflict situations".[34] In 1997, it emphasized that postconflict reconstruction is a central issue and that "the Bank has a critical role to play in the early stages of post-conflict reconstruction".[35] In fact, a 1998 World Bank report on experience with postconflict reconstruction established a direct link between peace and development, assuming that "in post-conflict countries sustained peace is essential to sustained development" where "broad-based development in its own right also contributes to sustainable peace".[36] The report expounds that "[c]ulture is not a luxury"[37] in postconflict situations, asking, "What is the justification for assisting in the protection and conservation of cultural heritage in situations of complex emergencies?" and explaining that

> [a]pplying scarce resources to conserving cultural heritage in a post-conflict situation may seem frivolous at first glance. However, cultural heritage has the power to inspire hope and remind people of their creativity. [It can be] viewed as integral to the transition from war to sustainable peace and as a prerequisite for economic and social development.[38]

The World Bank report on postconflict reconstruction and development prominently refers to Eritrea as a case study.[39] Simultaneously with the publication of this report, the World Bank encouraged the Eritrean government to apply for an LIL in order to develop its CARP. The bank welcomed the Eritrean request, which, it stated,

> comes coincident with the progress which is being made in launching post-conflict activities which are oriented toward economic reconstruction and recovery, and other social and economic programs with poverty reduction objectives.

However, work on the specifics of a loan application began shortly before a renewed war between Eritrea and Ethiopia started in 1998, which led to a waning image of Eritrea as "a model newly independent state"[40] and halted development activities until 2001.

Barely a year after the official cease-fire, the World Bank would approve funding for CARP, with two individuals formatively influencing the successful funding application. On the bank's side, it was the task team leader Peter Dewees who had experience with a similar heritage project in Ethiopia, and on the Eritrean side, it was Naigzy Gebremedhin, a trained architect and former employee of the UN Environment Program (UNEP). While Gebremedhin had been happy about the early economic success of postindependence Eritrea, he had grown increasingly skeptical about the ensuing building construction in Asmara.[41] He had noticed that some of the most prominent new buildings did not match the existing structures' scale and endangered the integrity of the city's modern architectural heritage. Gebremedhin calls it a "realization that development was going the wrong way. People started to think: this doesn't look right."[42] In cooperation with Dewees, Gebremedhin thus set out to write a concept paper arguing for the protection of Asmara's modern heritage. Endorsed by the Eritrean government, this document constitutes the foundation of CARP.[43]

Gebremedhin and Dewees's concept paper followed the then-recent World Bank policy's move from a 'do-no-harm' to a 'do-good' approach to cultural heritage.[44] In Gebremedhin's words,

> [t]here were two reasons to preserve heritage [. . .]. The number one reason is that you preserve heritage because it is an affirmation of national identity. [. . .] The second reason is very practical, in the sense that heritage preservation can be linked very strongly to economic development. And the World Bank was adamant in making sure that this link was made clear, operational and measurable.[45]

The eventual World Bank Project loan appraisal document for CARP indeed harks back to the 'do -good' notion of economic development, explicitly mentioning the potential of cultural heritage investments for postconflict reconstruction, nation building, economic development and poverty reduction in Eritrea.

In 2001, CARP was successfully launched on a loan of US$5 million, with Gebremedhin assuming its management for the Eritrean government. He came to coordinate the project together with a steering committee formally placed under the Eritrean ministry of finance but initially operating relatively autonomously. The World Bank's Peter Dewees, meanwhile, was reassigned, and Arlene Fleming took over as World Bank Team Task Leader. She had a record as a consultant in cultural heritage policy making and emphasizes the value of the LIL, which according to her "for the bank is small, but for the cultural heritage field is enormous".[46] Moreover, Fleming recognizes a pattern in the use of World Bank LILs for cultural heritage:

> What is interesting to mention is that these small loans for cultural heritage tended to be taken, not entirely, but frequently by countries who were newly free, newly independent. For instance there was one in Georgia, one in Romania, there was one in Eritrea; Azerbaijan, also. So you see that these countries have a particular interest in developing awareness and attending to their own cultural heritage, which had not been possible under the previous regimes. And that I think was an interesting feature, which is not often mentioned.[47]

Besides as an attempt to generate economic development through cultural heritage in financing CARP, the World Bank thus clearly supported an attempt to "reestablish Eritrea's identity",[48] as Naigzy Gebremedhin puts it.

Gebremedhin's ambition to forge Eritrea's national identity through the valorization of its modern built heritage coincided with rising interest in Africa's colonial architecture among global heritage organizations. In 2001, for instance, the very year CARP was launched, ICOMOS published a report considering modern architecture in Africa a "shared colonial heritage at risk".[49] The report urged the inventory and protection of modern heritage in Africa, suggesting joint responsibilities for former colonizers and colonized alike.[50] Moreover, ICOMOS in 2004 presented an advisory report to UNESCO titled *Filling the Gaps—An Action Plan for the Future*, identifying modern architecture in Africa as a category of heritage that combines thematic and regional shortcomings of the UNESCO World Heritage List.[51]

Against the backdrop of a concept of shared heritage, CARP's emphasis on Asmara's colonial architecture proved a powerful means to create interest in the newly independent state of Eritrea abroad. Realizing this potential, one of Gebremedhin's first decisions as CARP manager was to hire as foreign consultants Edward Denison and Guang Yu Ren, a British-Chinese couple with a background in design who had traveled in Eritrea.[52] Gebremedhin, Denison and Ren started to work vigorously in order to raise international awareness of Asmara's modern heritage, even though this was not a primary objective of CARP under the specifications of the World Bank loan. Denison described their consultancy for CARP as follows:

> A big part of our work [. . .] was about getting [the modern heritage of Asmara] out into the international domain: We have got to get the support of UNESCO, we have got to get the support of the World Monuments Fund, [the] Aga Khan [Foundation] was another one. So we sent out masses of emails to these organizations.[53]

One result was that the UNESCO World Heritage Center in Paris chose Asmara as the venue of a 2004 regional meeting of its Modern Heritage Programme. This programme was set up in 2001 in order to facilitate the identification and documentation of modern architectural heritage and to stimulate World Heritage List nominations.[54] UNESCO considers modern heritage in Africa "a source of identity and economic development"[55] but a particularly vulnerable one. During the conference in Asmara, the World Heritage Center, needless to say, then, complimented CARP's engagement with the city's modern architecture. In fact, it encouraged a tentative World Heritage List entry of Asmara's 'historic perimeter', which Denison and Ren wrote and submitted to UNESCO on behalf of CARP in 2005. This entry describes Asmara as the "most concentrated and intact assemblage of Modernist architecture anywhere in the world".[56]

Already in 2003, Denison, Ren and Gebremedhin had coauthored *Asmara: The Secret Modernist City*. In Denison's words, this book was meant to "get this material into the international domain, to celebrate Asmara".[57] Based on research conducted for CARP, the book advertises a "sublime urban environment that has miraculously survived to the present day" and refers to a "definite urgency in extolling Asmara's beauty".[58] In the preface, Denison writes that

> if one aim alone might be achieved through this publication, it would be that, by granting Asmara the recognition it rightfully deserves as one of the worlds architecturally magnificent cities, broader development in Eritrea may be encouraged.[59]

In fact, *Asmara: The Secret Modernist City* reads like a call for support. The mayor of Asmara, for instance, writes in his foreword,

> Eritreans are able to present to the world a heritage that is worthy of international acclaim and of which they should all be proud. This book therefore appeals to all Eritreans to offer an unending commitment to future generations that this legacy is preserved and to rise to

the challenge of nurturing and involving themselves in the positive development of their capital, which will serve to make it one of the world's most atmospheric, interesting and, importantly, safe cities. With an agenda based firmly on the needs of the Eritreans, including the alleviation of poverty and nurturing a balanced and equitable society, we are seeking to achieve these aims. Therefore I call upon individuals, communities and organizations, domestic and international, to collaborate in achieving these aims, and to assure that it is not only Asmara's fascinating history that is recognized, but also its bright future.[60]

This rhetoric combined with the aesthetic appeal of the highly visual content of *Asmara: The Secret Modernist City* can explain why Roxanne Hakim, Arlene Fleming's successor as World Bank Task Team leader for CARP in 2006, claims that the book "single-handedly brought Asmara on the international agenda".[61]

Indeed, CARP capitalized on the popular reception of the book to drum up support.[62] According to Hakim, the generation of an image of Asmara as "Africa's secret modernist city" made CARP "fantastic with partners":[63]

I've never seen a World Bank project that partnered so much with other organizations. The Alliance Française, a little NGO somewhere, the Italians, this project really did well in this respect. [. . .] CARP began to be seen as a body in Eritrea, which was a state channel to put your money in if you wanted to support culture. [. . .] This project, the topic, the sector we worked in; every kind of embassy in a country has a little fund somewhere, the sole aim of which is to do little stuff like this. [. . .] Now suddenly that pot of money found this huge bandwagon to jump on. [. . .]. Because [CARP] provided a structure and while not many government institutions were very efficient it had already identified things worthwhile to do.[64]

Effectively then, CARP facilitated a global heritage assemblage around the modern architecture of Asmara. CARP's mission of the "reestablishment of Eritrean national identity"[65] was joined together with the transnational appeal of Asmara's 'historic perimeter' as shared colonial heritage and the city's tentative UNESCO World Heritage status. CARP's conspicuous emphasis on global responsibilities of postconflict reconstruction, nation building, economic development and poverty reduction, however, caused opposition from the Eritrean president's office.

Asserting Sovereignty and Security

Widely recognized as bringing CARP's activities to the attention of a global audience, Gebremedhin only reluctantly coauthored *Asmara: The*

Secret Modernist City in his function as CARP's director. Denison and Ren privately took the initiative to find a publisher for the book and although its acknowledgment states "if there would be a single name under which the greatest number of contributors might willingly be represented, it would be that of CARP",[66] the Eritrean government did not officially endorse the book. According to Denison, this was because of what he describes as the incredibly protective attitude taken by the Eritrean regime:[67]

> The President's office didn't know about the book. [This] paranoia of needing to be in control of everything! CARP was almost an autonomous project, kind of governmental, but kind of not. Its global visibility made people suspicious, so if the president's office had known [about the publication], it would have been stopped.[68]

Though Denison and Ren knew that bypassing the highest political authorities when submitting the manuscript to their publisher, Merrel, in London, their publication would not be well received in Eritrea, they were surprised by the intensity of the resultant repression of CARP:

> At the point of publishing the book, CARP started to be questioned for its autonomy [. . .]. When the book came out, Naigzy [Gebremedhin] got under a lot of pressure from the government, almost to the point of house arrest. I mean, he was allowed to go to the office but he was put under strain. It became really uncomfortable to work in the later stages at the end of 2003. [Guang Yu Ren and I] finished our work in Eritrea in May 2004.[69]

In effect, Denison's account of the governmental reaction to the publication of *Asmara: The Secret Modernist City* reveals a fundamental opposition to CARP's policy of creating a sense of globally shared ownership of Asmara's modern architectural heritage. Eager to assert its newly won national sovereignty and pursing a radical policy of self-reliance, the Eritrean government cracked down on CARP's rallying of international assistance.

The Eritrean government's suspicion was not limited to CARP and generally affected foreign intervention at the time. Whereas in the early 1990s, Eritrea presented itself as "the darling of the western world",[70] its authorities became more and more apprehensive about foreign influence. From the late 1990s onward, this made it increasingly difficult for development organizations to work in Eritrea, and the German Gesellschaft fur Technische Zusammenarbeit, the World Food program and the US Agency for International Development all left the country because of Eritrean obstructions. Moreover, the number of NGOs active in Eritrea sharply decreased from 38 in 1993 to 3 in 2010.[71] Even the United

Nations Mission in Ethiopia and Eritrea (UNMEE), the UN peacekeeping mission installed after the 1998 war between the two countries, was forced to leave. First the Eritrean government withheld it gas to fuel its vehicles on account of alleged lack of gas supplies, then, when the mission's equipment had been exchanged for diesel-fueled cars, the Eritreans pretended there was a diesel shortage.[72] Among diplomatic personnel in Asmara it has become common to refer to this blunt expulsion of the UN mission when describing one's own experiences of the Eritrean government's indirect but effective sanctions against aid work; "Having been UNMEEed"[73] became a standing expression.

Apparently the publication of *Asmara: The Secret Modernist City* was reason enough to lead the Eritrean government to 'UNMEE' CARP until the termination of the World Bank loan in 2007. In fact, the World Bank *Implementation Completion and Results Report* about CARP, published in 2008, describes in diplomatic language how in the later phase of the project "there were difficulties in reaching decisions in a timely manner on some key matters" with an "ambivalent" government.[74] CARP activities were delayed or otherwise subjected to "changing and unpredictable government priorities".[75] According to the bank, the premises upon which the project was designed to achieve economic development and poverty reduction changed drastically as a result of "the changing political environment in Eritrea".[76] Originally, the World Bank's objectives for CARP established a crucial link between the preservation of the historic built environment of Asmara and economic growth. Among the so-called key indicators was a "growth-oriented planning process for urban and architectural management and conservation" and a "conservation fund [. . .] designed to stimulate the private sector and to engage communities".[77] Furthermore, the World Bank assumed that "low-income groups are targeted for training in specialized building trades related to conservation" and that the "conservation of priority sites in Asmara [. . .] is completed with a particular emphasis on improving community access to public services and spaces".[78] However, the Bank observed "three main shifts [. . .] in government orientation that affected the project activities and achievement of development objectives".[79] These main shifts compromised the initial key indicators regarding the preservation of Asmara's modern architecture, none of which was satisfactorily met, according to the Bank's final CARP evaluation.

The first political shift identified by the World Bank concerns the private sector, which was deemed crucial in attaining CARP's poverty reduction and growth objectives. The Eritrean government is reported to have "eliminated or greatly reduced" activities "in support of the private sector".[80] One example is the Eritrean Conservation Fund (ECF), which was to allow private owners of real estate in Asmara to engage in necessary maintenance and conservation works and was designed to "ensure a healthy post-Project afterlife" of CARP, though it is yet to be established. According to the World Bank "it is unclear when or if the ECF will become operational through a legal proclamation, in part due to the government's declining support of the private sector".[81] Meanwhile, Medhanie Maria from the Eritrean Department of Infrastructure euphemistically sums up government policy as a

> sort of embargo of building permits: for the past 10 years we didn't issue permits for new building construction. We tell the applicants: please wait until guidelines are fully established, for example the appropriate height of buildings. There is a great awareness of the heritage among the Eritreans. People are very cooperative. Many people are suspending their projects, because they want to wait until decisions have been made.[82]

The Eritrean government then has effectively halted private building activity on the pretext of cultural heritage preservation.

The second political shift the World Bank notes is that throughout the loan period for CARP "the scope to work with community groups was greatly restricted".[83] For instance, while according to Fleming the "empowerment of local people" was high on CARP's agenda and "there was a lot of attention in the early phases of the project to citizen involvement and creating enthusiasm among the people who owned property in Asmara", later this came to a halt.[84] She claims "no one really knew why, but the assumption was that the order came from the very top. They didn't want this in Eritrea, this citizen engagement, it had to stop."[85] A case in point is the Restore Asmara Campaign, which gathered Asmarinos for voluntary building conservation projects. According to the World Bank report, the Restore Asmara campaign was "a wonderful example of building social capital through cultural restoration", though "the stop put to [it] gave a strong message to the project regarding working directly with community groups" that the Eritrean government was opposed to civic engagement around cultural heritage projects.[86]

The third political shift that the World Bank identifies as having substantially compromised CARP concerns the Eritrean nationalization of the building trades. According to the World Bank,

> the withdrawal of construction contractors' licenses imposed by the government in the last few years [resulted] in delays in activities involving civil works, many of which remained undone at project closure.[87]

The practical monopoly created by this nationalization clashed with the procurement rules of the World Bank, which demand competitive bidding for contracts. As Roxanne Hakim indicates,

> [the Eritrean] government wanted to see something physical, they wanted us to restore a building. Now, the purpose behind that was

political. They wanted to restore Cinema Asmara and Cinema Capitol, but [we had] a huge, huge problem with procurement. [. . .] So we wasted a long time. Also, the government didn't want foreign companies to bid.[88]

This conflict between the Eritrean state ownership of industries and the World Bank's procurement rules concerning construction works is emblematic of CARP's failure to satisfy both parties' interests.

Actually, the World Bank's *Implementation Completion and Results* report on CARP arrives at a rather damning final evaluation of the project. The Bank frankly admits that the primary objectives of CARP were not met to its satisfaction, stating that "it is difficult to assess [. . .] the contribution of cultural assets to economic growth in the present circumstances of Eritrea" and that the "poverty impacts [of CARP] are primarily anecdotal".[89] Furthermore, the World Bank states that "a weak point in the design [of the loan for CARP] was the underestimation of risks and their mitigation. Several important risks, especially political risk, were underestimated."[90] Hakim explains:

In hindsight I think we really should have taken a step back and taken a little more drastic look at the design, to see if it would extend into the new situation. Remember, at the time of [project] design Eritrea was doing relatively well; 7% GDP, it was a really new country. When we actually implemented the project; it was after the war, but as you know the war was still going on. We were coming into a new dictatorial government in the country, communist philosophy, no private sector, not really an environment where creative heritage stuff was a priority.[91]

The far-reaching conclusion of the World Bank's CARP report is that "in retrospect, it may have been more realistic to *eliminate* [emphasis added] the poverty reduction and growth aspects of the development objective".[92]

Intriguingly, however, whereas the World Bank's evaluation complains about CARP's failure to achieve its economic development and poverty reduction objectives, on another front it credits the project as having positively "demonstrated that investing in cultural assets is an element of nation building [. . .] and post-conflict reconstruction".[93] This conclusion is largely based on CARP's effects on institutional cooperation and capacity building in Eritrea, as well as on the bank's insight that nationally and globally the "awareness raising on historic architecture [of Asmara] exceeded expectations".[94] The World Bank also notes that "media attention on Eritrea's cultural heritage has created a positive image of Eritrea"[95] abroad. Finally, CARP's initiative to add Asmara's 'historic perimeter' to the tentative UNESCO World Heritage List is credited as a success. But whereas internationally these events indicate an overwhelmingly positive interest in CARP, domestically they had a rather different resonance, as already hinted at. In fact, the Eritrean government fundamentally contradicts the World Bank when it comes to interpretations of nation building and postconflict reconstruction through cultural heritage.

A case in point is the Eritrean government's initial unwillingness to further participate in the UNESCO World Heritage program. While the World Bank portrays the drafting of the tentative World Heritage List entry under CARP as a major achievement and claims that so far an actual nomination has not been filed only because "the country lacks legal and management requirements",[96] Naigzy Gebremedhin talks about a conscious decision on the Eritrean government's part not to officially nominate Asmara:

> With the designation as World Heritage Site comes responsibility. There is an erosion of your sovereignty. [. . .] But Eritreans are terribly, terribly sensitive about an erosion of their sovereignty. And they have not yet made an application.[97]

The Eritrean government's refraining from a definite World Heritage List entry of the 'historic perimeter' of Asmara until 2016, when the Eritrean delegation confirmed the candidature of the city of Asmara at the 40th World Heritage Committee meeting in Istanbul, was an act of defiance against transnationally 'shared' responsibilities for Asmara's modern architectural heritage, denoting fundamental tensions between the national assertion of politics of sovereignty, on one hand, and transnational appeals to postconflict reconstruction, nation building, economic development and poverty reduction on the other.

Above all else, the Eritrean dictatorial regime valorizes Asmara's modern heritage with fervent nationalism and a calculated vision of political and economic self-determination, using the architectural heritage to ensure its national sovereignty very pragmatically. During my fieldwork in Asmara, I interviewed Samson Haile from the Eritrean Ministry of Information about his government's policy concerning Asmara's modern heritage. Haile's answers betray an understanding of cultural heritage as crucial for the establishment of Eritrean national sovereignty as he quickly referred to the many martyrs of war as a reminder of the "importance of preserving Eritrea's independence"[98] and continuously emphasized an imperative for Eritrean "self reliance",[99] always with an eye on the ongoing conflict with Ethiopia. After all, the authority of the Eritrean government depends on this conflict as it provides president Isaias with an excuse to neither pass the democratic constitution nor hold democratic elections.[100]

Whereas the World Bank complains about lost chances to ensure economic development and poverty reduction through cultural heritage preservation, Haile displayed a certain cynicism, maintaining that "we can be hungry, but we will work for Eritrea". He claimed that his country "may be poor economically, but it is rich in social and cultural values. Life is not only economy. Our community ties, that's what makes us strong."[101] Yet Haile's community ties are put under strain by the current circumstances in Eritrea, which, analysts warn, is repeatedly threatened by a major food crisis.[102] Because of hunger and widespread poverty, as well as the national service, which is mandatory from the age of 18 to 40 and likened by a high foreign diplomat in Asmara, as well as by Human Rights Watch, to a form of slave labor, more and more young Eritreans choose to leave their country.[103] Although Haile has nothing but disdain for "those who flee to Europe",[104] the Eritrean government is obviously hard pressed to appeal to social cohesion. Little wonder then, that Haile claims that "every Eritrean should be proud of Asmara"[105] and that the Eritrean government employs cultural heritage to instill a sense of national obligation.

The call to preserve Asmara's modern architectural heritage has effectively provided the Eritrean government with concrete means to discretely exercise disciplinary power domestically. For instance, the government launched an orchestrated press campaign to reduce the height of walls around private houses in Asmara. According to Samson Haile, who has published a book about Asmara's modern heritage in Tigrinya, the local language, of which 5,000 copies have been distributed in Eritrea:

> Asmara is an open city, so walls should only be 1,20m high. The 1938 master plan dictates this. During the Ethiopian period, walls were heightened for security because everybody was being killed. The government is now urging to abolish the walls. In my book and in other media we are campaigning for the reduction of the heights of walls. I devote one chapter to this in my book. [. . .] If they want privacy, they should plant hedges.[106]

Whereas Haile advertises lowering the walls for the sake of preserving the colonial built environment of Asmara, a main goal of his campaign is clearly to assist in the rounding up of draft dodgers.[107] Indeed, the Eritrean government enforces the national service with frequent raids, so called *gffa*. The cultural secretary of the Eritrean People's Front for Democracy and Justice, Zemeret Yohannes, states that "when our young people are defending our country, it is morally and socially unacceptable to hide from the duty of citizenship".[108] During *gffa*, though, it is common to hide to avoid arrest "until the provisional prisons—police stations, cinemas, backyards, and sometimes the stadium—are crowded".[109] Seen against this backdrop, the campaign to reduce the height of walls plays into the hands of the Eritrean government.

To illustrate the regime's brutality, the Italian newspaper *Corriere della Sera* recently published three photographs covertly taken from inside a diplomatic car in the city center of Asmara. The pictures show the 2004 shooting of a young man trying to escape his arrest. Wounded by bullets already, the man was publicly executed while lying on a busy street.[110] In this context, Haile's reference to Asmara as an 'open city' retains a very different connotation than the one from Guang Yu Ren and Edward Denison's expressed hope, in *Asmara: The Secret Modernist City*, that Eritrea would become more "open to the world";[111] it is clear that the Eritrean government means to do the opposite, doing all it can to close Eritrea from the world. As a matter of fact, *Asmara: The Secret Modernist City* is not available for sale in Eritrea and the book's censorship perfectly illustrates Eritrea's repeated ranking as the very last country on the World Press Freedom Index, behind North Korea.[112]

The Eritrean government thus coordinates the preservation of Asmara's architectural heritage through violations of fundamental human rights. And this puts the World Bank's admittance of underestimating the political risk of CARP in a critical light. Indeed, the bank's *Implementation Completion and Results* report notes,

> in retrospect, the risk assessment [for CARP] was overly optimistic and should have been Moderate (M) rather than Negligible (N). [. . .] During implementation [. . .] risk factors [previously not accounted for] seriously affected [the project's] implementation [such as a] change in government support for the involvement of the private sector, a downturn in tourism as a result of regional instability and border conflict [as well as a] depleting human resource base with out-migration and army enrollment.[113]

Still, such self-reflection has to be taken with a grain of salt. Not least because overall the World Bank rates CARP "MS", or moderately satisfactory, a rating which it claims is "fully justified as the project demonstrates extensive achievements and lessons learned".[114] In a strange move, the bank report maintains that CARP

> clearly contributed to increased recognition of the importance of cultural heritage in Eritrea. Among other achievements, it has led to the production of a number of important publications and studies of Eritrean cultural heritage, particularly related to old districts of Asmara [. . .]. These publications and studies have become popular among both tourists and scholars and have increased awareness of the cultural heritage of the country. The potential for increased tourism and international interest in historic sites and local culture provide important opportunities for building social capital and for contributing to economic growth. The project has also successfully provoked increased cooperation among municipalities and other Government bodies, urban planners, the private sector and cultural heritage professionals [. . .] directed towards the preservation and protection of cultural heritage of the country. This has included new zoning and

frontage regulations designed to preserve the historic [perimeter] of Asmara.[115]

Knowing just how the Eritrean government responded to the increased recognition of the importance of cultural heritage, how it censored the important publications, and how it interpreted the frontage regulations in terms of its campaign to lower the walls, it is hard not to read the report with a cynical eye. The World Bank rhetoric of political risk certainly underplays the Eritrean government's structural violations of human rights as a consequence of its radical politics of sovereignty. The World Bank even lauds the creation of "a positive image of Eritrea"[116] as a result of CARP's activities, maintaining that CARP, despite its shortcomings, has shown that "culture should be recognized as a unifying force in a post-conflict situation".[117] Clearly such statements play favorably into the hands of the Eritrean government and what Cultural Secretary Yohannes calls its "propaganda machinery", "the main element of [which] is a continuation of the old liberation struggle [against Ethiopia]. It is our heritage."[118]

In this respect, the global heritage assemblage around the modern architecture of Asmara appears to be a case in point of what the anthropologist James Ferguson has called an "anti-politics machine". For Ferguson, the antipolitics machine of development depoliticizes "everything it touches, everywhere whisking political realities out of sight, all the while performing, almost unnoticed, its own pre-eminently political operation of expanding bureaucratic state power".[119] When the World Bank ignores the political capital that the heritage valorization of Asmara's modern heritage creates domestically for the Eritrean government, this is exactly such an act of depoliticization through development.

Significantly, however, the heritage valorization of Asmara's modern architecture has not just served the Eritrean state well in its politics of national sovereignty. At a time when according to one foreign diplomat in Asmara "development work in Eritrea is like jumping out of a plane without a parachute",[120] the modern architectural heritage of Asmara presented an emergent transnational apparatus of government with a welcome opportunity to justify its pursuit of politics of security on the Horn of Africa.

Indeed, an immediate follow up to the World Bank's involvement in CARP is the 2009 European Union delegation's National Heritage Programme. Worth €5 million of direct investments in architectural heritage preservation, this programme is part of a €120 million development aid package for Eritrea that mainly focuses on food security and infrastructure. Its overall goal is

> to effectively support the ongoing efforts of the Government of the State of Eritrea in protecting or rehabilitating Eritrea's rich cultural and architectural heritage in order to sustain long term socioeconomic objectives.[121]

The programme is thus in line with the 2005 European Union Consensus on Development, which holds that "economic, social and environmental dimensions of poverty eradication in the context of sustainable development include many development activities", prominent among which is "culture".[122]

Like CARP, the EU National Heritage Programme focuses on Asmara's modern heritage in an attempt at "urban rehabilitation of Eritrea's capital city".[123] Its Terms of Reference state that

> Asmara possesses an internationally recognized urban ensemble which stands among the highest concentrations of Modernist buildings anywhere in the world, which has suffered a period of decades of neglect brought about by a lack of resources mainly caused by war. This built heritage not only constitutes a fundamental pillar of Eritrean identity, but also a rich resource for its urban public domain. If well maintained, this built heritage would offer further potential for social and economic projects, street market activities, the enactment of cultural events such as theatre, cinema and dance, and would also contribute to better attract international tourism.[124]

The EU delegation acknowledges the World Bank's cautionary *Implementation Completion and Results* CARP report. For instance, the Terms of Reference for the National Heritage Programme warn that "lack of assured dialogue and cooperation between stakeholders could lead to a halt in the urban rehabilitation project".[125] Still, the World Bank presented CARP as "highly relevant" and "good value for money [. . .] although its implementation was uneven",[126] and whether or not CARP yielded measurable economic development and poverty reduction results seems to be irrelevant to the project in the short term. Similar to the World Bank, then, the EU delegation to Eritrea with its National Heritage Programme pursues long-term interests of global governance and politics of security on the horn of Africa.

The EU has explicitly committed itself to preventing food shortages and to contain Eritrean immigration. Employees of the EU delegation to Eritrea, as well as diplomats from EU member states working in Asmara, however, doubt whether investment in the modern architectural heritage of their host city is effective. My expatriate interviewees in Asmara point out an essential tension between politics of sovereignty and security in Eritrea, especially considering the government's policy of self-reliance and its structural violations of fundamental human rights. They describe the Eritrean regime as fostering a "strange national pride, a *couleur nationale*, which is difficult in an environment of poverty when you should first feed your people".[127] They claim that the Eritrean government mistakenly thinks that it is "at the center of international attention",[128] "full of conspiracy theories about everybody who is advertising for cultural heritage abroad".[129] Above all else, though, my contacts spoke of Eritrea as a "notoriously unpredictable recipient of aid".[130] What then explains the urgency of continued transnational appeals to the development potential of the valorization of Asmara's modern heritage?

Restorative Nostalgia/Reflective Nostalgia

For the World Bank, CARP's LIL for was a relatively small investment. Similarly, for the EU delegation's development aid to Eritrea the National Heritage Programme merely constitutes a 'non-focal sector'. Still, the "restoration of national heritage" is said to provide "a substantial platform for European Union visibility in the country".[131] In fact, the EU delegation considers attention to cultural heritage particularly image friendly:

> The [EU delegation], as a potential lead donor, is ideally positioned to deliver a flagship project in an internationally renowned setting that other donors can replicate. Representatives of almost all [EU] member states in Asmara have expressed an interest in supporting future rehabilitation programmes bi- or multi-laterally if the Heritage Programme proves successful. This places the [European Union] in a unique position of taking the lessons learnt from [CARP] and assuming a lead role in Eritrea in this sector in the long term.[132]

Apparently transnational organizations consider Asmara's reputation as a City of Dreams, the title of a documentary movie, or Africa's secret modernist city to be a good advertisement for their interventions in Eritrea.[133] Ultimately both the World Bank and the European Union delegation crucially rely on a particular fascination with Asmara for their cultural representation of authority in Eritrea.[134]

Among the expatriate community in Eritrea there seems to be a very personal fascination with Asmara's modern architectural heritage and most believe it is ultimately well equipped to distract from the real dangers faced by the Eritrean population. One example is Edward Denison, whom the EU National Heritage Programme hired as a principal consultant, not least because of his experience with CARP. Denison says that one of the motivations for him to return to Asmara on the EU bill, despite his negative experience with the Eritrean government, was his conviction that

> [h]eritage is always going to be key to Eritrea's development. Even if that is just bringing people in, building relationships that lead to other things. [. . .] To ensure that it's going to remain a nice place to live. You know, it's certainly one of the safest cities in Africa, I mean socially as an anthropologist you'll be struck by that. So this is important in terms of development, I think.[135]

Here, Denison attributes the development potential of Asmara's modern heritage to his perception of the city as a nice and safe place to live. In his *Asmara: The Secret Modernist City*, he similarly characterizes the city as a "convivial urban idyll".[136] Several of my other expatriate interviewees in Asmara also pointed out the "nice atmosphere" in Asmara.[137] They claim it explains why for them "there is no way around being sympathetic to cultural heritage in this town".[138] Unanimously, they considered Asmara a pleasant and familiar environment and experienced it as safe. In addition to that, they pointed out Asmara's "Un-Africanness"[139]. Denison even referred to a certain "Europeanness", claiming that in Asmara "as Europeans and as Westerners, that's what we see Europe in Africa, the West in Africa".[140] This kind of fascination with the modern architectural heritage of Asmara might go a long way toward explaining the EU delegation's decision to launch a CARP follow-up.

Off the record there is great disillusionment among diplomats in Eritrea, several of whom express the belief that "the country really doesn't do anything with the potential of the modern heritage of Asmara"[141] and that "in order to stay in power, the [Eritrean] president needs to obstruct development".[142] Denison, however, told me,

> Jesper Pedersen at the EU [in Asmara] initiated the €5 million project. He felt, I think personally that heritage should be part of these €120 million [of development aid]. I think he's right. I think many people think he's right. And if the present situation wasn't as bad with the Eritrean government I think anyone who's passionate about this architecture would accept any money to preserve it.[143]

While Denison acknowledges "criticism of the €120 million aid package that it will only serve the [Eritrean] government to stay in power", he adds that "the heritage issue doesn't bother me morally, because I think that buildings will be around longer than any government".[144]

This statement implies more than a mere downplaying of political problems, however. When the image of Asmara is that of a 'European' colonial city, engagement with its modern heritage under Denison's motto that "buildings will be around longer than any government" also betrays a certain nostalgia. According to the comparative literature scholar Svetlana Boym,

> nostalgia like progress is dependent on the modern conception of unrepeatable, irreversible time. [. . .] Nostalgia remains unsystematic and unsynthesizeable, it seduces, rather than convinces.[145]

Somewhat paradoxically then, for transnational organizations and their staff, the appeal of Asmara's modern architectural heritage appears to be rooted in nostalgia for colonial utopias of progress. Against all odds, there is a belief in the capacity of cultural heritage, to, though not rapidly,

(re)transform Asmara into the progressive city it is said to have constituted a century ago.[146]

Nostalgia for colonial Asmara, claimed once to have been "the world's
prime building ground for architectural innovation during the Modernist Movement",[147] may explain a hope that its 'untouched' historic built
environment can reconstitute the "ideal blank canvas" allegedly available to colonial architects in the past. Only this time Asmara would be
a field of experimentation for transnational organizations to test out
new approaches to economic development, poverty reduction, nation
building and postconflict reconstruction through cultural heritage preservation. Indeed, if Boym understands heritage as "institutionalized nostalgia",[148] a way of "giving shape and meaning to longing",[149] clearly the
valorization of Asmara's modern heritage institutionalizes a nostalgia for
colonialism, a time when the colonial state introduced politics of security through modern architecture and urban planning. It is telling that
the tentative UNESCO World Heritage List entry of Asmara's 'historic
perimeter' refers to the colonial era as a time when "Italian architects
could practice and realize [. . .] modern ideals" on an "ideal blank canvas", transforming the city "from a relatively minor town into Africa's
most modern and sophisticated city at that time".[150]

Guang Yu Ren and Edward Denison's vision of "forward progress"[151]
for Eritrea through heritage preservation in Asmara also hinges on colonial nostalgia, as

> the implications for Eritrea evidently go far beyond extolling its colo-
> nial architectural heritage. The possibilities for all manner of initia-
> tives to encourage development largely through tourism, awareness
> and education are now more attainable than ever before.[152]

Denison admits that "it would be devious for Europeans to just focus
on tourism because it is us [Europeans] going there".[153] And indeed, the
fact that Asmara's modern heritage is continuously credited with a high
potential for international tourism, this may be the result of a nostalgia
for a colonial "age of travel and adventure [. . .] embodied in [the] new
architectural forms of Asmara", as it is literally described in the tentative UNESCO World Heritage List entry.[154] Today, globalization is said
to give rise to a new age of travel, and for Eritrea, the preservation of
Asmara's colonial built environment is presented as an opportunity to
finally join the rest of the world—through tourism and by capitalizing on
the link to global resources initially established by CARP.

The Strategic Urban Development Plan for Asmara, credited as a major
result of CARP and financed by the African Union, for instance formulates
a future vision under the heading "a convivial city, proud of its heritage":[155]

> In 2025, Asmara is a city which has succeeded in protecting its mod-
> ern heritage [. . .] Asmara has managed to place itself on the Tourist

map of the sub region. It is widely visited by specialized tours. [. . .] It
has managed to avoid the mass tourism which has proven so destructive of heritage.[156]

The Heritage and Tourism strategy expounded in the plan does, however,
remark that a necessary international promotion campaign for tourism
to Asmara can only be realized after "the normalization of relations with
neighboring countries".[157] That such normalization is not imminent is
illustrated by the 2009 UN resolution against Eritrea, responding to "a
threat to international peace and security" because of "the ongoing border dispute between Djibouti and Eritrea, as well as Eritrea's support
of armed groups destabilizing and undermining peace and reconciliation
in Somalia".[158] Only nostalgia for the relative geopolitical stability and
global dominance that allowed for a colonial "age of travel and adventure" on the Horn of Africa may obscure such realities.

Of course, the Eritrean government indulges in its own version of colonial nostalgia, one largely opposed to the one informing the agendas of
transnational organizations. After decades of fighting for national sovereignty and independence from Ethiopia, the Eritrean regime fundamentally depends on references to Italian colonialism for its legitimacy. In
fact, compared to the hated Ethiopian occupation, Eritreans regard the
Italians as 'the good colonizers'.[159] After all, as the anthropologists David
O'Kane and Tricia Redeker-Hepner note, it was during the period of
Italian rule that the Eritrean population "began groping towards a common identity".[160] Even if such a common identity was the result of brutal
colonial policies of racial segregation, it did make the Eritrean pursuit of
an independent nation-state possible in the first place.

Today, as a legacy of Italian colonialism, Asmara's modern architectural heritage stands as a symbol of Eritrea's cultural and political
borders. Not only do the contested borderlines of today's Eritrea more
or less coincide with those of the former Italian colony; it is also difficult to establish differences between Eritrea and its enemy Ethiopia that
reach further back than the period of Italian colonialism. In this respect,
Denison may be right to claim that "Asmara is adamant to break the
traditional African hostility to an acceptance of the continent's colonial
history".[161] But for the Eritrean government to embrace its Italian colonial heritage does not equal a willingness to 'share' its ownership transnationally. Instead, the Eritrean government exploits globalization trends
and mechanisms to assert the newly won Eritrean national sovereignty
with a sense of colonial nostalgia.[162]

Now, Svetlana Boym distinguishes between restorative nostalgia and
reflective nostalgia. According to Boym, restorative nostalgia manifests
itself in the total reconstruction of monuments of the past. For the restorative nostalgic, the past is a value for the present—it is not a duration
but a snapshot of an 'original image'.[163] As a consequence, restorative

nostalgics do not think of themselves as nostalgic; instead, they believe that their project is about truth.[164] Clearly such restorative nostalgia—instead of reflective nostalgia, which I define further on—informs Eritrean governmental reasoning. After all, the Eritrean government lists among the most important lessons learned from CARP "the empowerment to identify, know and write Eritrean ancient history free from Axumite hegemony and excessive Sabean [read: Ethiopian] influence", as well as the "improved interpretation of Eritrean history by Eritreans".[165]

The transnational occupation with Asmara's modern architectural heritage, however, is also fueled by restorative nostalgia. One of my diplomat interviewees in Asmara, for instance, admitted that he likes to "imagine sometimes how it must have been when the Italians were still here", claiming that "a splash of paint would make a world of difference".[166] Evidence of this type of nostalgia can be found in the funding of the EU National Heritage Programme, which is limited to two restorations. Edward Denison explains

> that 5 million, we decided in the end, will go two projects. One is the restoration of Cinema Capitol, which was part of the CARP project, contentiously so because it is opposite the government palace and there were criticisms that that would be beautifying it [. . .] the other is the rehabilitation of Medebar Market Square.[167]

One way or another, this isolated restoration of two monuments will result in the creation of two perfect snapshots of the past, feeding the different restorative nostalgias behind the valorization of Asmara's modern heritage.

Though transnational organizations ascribe much of the development potential of Asmara's modern heritage to tourism, the vision of a meticulously restored, monumental Asmara—although obviously far from attainable in the near future—does not seem to attract tourists from abroad. Rather, the few foreigners who do make it to Asmara for reasons of tourism often come because of the crumbling patina of its colonial built environment. If they are not put off by the Eritrean government's restrictive foreign visa regulations and international warnings about instability and violent conflict in the Horn of Africa region, they visit Asmara because of its exotic allure of secrecy.

When I waited at Asmara International airport's baggage claim on the eve of the Eritrean Christmas holiday together with many people from the Eritrean diaspora and just a handful of Asians and Europeans, I met Michael Baer, a Viennese historic preservationist who had come to spend his vacation in Asmara. Baer told me that he had first gotten to know about the city through *Asmara: Africa's Secret Modernist City*. He had even taken the book with him as a travel guide. Now that he had arrived, Baer feared he would not be able to experience the city as presented in the book, patina and all. Having read about the many international initiatives launched to restore Asmara, he was anxious that much of the façades would be hidden behind scaffolding.[168] Of course, when I met him again a couple of days later, he readily admitted that this worry had been ungrounded, given the virtual lack of any building construction, as well as perhaps even inappropriate, considering the poverty visible in Asmara.

This story captures Boym's notion of an alternative to restorative nostalgia, as reflective nostalgics

> are aware of the gap between identity and resemblance; the home is in ruins or, on the contrary, has just been renovated and gentrified beyond recognition. This defamiliarization drives [reflective nostalgics] to tell their story, to narrate the relationship between past present and future.[169]

As far as Baer was "longing for a different place" and "yearning for a different time",[170] he certainly displayed a nostalgia for Asmara's modern heritage. But, his actual experience of Asmara resembles the reflective nostalgia described by Boym: "[I]t reveals longing and critical thinking are not opposed to one another, as affective memories do not absolve one from compassion, judgment or critical reflection".[171] Though Boym acknowledges a need to accommodate a sense of longing for the past, for her, "the past is not made in the image of the present or seen as foreboding of some present disaster; rather the past opens up a multitude of potentialities, nonteleological possibilities of historic development".[172] As a consequence, "a modern nostalgic can be homesick and sick of home at the same time",[173] which may be how Baer felt once he had landed in Asmara.

Conclusion

In this chapter I attempted to narrate relationships between Asmara's past and future. I have tried to illustrate the multitude of possibilities opened up by the heritage valorization of Asmara's modern architecture. My analysis of the global heritage assemblage around Asmara can be read as a plea for a reflective nostalgia of the modern. With Foucault and Rabinow, I have shown how changes in the modern built environment have had an effect on the development of modern governmental reason, particularly the politics of sovereignty and security. I contend that contemporary governmental rationalities, rather than indulging in restorative nostalgia for the colonial politics of a recent past, need to reflect on how the global fascination with Asmara's modern heritage problematizes Eritrea's politics of sovereignty and security today. As my example shows, the Eritrean government instrumentalizes the colonial built environment of Asmara in order to establish its newly won national sovereignty, all the while violating fundamental human rights and obstructing transnational politics of security. The World Bank and the European Union, however, cast these problems aside, as their interventions in Eritrea depend on positive references to the potential of Asmara's modern heritage for global development.

In effect, this transnational nostalgia for Asmara's modern architecture obscures poverty, hunger and militarism on the Horn of Africa. The tentative UNESCO World Heritage List entry, for instance, considers it ironic that postcolonial "turbulence" and "continuous unrest" should have "served to protect Asmara's unique urban heritage" so that its buildings have "remained untouched".[174] Moreover, a foreword to the book *Asmara: The Frozen City* somewhat cynically states that for "a mysterious, slightly crumbling, ideal city of modernism [. . .] poverty is the best way to protect monuments".[175]

Still, Edward Denison maintains the success of his engagement with CARP and the National Heritage Programme:

> Although it may not be earth shattering in its wider significance, it tells good news from Africa. That is a welcome rarity in itself and represents an attempt to seek alternative approaches to development that have not been given much hearing. [A problem is that] the timeframe required measuring the success of cultural preservation, which often far exceeds the limited schedules of today's mega-donors. Cultural preservation cannot be ascribed an annual figure to demonstrate improvement. And it might sometimes only involve maintaining the status quo in the face of widespread change. When successful, it underpins the broader aims of development, linking the past with the present—and the present with the future.[176]

Denison may be right when he states that "slowly but surely Eritrea is learning to exploit the Western fascination with Asmara to support other development programs", but an important question to ask would be, 'How does it do so and to what ends?'

In the preceding discussion, I analyzed how the Eritrean government bases its problematic politics of national sovereignty on a kind of restorative nostalgia. Svetlana Boym likens nostalgia in general to

> a transformation of fatality into continuity, contingency into meaning. Yet this transformation can take different turns. It may increase the emancipatory possibilities and individual choices [. . .]. It can also be politically manipulated through newly recreated practices of national commemoration with the aim of reestablishing social cohesion, a sense of security and an obedient relationship to authority.[177]

It is not that the Eritrean government's domestic repression is completely ignored because many of my expatriate interviewees in Eritrea have doubts about the 'development impact' of the preservation of the modern architectural heritage of Asmara and say they would have spent the money otherwise.[178] Paradoxically, however, the obvious contingency of politics of national sovereignty and transnational security does not seem to reduce the colonial nostalgia for Asmara's modern built environment.

Certainly some reflect on what happens when a young African nation-state is forced to operate in a global space of transnational governance. Denison, for instance, claims that

> Eritrea, to be fair to their government, they've always taken the line of self-reliance. And they've also shot themselves in the foot probably more times than not, but they at least are a developing country that has taken that line consistently, and if that means building a wall around their border and saying we're on our own, they'll do it. And it might ruin ties with the nations but they'll do it, they've got that sort of headstrong mentality. And that pisses the West off, because the West knows ultimately they're right. You know why should a country exist on favors by the West?[179]

But such critical views of contemporary norms and forms of government are hardly represented in official policy documents. In fact, as James Ferguson has pointed out, in a different, yet applicable, context, "there are a host of statements, which are, if not actually forbidden, at any rate profoundly unhelpful in the discourse of a development agency".[180] Against this background, I would like to close with one of my expatriate interviewees' comments on the political situation in Eritrea: "There is reason to believe that things can't possibly stay as they are."[181]

Notes

1. Kreszentia Duer, *Culture and Sustainable Development: A Framework for Action* (Washington, DC: The Worldbank, 1999); Alcira Kreimer et al., *The World Bank's Experience with Post-Conflict Reconstruction* (Washington, DC: The World Bank, 1998); James D. Wolfensohn, *The Challenges of Globalization: The Role of the World Bank/Address to the Bundestag* (Berlin, Germany: The World Bank Group, 2001); Worldbank, "Implementation Completion and Results Report on a Learning and Innovation Loan to the State of Eritrea in the Amount of SDR 4.0 Million (US$ 5 Million Equivalent) for a Cultural Assets Rehabilitation Project."
2. David O'Kane and Tricia Redeker-Hepner, eds., *Biopolitics and Militarism and Development: Eritrea in the Twenty-First Century* (New York: Berghahn, 2009). xiv.
3. For example, Saskia Sassen, *Losing Control? Sovereignty in an Age of Globalization* (New York: Columbia University Press, 1996); Sassen, *Territory, Authority, Rights: From Medieval to Global Assemblages*.
4. Edward Denison, Naigzy Gebremedhin, and Guang Yu Ren, *Asmara: Africa's Secret Modernist City* (London: Merrell, 2003).
5. For example, Ofori, Ruby, and Scott, Edward. *Asmara: City of Dreams* (New York: Custom Flix, 2006).

6. Michel Foucault, *Security, Territory, Population: Lectures at the Collège de France*, vol. 4 (London: Macmillan, 2007). 313.
7. Jonathan Xavier Inda, *Anthropologies of Modernity: Foucault, Governmentality and Life Politics* (London: Blackwell, 2005); Michel Foucault, *The Birth of Biopolitics: Lectures at the Collège de France*, vol. 5 (London: Macmillan, 2010).
8. Inda, *Security, Territory, Population: Lectures at the Collège de France*. 4.
9. Ibid., 65–66.
10. Inda, *The Birth of Biopolitics: Lectures at the Collège de France*, 5– 308.
11. Ibid., 30.
12. Ibid., 296.
13. Inda, *Anthropologies of Modernity: Foucault, Governmentality and Life Politics*. 4.
14. Foucault, *Security, Territory, Population: Lectures at the Collège de France*. 4.
15. Paul Rabinow, *French Modern: Norms and Forms of the Built Environment* (Chicago: University of Chicago Press, 1989).
16. Ibid., 289.
17. Compare, for example, Nezar AlSayyad, ed. *Forms of Dominance: On the Architecture and Urbanism of the Colonial Enterprise* (Aldershot: Avebury, 1992); Lawrence J. Vale, *Architecture, Power, and National Identity* (London: Yale University Press, 1992); Jyoti Hosagrahar, *Indigenous Modernities: Negotiating Architecture, Urbanism, and Colonialism in Delhi* (London: Routledge, 2005); Rabinow, *French Modern: Norms and Forms of the Built Environment*.
18. Mia Fuller, *Moderns Abroad: Architecture, Cities and Italian Imperialism* (London: Routledge, 2007). 70.
19. Thomas Pakenham, *The Scramble for Africa: White Man's Conquest of the Dark Continent from 1876–1912* (London: Avon Books, 1992).
20. Fuller, *Moderns Abroad: Architecture, Cities and Italian Imperialism*. 212, 141.
21. Ibid., 138.
22. Ibid., 142.
23. Ibid., 144.
24. Fuller, *Moderns Abroad: Architecture, Cities and Italian Imperialism*; Denison, Gebremedhin, and Ren, *Asmara: Africa's Secret Modernist City*; Fouad Makki, "Imperial Fantasies, Colonial Realities: Contesting Power and Culture in Italian Eritrea," *South Atlantic Quarterly* 107, no. 4 (2008). 735–754.
25. Frederico Mayor Zaragoza, "The World Decade for Cultural Development," *UNESCO Courier*, November 1988.
26. Wolfensohn, *The Challenges of Globalization: The Role of the World Bank/ Address to the Bundestag*. 7.
27. Ibid., 15.
28. Interview of the author with Arlene Fleming.
29. Robert Picciotto, "Cultural Properties in Policy and Practice: A Review of World Bank Experience," Policy 23369, http://documents.worldbank.org/curated/en/310631468762018373/pdf/multi0page.pdf
30. Duer, *Culture and Sustainable Development: A Framework for Action*. 21.
31. Picciotto, *Cultural Properties in Policy and Practice: A Review of World Bank Experience*. 6.
32. Wolfensohn, *The Challenges of Globalization: The Role of the World Bank/ Address to the Bundestag*. 7.
33. Duer, *Culture and Sustainable Development: A Framework for Action*. 8.
34. Kreimer et al., "The World Bank's Experience with Post-Conflict Reconstruction." 6.
35. Ibid., xii.
36. Ibid., 21.

37. Ibid., 32.
38. Ibid.
39. Ibid., 2.
40. Interview of the author with Fleming.
41. Interview of the author with Gebremedhin.
42. Ibid.
43. Also compare Naigzy Gebremedhin, ed. *Asmara: A Guide to the Built Environment* (Asmara: CARP, 2003).
44. Picciotto, *Cultural Properties in Policy and Practice: A Review of World Bank Experience*. 3.
45. Interview of the author with Gebremedhin.
46. Interview of the author with Fleming.
47. Ibid.
48. Interview of the author with Gebremedhin.
49. ICOMOS, "Heritage at Risk 2001–2002: Shared Colonial Heritage".
50. Ibid.
51. Jokilehto, *The World Heritage List: Filling the Gaps—An Action Plan for the Future*.
52. Interview of the author with Gebremedhin.
53. Interview of the author with Denison.
54. van Oers, *Meeting on Modern Heritage for Africa: Asmara, Eritrea, 4–7 March 2004*. (Moreover: Interview of the author with van Oers)
55. Ibid., 1; 3.
56. Interview of the author with van Oers; Interview of the author with Densison.
57. Interview of the author with Denison.
58. Denison, Gebremedhin, and Ren, *Asmara: Africa's Secret Modernist City*.
59. Ibid., 17.
60. Ibid., 11.
61. Interview of the author with Hakim.
62. Travelling exhibition, Asmara—Africa's Secret Modernist City. Various locations starting 2006; for example, Ofori, Ruby, and Scott, Edward, *Asmara: City of Dreams* (New York: Custom Flix, 2006).
63. Interview of the author with Hakim.
64. Ibid.
65. Interview of the author with Gebremedhin.
66. Denison, Gebremedhin, and Ren, *Asmara: Africa's Secret Modernist City*. 6.
67. Interview of the author with Denison.
68. Ibid.
69. Ibid.
70. Ibid.
71. Interview of the author with Anonymous.
72. Ibid.
73. Ibid.
74. Worldbank, "Implementation Completion and Results Report on a Learning and Innovation Loan to the State of Eritrea in the Amount of SDR 4.0 Million (US$ 5 Million Equivalent) for a Cultural Assets Rehabilitation Project." 22.
75. Ibid.
76. Ibid.
77. Ibid., 2.
78. Ibid.
79. Ibid., 8.
80. Ibid.
81. Ibid., 13.

82. Interview of the author with Medhanie; also compare "Executive Summary of the Strategic Urban Development Plan for Asmara," ed. Department of Infrastructure, Asmara, 2006.
83. Worldbank, "Implementation Completion and Results Report on a Learning and Innovation Loan to the State of Eritrea in the Amount of SDR 4.0 Million (US$ 5 Million Equivalent) for a Cultural Assets Rehabilitation Project." 8.
84. Interview of the author with Fleming.
85. Ibid.
86. Worldbank, "Implementation Completion and Results Report on a Learning and Innovation Loan to the State of Eritrea in the Amount of SDR 4.0 Million (US$ 5 Million Equivalent) for a Cultural Assets Rehabilitation Project." 18.
87. Ibid., 8.
88. Interview of the author with Hakim.
89. Worldbank, "Implementation Completion and Results Report on a Learning and Innovation Loan to the State of Eritrea in the Amount of SDR 4.0 Million (US$ 5 Million Equivalent) for a Cultural Assets Rehabilitation Project." 17.
90. Ibid.
91. Interview of the author with Hakim.
92. Worldbank, "Implementation Completion and Results Report on a Learning and Innovation Loan to the State of Eritrea in the Amount of SDR 4.0 Million (US$ 5 Million Equivalent) for a Cultural Assets Rehabilitation Project." 10; 3.
93. Ibid., 17.
94. Ibid.
95. Ibid., 19.
96. Ibid.
97. Interview of the author with Gebremedhin.
98. Interview of the author with Haile.
99. Ibid.
100. O'Kane and Redeker-Hepner, *Biopolitics and Militarism and Development: Eritrea in the Twenty-First Century*; Tricia Redeker-Hepner, *Soldiers, Martyrs, Traitors, and Exiles: Political Conflict in Eritrea and the Diaspora* (Philadelphia: University of Pennslyvania Press, 2009).
101. Interview of the author with Haile.
102. UN, "World Food Programme: Report on Eritrea," http://www.wfp.org/countries/eritrea.
103. Interview of the author with Anonymous, also compare: *Service for Life: State Repression and Indefinite Conscription in Eritrea* (New York: Human Rights Watch, 2009). Redeker-Hepner, *Soldiers, Martyrs, Traitors, and Exiles: Political Conflict in Eritrea and the Diaspora.*
104. Interview of the author with Haile.
105. Ibid.
106. Ibid.
107. BBC, "Eritrea 'Rounds up Draft-dodgers,'" http://news.bbc.co.uk/2/hi/africa/323436.stm.
108. Ibid.
109. Magnus Treiber, "Trapped in Adolescence: The Postwar Urban Generation," in *Biopolitics, Militarism and Development: Eritrea in the Twenty-First Century* ed. David O'Kane and Tricia Redeker-Hepner (New York: Berghahn, 2009). 97.

110. Ibid., 98.
111. Edward Denison and Guang Yu Ren, "Africa's Secret Modernist City," www.theglobalist.com/StoryID.aspx?StoryId=4115.
112. "Reporters Without Border: World Press Freedom Index 2010," http://en.rsf.org/press-freedom-index-2010,1034.html.
113. Worldbank, "Implementation Completion and Results Report on a Learning and Innovation Loan to the State of Eritrea in the Amount of SDR 4.0 Million (US$ 5 Million Equivalent) for a Cultural Assets Rehabilitation Project." 15.
114. Ibid., 17.
115. Ibid.
116. Ibid., 19.
117. Ibid., 24.
118. *Zemeret Yohannes cited in* Lucy Hannan, "Desert War of Rusty Weapons and Sophisticated Words," *The Independent*, 1999.
119. James Ferguson, *The Anti-Politics Machine: 'Development,' Depoliticization, and Bureaucratic Power in Lesotho* (Minneapolis: University of Minnesota Press, 1994). xv.
120. Interview of the author with Anonymous.
121. Commission EU, *European Commission Delegation to Eritrea: Policy Plan National Heritage Programme* (2009). 2.
122. Commission EU, "The European Consensus on Development," http://ec.europa.eu/europeaid/what/development-policies/european-consensus/; EU, *European Commission Delegation to Eritrea: Policy Plan National Heritage Programme*. 1.
123. EU, *European Commission Delegation to Eritrea: Policy Plan National Heritage Programme*. 3.
124. Ibid.
125. Ibid., 6.
126. Worldbank, "Implementation Completion and Results Report on a Learning and Innovation Loan to the State of Eritrea in the Amount of SDR 4.0 Million (US$ 5 Million Equivalent) for a Cultural Assets Rehabilitation Project." 14; 16.
127. Interview of the author with Anonymous.
128. Ibid.
129. Ibid.
130. Ibid.
131. EU, *European Commission Delegation to Eritrea: Policy Plan National Heritage Programme*. 1.
132. Ibid. 2.
133. Ofori, Ruby, and Scott, Edward. *Asmara: City of Dreams* (New York: Custom Flix, 2006).
134. Today, there is even competition among employees of transnational organizations to engage in high visibility cultural heritage projects in Eritrea. One of the EU delegation officials in Asmara made me promise to quote his claim that "we [from the EU delegation] are quicker than the World Bank and the UN."
135. Interview of the author with Denison.
136. Ibid.
137. Interview of the author with Anonymous.
138. Ibid.
139. Ibid.
140. Interview of the author with Denison.
141. Ibid.
142. Ibid.

143. Interview of the author with Denison.
144. Ibid.
145. Svetlana Boym, *The Future of Nostalgia* (New York: Basic Books, 2001). 13.
146. UNESCO, "Tentative World Heritage List Entry: The Historic Perimeter of Asmara and Its Modernist Architecture," http://whc.unesco.org/en/tentativelists/2024/.
147. Ibid.
148. Boym, *The Future of Nostalgia.* 15.
149. Ibid., 41.
150. UNESCO, "Tentative World Heritage List Entry: The Historic Perimeter of Asmara and Its Modernist Architecture".
151. Edward Denison and Guang Yu Ren, "Supporting Africa's Secret City," www.theglobalist.com/StoryID.aspx?StoryId=3761.
152. Ibid.
153. Interview of the author with Denison.
154. EU Commission, *European Commission Delegation to Eritrea: Terms of Reference National Heritage Programme* (2009). 3.
155. DUD Ministry of Public Works, "Final Strategic Urban Development Plan: Executive Summary," (Asmara, Eritrea 2006). 15.
156. Ibid.
157. Ibid., 22; 23.
158. UN, "Security Council Resolution 1907, December 2009," http://www.dfat.gov.au/un/unsc_sanctions/eritrea.html.
159. Interview of the author with Gebremedhin.
160. O'Kane and Redeker-Hepner, *Biopolitics and Militarism and Development: Eritrea in the Twenty-First Century.* xviii.
161. Denison and Ren, "Africa's Secret Modernist City"; Denison, Gebremedhin, and Ren, *Asmara: Africa's Secret Modernist City.*
162. O'Kane and Redeker-Hepner, *Biopolitics and Militarism and Development: Eritrea in the Twenty-First Century.* xiv.
163. Boym, *The Future of Nostalgia.* 49.
164. Ibid., 41.
165. Ibid., 46.
166. Interview of the author with Anonymous.
167. Interview of the author with Denison.
168. Interview of the author with Anonymous.
169. Boym, *The Future of Nostalgia.* 50.
170. Ibid., xv.
171. Boym, *The Future of Nostalgia.* 50.
172. Ibid.
173. Ibid.
174. Ibid.
175. Jochen Visscher and Stefan Boness, *Asmara: The Frozen City* (Berlin: Jovis, 2006). 10.
176. Interview of the author with Denison.
177. Boym, *The Future of Nostalgia.* 42.
178. Interview of the author with Anonymous.
179. Interview of the author with Denison.
180. Ferguson, *The Anti-Politics Machine: "Development," Depoliticization, and Bureaucratic Power in Lesotho.* 68.
181. Interview of the author with Anonymous.

6 Modern Trophy

Contesting Technologies of Authenticity and Value in Niamey, Brazzaville, Paris, New York and Venice

In 1993, the French government commissioned research on the colonial architecture of Brazzaville, the capital of the Republic of the Congo. This research was cofinanced by the French ministries of Foreign Cooperation and Culture and would take place over two years. In 1996, the project yielded two brochures published in a government series on French heritage,[1] *Brazzaville Decouvertes* and *Brazzaville la Verte*. These brochures featured photographs of two so-called *Maisons Tropicales*, prototypes of a prefab design by French industrial designer Jean Prouvé in the mid-20th century. This system of standardized aluminum modules could construct colonial buildings ranging from expeditionary shelters to school complexes and went by various names, such as *Maison Colonial, Maison Equatorial* and *Maison Tropicale*.[2] In 1949, Prouvé's company Maxeville first shipped the modules for a Maison Tropicale prototype via air-cargo from Nancy in metropolitan France to Niamey, the capital of the French colony of Niger. There, the separate parts were assembled to serve as a home for colonial officials. Two years later, the two Brazzaville Maisons Tropicales followed suit as demonstration models to acquire government contracts. Shortly thereafter, however, Prouvé was forced to abandon his project in the wake of decolonization in French West Africa.

After the French Niger and Congo achieved political independence, the Maisons Tropicales prototypes saw half a century of local use for purposes of accommodation and commerce until their 'rediscovery' as a result of the French heritage inventory in Brazzaville, which coincided with art market excitement around Prouvé's modern industrial design in the mid-1990s. After the publication of photographs of the Maisons Tropicales, an American collector actually commissioned a French gallery owner to remove the Maisons Tropicales from postcolonial Niamey and Brazzaville as 'collector's items'. In 2001, they were successful and dismantled all three Maisons Tropicales, shipping them to France for restoration, despite prominent calls to preserve the houses *in situ* from the French Ministry of Culture, as well as the Africa section of the UNESCO World Heritage Center in Paris. Since 2005, one of the Maisons Tropicales is on permanent loan to the Centre Pompidou. Christie's in New York sold a second Maison Tropicale to a private buyer for a reported

US$4.97 million in 2007. The auction coincided with the 52nd Venice Biennale, where it received much critical attention. The third Maison Tropicale remains in private gallery ownership.

In this chapter, my inquiry concerns the case of the rediscovery, translocation, commoditization and display of these Maisons Tropicales. I draw on multisited anthropological fieldwork to describe the connections and disconnections between the various actors involved and argue that the removal of the Maisons Tropicales from Africa problematizes contemporary norms and forms of collecting objects of art and culture. With this argument, I add to current anthropological scholarship on global exchanges of material culture, including art objects, as well as on the production of artistic and cultural value under conditions of globalization.[3] My particular interest is in the emergence of a contested global heritage assemblage around the Maisons Tropicales, seeking to understand the rediscovery of the Maisons Tropicales as modern architectural heritage, as well as their translocation, commoditization and display as modern works of art. Specifically, I ask how alternative valorizations of the Maisons Tropicales are related to the changing global relations concerning objects of art and culture.

My analysis zooms in on powerful practices of collecting art and culture. On one hand, officials from the field of cultural heritage argue for the fundamental site specificity of the Maisons Tropicales, emphasizing the structures' integrity to the urban built fabrics of Niamey and Brazzaville. On the other hand, actors from the field of modern and contemporary art present Jean Prouvé's prefabricated system as essentially 'nomadic' modern industrial design.[4] They celebrate the recovery of the Maisons Tropicales from alleged neglect and decay in Africa.

In the following, I reflect on this contestation of different notions of authenticity and value. I argue in particular that defining the Maisons Tropicales as modern architectural heritage in need of international protection and local preservation is reminiscent of certain colonial exchanges of culture. I also claim that the appropriation of the Maisons Tropicales as modern works of art problematically transforms them into a kind of modern trophy. Ultimately, I assert that the Maisons Tropicales are in need of recontextualization regarding their colonial and postcolonial legacies. For this purpose, I consider the conceptual artist's Ângela Ferreira's work, which revolves around the Maisons Tropicales, as well as the documentary by filmmaker Manthia Diawara that accompanies Ferreira's work. I claim that these artistic treatments amount to a valuable remediation of the dominant technologies of authenticity and value that are at stake.

Technologies of Authenticity and Value

In the following, I draw on the sociologist Niklas Luhmann's definition of technology as functional simplification, a form of reduction of complexities that can enable the self-description of contemporary society.[5]

Luhmann's systems theory specifically emphasizes the importance of artistic technologies for the purpose of making "observations on modernity", distinguishing between what he calls first- and second-order observations.[6] First-order observations are ordinary realist attempts to describe the world, ways of grasping a referent by establishing a context and assuming a specific perspective on it—which is what most actors in the social world are content to do. Second-order observations, then, are observations of first-order observations. Such meta-observations take a given first-order observation as their referent, making it possible to reflect on certain blind spots resulting from the necessary arbitrariness of the first-order observers' choice of perspective.[7] As a consequence, first-order observations are directed at one context while second-order observations are directed toward more than one context. In Luhmann's terms, second-order observations include the observation of observers observing a context, as well as the fact that they are observing them. Luhmann notes that much art provokes its audience by insisting on being observed as observant; it calls for second-order observations. According to him, art is thus a particularly effective technology of distinction between contexts and their observations.[8]

Luhmann refers to the artist as a machine that produces contingencies by encouraging specific second-order observations, claiming that when one observes artists resorting to their means, one observes the marking of difference on an initially empty time, as well as on an empty space.[9] As a result, artists use second-order observations to develop self-reflexive forms, which Luhmann believes make for an archetypically modern problem.[10] For example, many artists experiment with novelty and chance to achieve viable forms. Luhmann argues that, if successful, such forms of art manage to direct observations while remaining visibly contingent; they generate time by differentiating between simultaneity and distinctions of before and after. Artists can thus problematize the present when they engage with the self-reflexive potential of different forms.[11] To speak in Luhmann's terms, they are capable of introducing new descriptions of objects as observations, for instance, based on the opposition between tradition and modernity.[12] He believes artistic technologies as a helpful in understanding the modernity of contemporary society's cultural situation.

Luhmann argues that the cultural technologies of authenticity and value that characterize present-day conceptions of modernity are predominantly shaped by a European tradition.[13] In the process, he largely neglects colonial and postcolonial legacies, which, as I reveal, matter significantly in the case of the Maisons Tropicales. The anthropologist James Clifford explicitly does trace those legacies. Similar to Luhmann, Clifford introduces a system of art, culture and authenticity, which he presents as a complex where cultural description is shown to proceed from specific assumptions about temporality, wholeness and continuity.

Clifford refers to his art–culture–authenticity system as a historical and political machine to create authenticity and value.[14]

Clifford is particularly interested in what Luhmann would call technologies of authenticity and value that depend on the opposition between tradition and modernity. For example, in his essay *On Collecting Art and Culture*, Clifford's focus is on the appropriation of traditional objects of material culture from the European colonies as so-called primitive art. Of course, modern histories of colonialism abound with the colonizers' appropriations of other cultures, and such appropriations either took the form of scientific inventory or of the actual removal of material culture.[15] Since the late 19th century, the colonizers registered and described exotic, archaic or tribal objects, which were frequently collected as trophies for the purpose of their display in the European metropolis. Clifford explains how initially only ethnographic museums exhibited such collections of primitive culture, mainly in order to prove the backward state of native cultural development. But soon art museums also celebrated this primitive aesthetic and gradually a new attitude developed toward the primitive as fine art equal in value to the greatest Western masterpieces.[16] By the mid-20th century, the aesthetic display of primitive art, out of time and out of context, had made an enormous impact on the development of avant-garde art in the West.[17] Western artists began to reflect on the appropriation and display of primitive art objects as observations on modernity in their own right. According to Clifford, though, such observations still relied on a limited set of technologies of authenticity and value. Essentially, Clifford argues, even today the art–culture–authenticity system remains a set of powerful ideological and institutional practices of contextualization and valorization that is dominated by the West.[18]

The anthropologist Sally Price agrees with Clifford's evaluation and, in her book *Primitive Art in Civilized Places*, describes "the plight of objects from around the world that [. . .] have been discovered, seized, commoditized, stripped of their social ties, redefined in new settings and reconceptualized to fit the economic, cultural, political and ideological needs of people from distant societies".[19] Price identifies five dimensions of Western control over the authenticity and value of primitive art today: First, the acclaim of a given object as primitive art tends to rely exclusively on the Western observer's discriminating eye. Second, Western collectors and institutions ignore local circumstances and act largely according to their own, limited priorities when engaging with primitive art. Third, Western connoisseurs assign themselves the job of interpreting the meaning and significance of artistic objects produced by peoples they regard as less equipped to perform the task. Fourth, Western experts employ considerable financial and communicative resources to bestow international artistic recognition and value on their personal favorites from the world of primitive craftsmanship. Fifth and finally, Price notes how Westerners are successful in determining the (re)production of primitive art in virtually every corner of the world today.[20]

Price's analysis of Western practices of collecting, classifying and circulating primitive art describes what Luhmann would term powerful technologies of differentiation. In defining the authenticity and value of primitive art, these technologies highlight the opposition between tradition and modernity as a problem of cultural difference. Price's account of the significance of histories of collecting primitive art also matches Clifford's, yet Clifford believes that such generous appropriations of Western categories such as primitive art are now much less stable than they used to be in the past.[21] In fact, Clifford emphasizes the current transience of the art–culture–authenticity system, linking it to the growing interconnection of the world's populations and to contestations of colonialism and Eurocentrism. As a consequence, for Clifford, collecting art and culture now inevitably takes place in "a changing field of counterdiscourses, syncretisms and re-appropriations originating both inside and outside the West".[22]

According to Clifford, categories of art and culture can no longer be simply extended to non-Western peoples and things, "they can at worst be imposed, at best be translated—both historically and politically contingent operations".[23] He hopes that contingency, which also appears to be characteristic of such contemporary exchanges of art and culture as the rediscovery, translocation, commoditization and display of the Maisons Tropicales, might challenge the dominant ramifications of the art–culture–authenticity system. In fact, he aims to situate cultural relations in a so-called contact zone, where "fundamental assumptions about relationships themselves—notions of exchange, justice, reciprocity—may be topics of struggle and negotiations".[24] Ultimately, Clifford argues, the art–culture–authenticity system must operate as a historically specific and contestable field of meanings and institutions.[25] But what exactly happens when established technologies of authenticity and value are contested today?

A Global Heritage Assemblage around the Maisons Tropicales

When the European colonizers arrogated themselves to be the rightful custodians of primitive art and culture, they considered modern architecture as an instrument of civilization and an effective development tool. The colonizers introduced modern regimes of building construction in exchange for the scientific inventory, collection and display of traditional objects.[26] It was assumed that the progressive nature of the modern built environment would emancipate the colonial population, a utopian idea that implied that living in a modern house would make one a civilized person.[27] During the colonial period, modern architecture and urban planning were also means to appropriate territory and effectively rule over the indigenous population.[28] In this respect, the former African colonies constituted significant fields of experimentation for the development of modern architecture and Jean Prouvé's Maisons Tropicales were no exception.[29]

Though Prouvé had started testing his modular designs for building construction in France in the 1920s, he quickly turned his attention to the French colonies in Africa, competing in the late 1930s for military contracts to build shelters for the French colonial troops and, in the early 1940s, for the corps of engineers.[30] It was not until 1948, after a number of rejected bids, that Paul Herbé, who had recently been appointed town planner to the colonial authorities in French West Africa, asked Prouvé to plan a college, the main government building and the law courts in Niamey. Herbé presented Prouvé with a tailor-made opportunity to test his prefabrication system, suggesting that "all possible interest should be shown, for a region so remote and deprived of transport, in the total contribution by metropolitan industry for pre-manufactured lightweight alloy materials".[31] And indeed, the industrial production of Prouvé's designs took place in his factory in Maxeville, France, which meant that the modules would be transported to the colonial periphery and assembled there by cheap, unskilled labor.

Prouvé's designs aimed to exploit a potentially profitable market in prefabricated housing for the French colonies in Africa, as he explained:

> in short, the problem of providing houses for regions with particular climatic conditions, unequipped regions, is that every instance of the supply and transportation of building materials, tools and labor force constitutes a substantial operation. And this leads to that: the house prefabricated, made of metal, well ventilated.[32]

One of Prouvé's primary objectives, then, was adapting his designs to the West African climate. This was imperative also because, according to him:

> an exhausting climate breaks the initial fighting spirit, and this does not encourage the 'building' process. And yet, an acceptable dwelling must be given to a man who has to live and work under difficult conditions: to create an 'environment' from the new requirements.[33]

Besides climatic concerns, Prouvé was very much aware of the specific requirements of French colonial rule, and he generally approved of the system of colonial dominance. He, for instance, took it for granted that "the Europeans will try to off-load most maintenance duties, hard or special, onto the natives".[34]

This attitude is also reflected in Prouvé's drawings and descriptions of the Maisons Tropicales. In his explanation of the floor plan of the

Brazzaville Maisons Tropicales, for example, Prouvé shows that he adapted his designs to the everyday realities of colonialism:

> The bed is very important to the daily rest cycle. Women, for instance, generally wake up at only about ten in the morning. Their sleeping quarters must be connected with the bathroom or with the children's bedroom without having to run across the 'boy' who is cleaning the living room or the annexes.[35]

Prouvé thus engaged in a classical colonial project and it should not come as a surprise that his very first drawings were appropriately titled designs for a series of *Maisons Coloniales*. Only later did Prouvé come up with alternative names such as *Maisons Equatoriales*, *Maisons Africaines* or the term most exclusively used in description of the project today, *Maisons Tropicales*.[36]

Yet despite Prouvé's extensive lobbying for the realization of Herbé's large-scale commissions in Niamey, in the end only one prototype of the Maisons Tropicales series was built there for demonstration purposes in 1949. And although the state-owned company Aluminum Francais installed two more houses in Brazzaville in 1951, this did not have the anticipated promotional effect either.[37] Apparently, Prouvé's design proved well suited for the specific climatic conditions, but the aluminum modules simply were too expensive for broader implementation.[38] Moreover, the French soon left their sub-Saharan territories.

After the French retreat from the Niger and the Congo in 1957 and 1960, respectively, the Maisons Tropicales received little attention in Western histories of modern architecture and industrial design. Local inhabitants, however, used the buildings for accommodation and business purposes. After political independence, one of the Brazzaville Maisons served as a copy shop and the Niamey house provided shelter for poor neighboring residents.[39] Nevertheless, until their so-called rediscovery in the wake of a French heritage mission, the Maisons Tropicales were said to be "forgotten" or "long lost" to the West.[40]

In 1993, the French Ministry of Foreign Cooperation decided to cofund research on the built heritage of Brazzaville and commissioned Bernard Toulier, a senior expert on 20th-century built heritage for the French Ministry of Culture, to conduct a two-year research project on the colonial architecture of Brazzaville's so-called European sector.[41] In an interview, Toulier explains that among the reasons for the French government's interest in Brazzaville's modern architectural heritage was the upcoming international recognition of the need to register and protect colonial heritage, which ICOMOS refers to as at-risk 'shared heritage'.[42] Furthermore, French officials unequivocally regarded modern architecture in the former French colonies as a distinctly 'national' inheritance, as also becomes clear from the fact that Toulier's research reports appeared in the context of an official series on the monuments and antiquities of

France, *Inventaire Général des Monuments et Richesses Artistiques de la France*.[43]

Toulier's two reports, *Brazzaville Decouvertes* and *Brazzaville la Verte*, both published in 1996, feature photographs of Prouvé-designed buildings, including the Maisons Tropicales.[44] Though, initially, Toulier was not aware of their existence in Brazzaville, shortly before his first visit he was tipped off to the existence of "a strange house" there.[45] Tristan Guilloux, at the time an architect based in Brazzaville, contacted Toulier with the description of a house that "looks like modern architecture, but it isn't listed anywhere".[46] As a result, Toulier and Guilloux started a search, both on the ground and in the archives. Toulier explains:

> Coincidently, at the time I had worked in Touraine with Jean Prouvé's daughter, Catherine Prouvé. [. . .] She told me go see the archives in Lorraine, and that's where I found a piece of information, and so this little piece [made the difference]: 'Jean Prouvé, constructeur in Nancy sent a prototype of a metallic house in 1949.' It was in 1993–94 that I had found this in the archives.[47]

When in Brazzaville, Toulier could then identify Guilloux's strange house as the twin prototypes of Prouvé's Maisons Tropicales. And Toulier made another rediscovery while in Brazzaville, reporting about a former Air France office building designed and furnished by Prouvé and his contemporary, the industrial designer Charlotte Perriand.

In retrospect, Toulier considers the public disclosure of his rediscoveries fateful, as he had not anticipated the impact of his heritage inventories, which coincided with hype around 20th-century industrial design on the art market in the 1990s. As a consequence of this hype, Toulier's publication of photographs of modern architectural heritage in Brazzaville actually led to the removal of modern furniture from Brazzaville, and ultimately to the removal of the Maisons Tropicales from Brazzaville and Niamey. For instance, Parisian gallerists Phillippe Jousse and Patrick Seguin, reacting to Toulier's publications, embarked on an expedition to the Republic of the Congo.[48] A trip that resulted in what was called the 'repatriation' to France of large quantities of industrial design such as chairs, shelves, tables and even solar protection panels ripped off façades.[49]

Joussee and Seguin's 1998 gallery catalogue *Jean Prouvé* features many images of the objects brought from Brazzaville and sold in Paris. It states,

> [I]n addition to what is still being said and written about [Prouvé's] oeuvre, and in addition to the passionate interest that oeuvre still generates among collectors and connoisseurs around the world, the true exemplar remains the man himself. [. . .] Prouvé offered a stringent, unadorned grace, yet anyone who takes the time to examine his furniture cannot fail to be struck by the technical sophistication, the meticulous choice of materials, the absolute rightness of proportion

and the unrelenting concern with producing a truly noble object. [. . .] Generous and humane, Prouvé transcended the merely functional: he offered beauty and intelligence and—the ideal of many of today's designers—made them available to all.[50]

Such praise of Jean Prouvé's 'unchallenged' standing as a modernist genius explains why his designs, once intended for cheap mass production, have become exclusive and expensive collector's items for sale on the art market. At the turn of the millennium, James Zemaitis, director of 20th-century design sales at Sotheby's even spoke of an "insatiable thirst for Prouvé furniture":

> The reason for the huge upswing in price is that Prouvé is now recognized as one of the most influential European architects of the 20th century—especially when you look at his contributions to low-income housing and mobile housing. He was vastly underrated until recently.[51]

It is no coincidence at all that Zemaitis's appraisal of Prouvé's designs features a specific reference to mobile housing, as, with Prouvé's furniture and fixtures yielding exorbitant prices on the art market, it did not take long before the Maisons Tropicales, of which Jousse and Seguin had published photographs in their gallery catalogue, became mobile indeed.[52] After noticing Joussee and Seguin's successful sales of Prouvé objects from Brazzaville, the wealthy American investment banker Robert Rubin had "the idea of perhaps repatriating the houses themselves", calling it "a daunting prospect for both political and financial reasons, but nonetheless an idea whose time would eventually come".[53]

As a man of means, Rubin collects vintage cars as well as modern architecture. He for instance owns the 1932 *Maison de Verre* by Pierre Chareau, a famous and now painstakingly restored piece of modern architecture tucked into the backyard of a Left-Bank residential complex. Until recently, Rubin was also enrolled as a student of architectural history at Columbia University, where he worked as an assistant to the renowned architectural historian Kenneth Frampton, a fact that indicates he takes his collections seriously.[54] The *New York Times* called Rubin a "born collector with the zeal of a scholar"[55] and he credits his initiative to get the Maisons Tropicales out of Africa as much to his impulses as a collector—"the basic competitive collector's urge to own the coolest Prouvé piece"[56]—as to his realization of the historical significance of Jean Prouvé's prefabricated architecture:

> It is true my original impulse to buy the house was a collector's impulse. To buy the most creative, the most complicated work of art by Jean Prouvé that you could find, and the tropical house is that. It's a famous house. [. . .] There are pictures of it in various books about Prouvé. And in 1996 there were two books that came out. One

was *Brazzaville La Verte*, and the other one was the Seguin catalogue with pictures in them, and Seguin got all this furniture. So well, I said one time: wouldn't it be great to get this house out, because this house is really typical of Prouvé's design. And, you see, I also thought that Prouvé is being compromised by his reputation as a furniture maker and that that means that his buildings are being torn down and recycled and his talents as a builder are being destroyed. [. . .] So that's how the project came about and there was a dealer, a furniture dealer. And, yeah, he said it's my dream to get these houses out, but of course it's a question of finances. So I said here you go and he went there and got them out.[57]

The furniture dealer that Rubin refers to as his collaborator is Eric Touchaleaume. Touchaleaume owns the Gallerie 54 in Paris and exclusively deals in modern furniture and industrial design. The Guardian calls him the Indiana Jones of furniture collecting and the *New York Times* mentions him "scouring the former French colonies—including Cameroon, Niger and Morocco—for two decades in search of lost Modernist works".[58] He is reported as "salvaging"[59] many tables and chairs from Algeria shortly before engaging with the Maisons Tropicales. No wonder then, that when Rubin encouraged Touchaleaume to embark for Brazzaville and Niamey in search of the Maisons, the latter enthusiastically referred to "those mythical houses"[60] as his "holy grail".[61]

Touchaleaume describes the process leading to the acquisition, dismantling and removal of the Maisons Tropicales from both Brazzaville and Niamey to France as follows:

> Six months of endless talks, joys, disappointments, dirty tricks, meetings with some amazing people and some vile ones, and lastly, our heads filled with fabulous memories and the tropical houses, all spruced up, displayed in Paris, just like in my dream.[62]

He claims to have paid a number of (self-)proclaimed proprietors of the houses, bribed government officials and leveraged what he calls "patrimonial claims",[63] which, according to Rubin, were obviously also being paid to extract bribes.[64] Touchaleaume explains that after acquiring and dismantling the houses,

> we packed the pieces in banana leaves, in 15 shipping containers, and took them by rail to the port with armed guards. At the last minute the government stopped us for one more 'petit cadeau'.[65]

Including this 'little gift', Rubin estimates the total expedition costs to have been $1 million.[66] In light of the successful commoditization and display subsequent to the translocation of the Maisons Tropicales, however, Rubin and Touchaleaume's expenses proved to be a great investment.

When Touchaleaume reports that "people [in Niamey and Brazzaville] were incredibly suspicious; no one could believe we had only come for 'old scrap iron' ",[67] this suspicion ultimately turned out to be very much justified, as old scarp iron this definitely was not. Robert Rubin kept one of the houses in return for his expenses, though Forbes.com claims "he could have sold the house for its parts, which might have fetched $10 million".[68] Instead, Rubin had his house restored by conservator Alain Banneel in Paris and soon thereafter launched a well-orchestrated campaign of publications and exhibitions about the Maisons Tropicales. He now fashions himself as the prime expert on the Maisons, publishing scholarly articles and lecturing widely about his collector's item. He has also displayed his Maison Tropicale at a number of prestigious institutions in the US and Europe: in 2005, it was shown to architecture students at Yale University and at the University of California.[69] Another notable exhibition was the 2008 "Home Delivery" show on prefabricated architecture by the Museum of Modern Art (MoMA) in New York, for which Rubin wrote a catalogue entry.[70] At the MoMA show, however, the house was not physically displayed because Rubin gave it on permanent loan to the Centre Pompidou in Paris earlier in 2007. He executed this loan through the US-based Centre Pompidou foundation, which Rubin revived for this purpose and over which he presided at the time.[71]

For Touchaleaume, as well, the attention Rubin generated for the Maisons Tropicales in the field of modern and contemporary art paid off well. Touchaleaume also had one of his Maisons Tropicales restored on their translocation to Paris. On completion, he first exhibited it on the banks of the Seine, as he says, "just like in my dream".[72] In 2007, however, Touchaleaume capitalized on the considerable fame that the Maisons Tropicales had acquired by then and sold one of his two prototypes through Christie's in New York. Press reports of the auction include articles in Vogue Interiors, as well as in architectural magazines and international newspapers such as the *New York Times*. Eventually the real estate and hotel magnate André Balasz bought Touchaleaume's Maison Tropicale for the spectacular sum—widely publicized—of $4.97 million.[73]

Acting on the momentum created by Rubin and Touchaleaume's series of exhibitions, Balasz immediately lent his "modernist gem"[74] for display in front of the Tate Modern in London. The Vitra company, which holds license rights to Prouvé's furniture designs, supported Balasz's show in London, as Vitra's own corporate museum curated an accompanying Prouvé retrospective in the Design Museum neighboring the Tate.[75] Afterwards, Balasz failed to relocate the house to Miami in time for the Art Basel Miami Beach fair, as initially planned. Already promoting his Maison Tropicale with a visually sophisticated website,[76] he now aims to turn the Maisons Tropicale into a luxury hotel in the Caribbean to be run by his company, Balasz-Properties.[77]

Ultimately, Rubin and Touchaleaume characterize their translocation, commoditization and display of the Maisons Tropicales as a rescue operation, a storyline prominently reiterated in their popular exhibitions as well as in the media, as for instance in a Guardian piece reporting on the Christie's auction, which is headed "Bullet Holes Extra: A Classic of Modern Design Has Been Saved From Squatters, Snipers and the Congolese Jungle".[78] Officials at governmental and intergovernmental cultural heritage organizations, however, did not share the welcoming reactions from the field of modern and contemporary art to the removal of the Maisons Tropicales from Africa and fiercely protested against it. In fact, Rubin and Touchaleaume removed the Maisons Tropicales from Brazzaville and Niamey in defiance of complaints from French authorities and the UNESCO World Heritage Center, which officially pleaded for their stay and protection on-site.

Contesting Authenticity and Value

Among Rubin and Touchaleaume's fiercest critics all along was Bernard Toulier, the initiator of the heritage inventories that inspired the translocation of the Maisons Tropicales in the first place. He now believes that it was a mistake to provide "the information, which benefited the Parisian speculators" and he has come to regret his initial "naiveté".[79] He says that when Seguin and Jousee were removing furniture from Brazzaville,

> I attempted to convince [the dealers] through idealism; talking as a conservator of heritage, not as a money-making man. I know that a lot of money can be made with it, but well, I have my salary at the end of the year, I am for patrimony, I am for education, via UNESCO, for the people. I went to their exhibitions and all, but I couldn't talk to them, I couldn't communicate. I couldn't put down this commercial system. And then I saw coming, coming, coming, coming wagons full of objects from over there and I felt sad in my heart. I felt very, very bad for a long time.[80]

But when Toulier was first informed of Rubin and Touchaleaume's plans to remove the Maisons Tropicales to France, he tried ways to "counter" the dealers.[81]

Toulier knew of the imminent translocation of the Brazzaville Maisons Tropicales to France early on. As an expert on Prouvé's architecture at the Association of Friends of Prouvé, he kept in touch with Catherine Prouvé, who, he claims, knew everything that was going on. As a result, Toulier immediately tried to intervene upon learning of Rubin and Touchaleaume's activities. He informed Lazare Eloundo Assomo, chief of the Africa section at the UNESCO World Heritage Center, who in turn alerted national authorities in Brazzaville. Eloundo Assomo warned about the "risk to lose the Maisons Tropicales because of collectors in the process of removing the houses from the Congo, and that they should remain there".[82] To his disappointment, however, the Congolese Ministry of Culture did not recognize such a risk, nor did it seem to be aware of any heritage significance of the Maisons Tropicales. It became clear that no steps could be taken at the ministerial level because no appropriate heritage legislation was in place. And although Eloundo Assomo tried to get involved again—at the "last minute" as he puts it—other people at another Congolese government institution, who apparently didn't know the value of the houses "but merely saw pieces of metal", eventually authorized the translocation.[83]

In the aftermath of the translocation, the Republic of the Congo received international assistance to draft effective national heritage legislation, which was signed into effect in 2009. Had it been in effect earlier this legislation would have actually prohibited the removal of the Maisons Tropicales.[84] Recently, the Congolese ministry of culture even discussed a motion—fundamentally based on Bernard Toulier's original heritage inventory—to list the modern architecture of Brazzaville as UNESCO World Heritage.[85] But in spite of this late and somewhat ironic recognition of the national and international heritage value of the Maisons Tropicales, Toulier thinks that "the majority of conservators of modern art and design do not care whether Prouvé is in Brazzaville or here [in France]".[86] Toulier's position as a heritage official in relation to the field of modern and contemporary art highlights the connections and disconnections among the various actors involved in the emergence of a global heritage assemblage around the Maisons Tropicales.

Toulier is for instance puzzled that during the translocation, commoditization and display of the Maisons Tropicales Seguin and Jousee, as well as Rubin and Touchaleaume, frequently approached him with requests for assistance. Apparently they did not realize how much Toulier objected to their art market practices:

> In the beginning, they went a first time to take the loose elements that were left, so they took the furniture, and a second time they went to take the house. The first time they made an exhibition and they wanted me to collaborate but I said: No, no, no! And later Eric Touchaleaume asked me to write the book, with photographs, I was proud, but no, no, no! So, it's really—they all think that I'm crazy![87]

Ultimately then, this apparent lack of understanding illustrates two competing and conflicting technologies of authenticity and value regarding the Maisons Tropicales.

For one, Toulier never had any doubt about the fact that the Maisons Tropicales should remain in Brazzaville and Niamey. He contends that they

> were prototypes in a series, but they were made for a specific environment. When they are in the Centre Pompidou it is not their

environment. The Maisons Tropicales were made for a small valley, a small river which passes in front the most ancient site of Brazzaville and flows towards the Congo. And that's where Prouvé was smart enough to put the houses. Because in order to have natural ventilation, there has to be a difference in temperature. So he put the houses on stilts above the river, and it can only work on this river; to put them somewhere else is to eliminate the very defining feature of this house. It can be considered as an industrial element, as furniture, but the person who made it knew perfectly well where to put it, and it's the place as much as the object which is important to make it heritage. This object cannot be put anywhere, not by the Seine, it will never breathe.[88]

Toulier's evaluation here echoes Lazare Eloundo Assomo's, who considers the exhibitions of the Maisons Tropicales in Paris scandalous and refuses all invitations to visit them. Eloundo Assomo does not want his name or that of UNESCO associated with the exhibitions. He argues that the removal of the Maisons Tropicales had "very negative consequences for our business of promoting awareness of modern heritage values in the Republic of the Congo and the preservation of colonial architectural heritage across Africa".[89] Thus, for Toulier and Eloundo Assomo, the authenticity and value of the Maisons Tropicales are inextricably entwined with the specific situation of the houses in the local urban fabric. Both argue for the preservation of significant buildings such as the Maisons Tropicales in their original location, as well as for an official listing of architectural heritage from 20th century as 'shared colonial heritage'.

Contrary to Toulier and Eloundo Assomo, who believe in the fundamental site specificity of the Maisons Tropicales, private collector Robert Rubin emphasizes what he calls the houses' nomadic or itinerant character. He considers them works of art and regards their authenticity and value as essentially not site specific. He claims that in the context of their displays as masterpieces of industrial design the Maisons Tropicales have recovered their "original identity".[90] Rubin counters criticism of the Maisons Tropicales's removal from Africa in the academic journal *Future Anterior*, which means to approach historic preservation from a critical perspective, writing that

[i]n the spirit of 'presentation' rather than any orthodox notion of 'preservation', the exhibition of the Tropical House seeks to capture its dynamic qualities. Preserving these prototypes where they happen to have landed hardly does justice to Prouvé's vision of an industrialized architecture. Each new venue for the Tropical House is intended to advance the historical resituation of Prouvé.[91]

For Rubin and his collaborators from the field of modern and contemporary art, it thus was neither strictly necessary nor a viable option to preserve the houses *in situ*. Instead, Rubin contends that

> [t]he tropical house is a unique case because it is a prototype of a building system. But it has a very famous and charged specific iteration. You know, I mean I can take pieces of the tropical house and put them together any way I like. [. . .] So it has a lot of flexibility and then of course you're taking it out of a spot, which is a freighted spot also. I mean, there is this whole postcolonial dialogue and discourse going on, and so on. I mean, I just thought to restore it at the moment before it came to Africa, which is one possible choice among many but probably the most logical choice for an architectural historian or another kind of art historian.[92]

Indeed, prominent institutions like the Centre Pompidou share Rubin's account of the uniqueness of the Maisons as works of art. After all, the Pompidou show of Rubin's Maison Tropicale on the Centre Pompidou's fifth-floor balcony celebrates its "frank modernity" without references to the structure's problematic colonial and postcolonial histories, conforming to Rubin's talk of the "coolest Prouvé piece".[93]

Arguably then, Rubin and Touchaleaume's practice of collecting the Maisons Tropicales as modern art through translocation, commoditization and display, on one hand, and Toulier and Eloundo Assomo's practice of 'collecting' the houses as modern architectural heritage through appeals to their inventory, listing, and preservation *in situ* on the other, both articulate competitive and conflicting technologies of authenticity and value. Nonetheless, I contend that these technologies invariably exhibit institutionalized areas of blindness and controversy, at the grounds of which lay specific expectations of temporality, wholeness, continuity and essence long built into Western ideas of art and culture.[94]

James Clifford maintains that in the wake of colonialism, objects collected from non-Western sources have predominantly been classified in two major categories: as (scientific) cultural artifacts or as (aesthetic) works of art.[95] I argue that this basic distinction, which I claim to be fundamentally based on the opposition between tradition and modernity, as well as notions of the primitive, informs the contestations of the significance of the Maisons Tropicales in ways reminiscent of colonial exchanges of culture.

First, the official rediscovery and scientific inventory of the Maisons Tropicales as modern architectural heritage during a French research mission to Brazzaville is reminiscent of colonial approaches to the traditional built environment. In fact, the emergence of the scientific discipline of historic preservation in Europe was formatively influenced by colonial encounters with 'other' forms of architecture. When the colonizers introduced their modern regimes of building construction, this went hand in hand with the expropriation of property and the destruction of natives' living quarters. Colonial architects and urban planners, however, frequently took to conserving isolated monuments. While the large-scale application of ideologies and techniques of modern architecture was to do away with the 'backward' ways of native dwelling once and for all, the incidental preservation of monuments underlined civilized modernity through opposition. As the historian Benedict Anderson puts it, for the colonial powers the monumentalization of traditional buildings constituted an effective means to govern an indigenous population. It suggested to the natives that "our very presence shows you that you have always been, or have long become, incapable of either greatness or self-rule".[96]

Against this backdrop then, the notion of a rediscovery of the Maisons Tropicales as modern architectural heritage is rather problematic. The unilateral French research into Brazzaville's colonial architecture suggests that the Congolese have not 'learned to appreciate modernity' as it was introduced by their former colonizers. The description of the Maisons Tropicales as a distinctly 'French' inheritance that was "long lost" or "forgotten" implies that the 'culture of modernity' is also lost in Africa, thus providing good reason for a French reappropriation of Brazzaville's colonial built fabric. Along these lines, even the removal of the Maisons Tropicales may suitably serve as proof of the necessity of such interventions.

Yet while the French government commends the rediscovery of the Maisons and urges the Congolese government to protect the (remaining) modern architectural heritage of Brazzaville according to Western standards, the removal of the houses from Africa is a different type of intervention reminiscent of colonial exchange of culture. When Rubin and Touchaleaume herald the translocation of the Maisons Tropicales as the buildings' "resurrection" from decay and misuse, such a discourse is analogous to justifications of colonial appropriations of so-called primitive art, where the natives were also not thought to appreciate the objects quite as much or as well as the Westerners.[97] Rubin and particularly Touchaleaume fashion themselves as saviors of the Maisons Tropicales, which they claim faced imminent destruction in the Congo and in Niger.

Touchaleaume told the Guardian that his "main passion is to be a kind of private curator, to make my contribution to save the heritage of the 20th century":

> [I]n a perfect world, we would keep the Maisons Tropicales *in situ*. But in [Africa], they can't afford to maintain or restore them and they would be lost. The important thing is to protect the artwork.[98]

Rubin admits that maybe it "would have been as valid to restore the house *in situ*"[99] but claims that his repatriation of the Maisons Tropicales came just in time since "public money for French modernism is becoming scarce".[100] In effect, Rubin and Touchaleaume present their removal of the Maisons Tropicales from Brazzaville and Niamey as a generous rescue operation; just like artifacts from primitive cultures, they consider the Maisons Tropicales legitimate collector's items.

Ultimately, this is a problematic attitude, treating the Maisons Tropicales like trophies. Similar to displays of primitive art, Rubin and Touchaleaume's museal displays of the Maisons Tropicales as icons of modern art present the houses as aesthetic objects, out of time and out of context. They fail to reflect on the relationships of domination, expropriation and exploitation that the Maisons represent as prototypes of a colonial building project. When Rubin and Touchaleaume speak of the removal of the structures from Brazzaville and Niamey in terms of their rescue and salvation, they uncritically acknowledge the colonial utopias of civilization, progress and development for which Jean Prouvé's designs once stood; they consider the Maisons Tropicales noble gifts of modernity spurned by the Africans. Consequently, when they appropriate the Maisons as works of art, they treat them as what I would like to call "modern trophy". As such modern trophy the Maisons Tropicales constitute Rubin and Touchaleaume's somewhat paradoxical attempt to collect a tradition of modernity; just as colonial collections of primitive art claimed to salvage objects from of a backward, nonrepeatable time, the translocation, commoditization and display of the Maisons Tropicales describes an attempt at collecting the future of a modern past.

Though Rubin and Touchaleaume appropriate the Maisons Tropicales as modern things, instances of a certain modern tradition, they do not critically reflect on the complex intertwinement of these modern things with problematic colonial histories. Neither Rubin and Touchaleaume's exhibitions nor their publications about the Maisons Tropicales, for instance, critically mention Prouvé's alternative designations for the structures, such as *Maisons Coloniales*. In the end, their aestheticizing approach to the Maisons Tropicales as modern trophy thus sanitizes the houses' colonial legacies. Furthermore, their treatment of the Maisons Tropicales as modern trophy denies the legitimacy of the houses' postcolonial local contexts. Whereas Rubin and Touchaleaume make many references to Jean Prouvé as the Western master artist responsible for the original design, their restorations reject later structural changes to the Maisons Tropicales made by local inhabitants.

In this respect, an apparent parallel to what Sally Price has called the "anonymization" of primitive art is relevant. According to Price,

> after a Primitive artifact has been removed from the field (whether by sale, theft, or some other variant of the transfer to Western ownership) it is customarily issued a new passport. The pedigree of such an object does not normally provide detailed information on its maker

or its original (native) owners; rather it counts only the Western hands through which the object has passed.[101]

Rubin and Touchaleaume's restoration of the Maisons Tropicales to their so-called original condition also bluntly rejects meaningful local alterations. All emphasis is on the collector and dealer's accounts of their adventurous rescue of the Maisons Tropicales as modern trophy. Rubin even claims that the only traces preserved of the structures' African habitat are the "bullet holes made by Kalashnikovs".[102]

In Africa, the Maisons Tropicales did not wait for their 'rescue' as works of modern art. Neither did they wait for their 'rediscovery' as modern architectural heritage. Instead, in postcolonial Brazzaville and Niamey the Maisons Tropicales fulfilled significant functions for their inhabitants, who changed them to suit their practical, everyday needs. But, as my analysis of the case of the rediscovery, translocation, commoditization and display of the Maisons Tropicales shows, the dominant technologies of authenticity and value ignored local circumstances. Though it is safe to say that the Maisons Tropicales were not locally appreciated as valuable in terms of cultural heritage or art—certainly not before the French heritage inventory and probably not even after their removal from the African continent—and though I have shown that the respective technologies of authenticity and value are contestable, there has been no reflection on matters such as local opposition, appropriate compensation or other issues that touch upon the ethics of the dominant Western collecting practices.[103] In its place, a lighthearted, realist attitude along the lines of 'boys will be boys' prevails.[104] The *International Herald Tribune*, for instance, posted a "Style Alert" on the Maison as "the biggest trophy in modern and contemporary design".[105] What is thus remarkable about the rediscovery, translocation, commoditization and display of the Maisons Tropicales is not so much that there are competing and conflicting technologies of authenticity and value involved. Instead, what is striking is that these originate solely "inside the West", excluding and marginalizing various residual and emergent contexts.[106] The case of the Maisons Tropicales seems to confirm James Clifford's insight that "one cannot avoid the global reach of Western institutions allied with capitalist markets and the projects of national elites".[107]

Recontextualization/Remediation

So far, my analysis has indicated that the rediscovery, translocation, commoditization and display of the Maisons Tropicales problematize genealogies of Western practices of art and culture collecting.[108] With Luhmann, I argue that the technologies of authenticity and value relating to the Maisons Tropicales as modern architectural heritage, on one hand, and as modern art, on the other hand, constitute different 'observations on modernity'. As I have described them, the dominant technologies of authenticity and value regarding the Maisons Tropicales appear as Luhmannian first-order observations: They grasp their referent by establishing a limited context and assuming a specific perspective on it. Although these two occupy competing and conflicting perspectives, they both imply specific temporal positions and forms of historical narration that essentially depend on the opposition between tradition and modernity.

As first-order observations, however, these technologies of authenticity and value relate to this opposition arbitrarily; they do not critically reflect on its complex and problematic colonial and postcolonial iterations. As a result, the Maisons Tropicales require a recontextualization of their colonial and postcolonial legacies; they are in need of second-order observations on modernity. In the following I analyze artist Ângela Ferreira and filmmaker Manthia Diawara's attempts at such a second-order recontextualization of the Maisons Tropicales.

During the 2007 Venice Biennale, Ferreira presented a critical conceptual artwork titled *Maison Tropicale* at the Portuguese Pavilion. The work's main component is a wooden structure that models Jean Prouvé's prefab prototype in transit. It configures the Maisons Tropicales's dismantled parts for transportation in a container, which mirrors the way the houses where shipped to and out of Africa. Ferreira's Venice audience was invited to walk through this life-sized container—it constituted the entry to the pavilion—in order to in a way experience the Maisons Tropicales's transitory existence. On the walls Ferreira displayed images of the Maisons's original sites left vacant after the houses' removal.

In preparation for her work Ferreira had traveled to Brazzaville and Niamey together with a photographer and the New York–based Malinese documentary filmmaker and anthropologist Manthia Diawara. His record of the trip is part of a documentary—also titled *Maison Tropicale*—about Ferreira's process leading up to the Biennale show. Diawara's film includes Ferreira's interviews with the former inhabitants of the Maisons Tropicales in Brazzaville and Niamey, providing a counterpoint to the dominant accounts of the houses' rediscovery, translocation, commoditization and display. As a result, Ferreira and Diawara jointly recontextualize the Maisons Tropicales in their colonial and postcolonial legacies.

Ferreira adamantly disagrees with Robert Rubin and Eric Touchaleaume on the alleged nonsite specificity of the Maisons Tropicales. Like Bernard Toulier and Lazare Eloundo Assomo, she considers the translocation of the houses a "kind of an amputation, not in terms of the objectness itself, but because of the landscape, the urban landscape":

> It was the prefabrication that helped moving [the Maisons Tropicales] from France because the house traveled in parts. But if you look for example at English Victorian houses, bungalows for example, or

all the row housing for South Africa in the 19th century, it was all made in England and transported in parts. It was an economical project. But the parts weren't built in parts so that you could take them there and bring them back. [. . .] That's what makes this particular object an interesting object, because its fabrication permitted that kind of mutilation and eventually revealed the kind of appropriation scam we are witnessing. [. . .] The houses were built for a place, they weren't built to be moved anywhere; they were rooted in a place. And it's with that in mind that Prouvé designed [them], he wants to show them off as best as he can. I mean, houses have roots, they have foundations, even prefab houses.[109]

For Rubin and Touchaleaume, however, the Maisons Tropicales's foundations, their roots, were uninteresting because they were unmovable. Left behind in Brazzaville and Niamey, they remained for Ferreira to engage with.[110]

Despite her criticism of the Maisons Tropicales's removal from Africa, Ferreira is cautious in her judgment. Although some cultural heritage experts speak of the Maisons as "stolen in bright daylight",[111] Ferreira explains that with her work she intends not only "to reveal a return to kind of a colonial practice" but also "to highlight the idiosyncrasies of these processes and to say we need to read this in a different way":

There's a lot of neo-colonialist approaches from the European side, but there is also a lot of very constructive approaches from Europe [. . .] because while they have a fraught lineage, the context changes the buildings, in a way. So there's a lot of genuine people and then there's a lot of misguided people from the European side. But, I think exactly the same is happening from the African side. I think that the issue of guilt, of right and wrong, is very murky here. I think that there are a lot of problems with the view of those buildings by Africans themselves. You know, there is a lot of expediency. This is about an incredibly complex melting pot that is really about the relationships between Europe and Africa.[112]

With her piece *Maison Tropicale* Ferreira reflects on what she calls the African side of this complex relationship.

Diawara's documentary shows Ferreira talking about the Maisons Tropicales with local interlocutors in Brazzaville and Niamey. These conversations reveal an interesting plurality of perspectives that play no role in the dominant narratives of the rediscovery, translocation, commoditization and display of the houses. On one hand, Artonnor Ibriahine, who used the Niamey house for shelter, expresses feelings of powerlessness and resignation in the face of the structure's removal. On the other, Mireille Ngatsé, the legitimate owner of the Brazzaville houses, fought European claimants in court for her right to sell the Maisons Tropicales. Ngatsé even used the revenue from her successful sale to redevelop the land left vacant and start a successful business, a remarkable achievement for a single Congolese woman "without contacts in the government".[113]

Diawara's film also illustrates how Ferreira's local contacts generally show little awareness of the Maisons Tropicales' valorization abroad as modern architectural heritage or modern art; they are genuinely surprised when presented with information of the current fate of the houses. There is one exception: When Ferreira asks Amadou Ousmane, one of her contacts in Niamey, whether he thinks it is a shame they bought and took the houses, Ousmane denies this, reminding the artist that the only reason she interviews him in the first place is the Maisons' prominent display outside of Africa. Ousmane claims that the Niamey house at least was not previously regarded as of heritage value, let alone of much value otherwise: "[P]eople wanted to get rid of it".[114] As far as the Brazzaville Maisons Tropicales are concerned, Ngatsé confirms Ousmane's estimation, believing that even if there had been local awareness of the Maisons Tropicales as cultural heritage or art, no government resources would have been made available to issue priority care for the houses. In any case, Ngatsé herself was unable to execute the necessary repairs, and she doubts the willingness and ability of the Congolese state to engage in any such work. When confronted with images of Eric Touchaleaue's Maison Tropicale on display in Paris, Ngatsé contends that "Africa isn't Europe. [. . .] We couldn't have kept it. It would never have become what it is now."[115]

Of Ferreira's interviewees, only the artist Besongo angrily demands the return of the Brazzaville *Maisons Tropicales* to the African continent and their valorization as Congolese national heritage:

> As a nationalist, I can say I'd like to see that house come back here and then that wealth would become a tourist attraction that people could visit. It also brings in money. I wish it were in my country, the expatriates would come back. Things would be more interesting. I am not happy to see the houses back in France, you see.[116]

Yet Besongo's opinion remains an exception. In fact, when Diawara says that as an African, he would like to see the *Maisons Tropicales* back in Africa, Ngatsé responds:

> Yes, it would be nice if they came back to Africa. But, who would look after them, that is the problem. [. . .] They can't look after things. I prefer that the house stays where it is now. It's better off there. They'll take better care of it and love it more. Here it would be abandoned and run-down.[117]

Thus, Ngatsé relativizes Besongo's anger as well as Ferreira and Diawara's criticism, questioning ideals of an *in situ* preservation of Brazzaville's modern architecture as cultural heritage.

In the end, Ngatsé's opinion indicates that there are alternative narratives of postcolonial appropriations and reappropriations to be told about the *Maisons Tropicales*. Ferreira and Diawara acknowledge this when they juxtapose Ngatsé's story of assuming agency to sell off the Brazzaville houses with the presentation of one of the *Maisons Tropicales* on the art market:

> The Touchaleaume presentation was a commercial exercise. It was selling a design object that you could be seeing in a gallery. And the presentation at Christie's; that was a commercial exercise, pure commercial exercise! It's money.

Against this background, Diawara's film projects Ngatsé's reaction to the information that her house is on sale for close to US$5 million in New York. Left speechless only for a short moment, she quickly goes on to say:

> This value of the house, it pleases me. I wish I could have sold it for its current price, but since it didn't work out, I am happy because at least it proves I wasn't sleeping in a shanty. It's one of those things that will become a story to tell. For me it's one of those jokes that turn against themselves.[118]

Arguably then, Ferreira and Diawara engage in an effective recontextualization of the Maisons Tropicales. Insofar as they provide a forum for Ngatsé's perspective—among others—they enable the projection of a kind of symmetry between local appropriations and reappropriations of the Maisons Tropicales and the dominant Western collecting practices.

Ferreira's conceptual artwork and Diawara's documentary movie thus invite second-order observations, breaking up a particular us/them opposition usually taken for granted in the case of the Maisons Tropicales. As I have shown, dominant Western collecting practices depend on technologies of authenticity and value, which in turn rely on the opposition between tradition and modernity and thus mark time on difference. Ferreira and Diawara's work vehemently criticizes these practices, while at the same time indicating how "creative recontextualization and indeed re-authorship may [. . .] follow from taking, from purchase or from theft".[119] Ngatsé testifies to such a re-authorship when she reflects on the postcolonial legacies of her own Brazzaville Maisons. Consequently, by providing a forum for Ngatsé through their art, Ferreira and Diawara remediate the dominant technologies of authenticity and value, enabling second-order observations on the contextualizations and valorizations of the Maisons Tropicales as modern architecture and modern art. Because

Ferreira and Diawara portray the rediscovery, translocation, commoditization and display of the houses as historically and politically contingent operations, they problematize the self-description of contemporary Western society as modern.

In the face of powerful Western collecting practices, the question arises whether Ferreira and Diawara's recontextualization and remediation can have a lasting impact. Although Diawara's movie is screened frequently and Ferreira's Venice Biennale show of *Maison Tropicale* was widely noticed in the field of modern and contemporary art, Ferreira has her doubts:

> I was incredibly lucky with my project because Christie's sale was going on at the same time, two days before the opening [of the Venice Biennale] and [the Maison Tropicale] sold for millions of dollars. I mean, we were installing the work in Venice and we were watching [the auction] online as the bidding was going on. I didn't plan it like that, It just happened. Anybody who was a buyer in Venice had been online watching this thing and they were all talking about this American hotel mogul, reporters and so on. It kind of worked in a very visceral way for me, because I didn't have to do much effort to enter the discourse: the discourse was in the air.[120]

Nonetheless, she cautions that her exhibition received considerably less public attention than Christie's auction in New York and points out that the major problem with the Christie's auction is that "it has depoliticized the whole thing".

But, while her ambition is to "re-politicize" the Maisons Tropicales, in the end she is hesitant to attribute a big impact to her work:

> The project had incredible reflections, Christoph. But you know; it's an art object. How much visibility does an art object have? It doesn't have a broad legibility. I am sure it contributes to the critical pool in various senses. But, art is not a huge public medium. It's not politics. I am not a politician, and I am not working on [becoming] that. [. . .] Within the art context the project had incredible visibility and reflection, and I think, still today, many people are very touched by looking at the photographs, and then by the object. You know, walking through it and then going to find out about the story. Falling in love with the kind of history of it and so on. You know, it was a good project for me, but I don't think that art is that powerful. I don't think it's going to change Robert Rubin.

In the aftermath of the Venice Biennale Rubin actually repeatedly tried to get in contact with Ferreira—he wanted to buy her *Maison Tropicale* too. Needless to say, Ferreira politely declined. As a result of his confrontation with the artist's work, though, Rubin has started to show a certain degree of self-reflexivity about his position as a collector. In an article for the Centre Pompidou he mentions Ferreira's "keen sense of modernism's colonial failures and their dystopian wakes",[121] if only in passing.

Conclusion

In this chapter, I have described the rediscovery, translocation, commoditization and display of the Maisons Tropicales. Zooming in on the connections and disconnections between the different actors involved, my analysis has shown how the dominant Western collecting practices are reminiscent of colonial exchanges of culture. I have argued that the case of the Maisons Tropicales problematizes contemporary norms and forms of collecting objects of art and cultural heritage. The dominant technologies of authenticity and value, which render the Maisons Tropicales as either modern architectural heritage or modern art, invariably amount to reductions of the houses' historical and political meanings. The removal of the Maisons Tropicales from Africa as modern trophy, which is conspicuously analogous to appropriations of primitive art, for instance, sanitizes the houses' colonial and postcolonial legacies.

But whereas powerfully institutionalized Western collecting practices rely on a problematic opposition between tradition and modernity when they engage with the Maisons Tropicales, the resultant contextualizations and valorizations are not totally immutable. Ângela Ferreira's *Maison Tropicale* and Manthia Diawara's documentary movie of the same name both prove the necessity and the critical potential of recontextualization and remediation. Together, Ferreira's artwork and Diawara's film capture what James Clifford means when he speaks of the transience of the current art–culture–authenticity system. He claims that the collecting of art and culture under current conditions of globalization tends to happen in a "contact zone". He believes that when artistic or cultural collections come to be perceived as made up of ongoing historical, political and moral relationships, as power-charged sets of exchanges of 'push and pull', then there is room to claim reciprocities. Ferreira and Diawara's work makes such potential for alternative exchanges of culture visible. Their artistic engagement with the Maisons Tropicales does not present authenticity and value as fixed and essential but as in flux and in need of negotiation. Their recontextualization of the Maisons Tropicales in specific colonial and postcolonial legacies thus emphasizes that dominant technologies of authenticity and value can (and should) be contested.

Ferreira and Diawara's remediations enable reflection on contemporary dynamics of global exchanges of art and culture today; they criticize exclusive accounts of the geographical, cultural and political identity of the Maisons Tropicales and question binary oppositions of home and abroad, staying and moving. They thereby shed new light on the prevalent debate about the site specificity of the Maisons Tropicales. Ferreira's artwork and Diawara's documentary show how displacement practices may emerge as constitutive of cultural meanings in their own right.[122] As a result, their work underlines Clifford's argument that there cannot be any automatic and privileged right to the contextualization and valorization of collections of cultural objects or to the narration of histories of colonial and postcolonial contacts:[123]

> [I]t is important to resist the tendency of collections to be self suf-
> ficient, to suppress their own historical, economic, and political pro-
> cesses of production. Ideally the history of its own collection and
> display should be a visible aspect of any exhibition [of culture].[124]

Ferreira and Diawara's work on the Maisons Tropicales invites such a reflexive approach to collecting because it captures so well what Clifford refers to as "the stuff of contemporary cultural politics, creative and virulent, enacted in the overlapping historical contexts of colonization/decolonization, nation formation/minority assertions, capitalist market expansion/consumer strategies".[125] In the end, the rediscovery, transloca-tion, commoditization and display of the Maisons Tropicales shows that Western practices of collecting art and culture remain problematic. My analysis reveals how dominant technologies of authenticity and remain inevitably contingent: the story of the Maisons Tropicales demonstrates that cultural or artistic authenticity and value has as much to do with an inventive present as with a past and its objectification, preservation or revival.[126]

As the anthropologist Nicholas Thomas once stated, objects of art and culture "are not what they were made to be, but what they have become".[127] I would like to reformulate this claim with the transitoriness of the Maisons Tropicales in mind: cultural objects are not what they were made to be, but they will always remain what they are becoming.

Notes

1. Bernard Toulier, ed. *Brazzaville-la-Verte: Inventaire Général des Monuments et Richesses Artistiques de la France* (Brazzaville/Nantes: Centre Culturel Francais, 1996); Bernard Toulier, ed. *Brazzaville Decouvertes*, Itinaires Du Patrimoine (Saint-Herblain: Imprimerie Le Govic, 1996).
2. Olivier Cinqualbre, ed. *Jean Prouvé: La Maison tropicale* (Paris: Centre Pompidou, 2009).
3. For example, Sally Price, *Paris Primitive: Jaques Chirac's Museum on the Quai Branly* (Chicago: Chicago University Press, 2007).
4. Centre-Pompidou, "Jean Prouvé: Maison tropicale, prototype de Brazzaville, 1953," http://www.centrepompidou.fr/Pompidou/Musee.nsf/Docs/ADFA69 FCEF2DD1D0C12576E7002D8B96?OpenDocument&salle=1N5TERSUD= salle&Key=1N5&L=1; Robert Rubin, "Jean Prouvé's Tropical House: Preservation,

Presentation, Reception," in *Jean Prouvé: La Maison Tropicale*, ed. Olivier Cinqualbre (Paris: Centre Pompidou, 2009). 117–132.

5. Niklas Luhmann, *Observations on Modernity* (Stanford: Stanford University Press, 1998). 6–7.
6. Niklas Luhmann, *Art as a Social System* (Stanford: Stanford University Press, 2000).
7. Rabinow, *Marking Time: On the Anthropology of the Contemporary*. 64.
8. Ibid., 65.
9. Luhmann, *Observations on Modernity*. 196.
10. Niklas Luhmann, *Schriften zu Kunst und Kultur* (Frankfurt am Main: Suhrkamp, 2008). 194.
11. Luhmann, *Observations on Modernity*. 207; 211; 219.
12. Ibid., 18ff, 209.
13. Ibid., 22.
14. Ibid., 224.
15. For example, Said, *Culture & Imperialism*; Said, *Orientalism*, Repr. / ed., Penguin history (London: Penguin Books, 1995); Nicholas Thomas, *Entangled Objects: Exchange, Material Culture and Colonialism in the Pacific* (Cambridge: Harvard University Press, 1991); James Clifford, *The Predicament of Cultures* (Cambridge: Harvard University Press, 1988). 222.
16. *Compare* Clifford, *The Predicament of Cultures*; Sally Price, *Primitive Art in Civilized Places* (Chicago: Chicago University Press, 1989). Fabian, *Time and the Other: How Anthropology Makes its Object*; George E. Marcus and Fred R. Myers, eds., *The Traffic of Culture: Refiguring Art and Anthropology* (London: University of California Press, 1995).
17. Clifford, *The Predicament of Cultures*. 222.
18. Ibid.
19. Price, *Primitive Art in Civilized Places*. 5.
20. Ibid., 68–69.
21. Clifford, *The Predicament of Cultures*. 235–236.
22. Ibid.
23. Ibid.
24. Ibid.
25. Ibid., 223.
26. AlSayyad, *Forms of Dominance: On the Architecture and Urbanism of the Colonial Enterprise*.
27. For an anthropological critique of the developmental ideologies of modern architecture and urban planning and an explanation of the concept of "inverted development" see Holston, *The Modernist City: An Anthropological Critique of Brasilia*.
28. AlSayyad, *Forms of Dominance: On the Architecture and Urbanism of the Colonial Enterprise*; Fuller, *Moderns Abroad: Architecture, Cities and Italian Imperialism*; King, *Colonial Urban Development: Culture, Social Power and Environment*; AlSayyad, *Urbanism, Colonialism, and the World-Economy: Cultural and Spatial Foundations of the World Urban System*; Rabinow, *French Modern: Norms and Forms of the Built Environment*.
29. Crinson, Empire Building: Orientalism and Victorian Architecture; Crinson, *Modern Architecture and the End of Empire*; Hilde Heynen, "The Intertwinement of Modernism and Colonialism: A Theoretical Perspective" (paper presented at the ArchiAfrica : Conference Modern Architecture in East Africa around Independence, Dar es Salaam, Tanzania, 2005).
30. Eric Touchaleaume, *Jean Prouvé: Les Maisons Tropicales* (Paris: Galerie 54, 2006); Cinqualbre, *Jean Prouvé: La Maison tropicale*.

31. Tristan Guilloux, "The Maison Tropique: A Modernist Icon or the Ultimate Colonial Bungalow?," *Fabrications* 18, no. 2 (2008). 10–11.
32. Quoted in Ibid.
33. Quoted in Ibid.
34. Quoted in Ibid.
35. Quoted in Ibid.
36. *Compare the captions of the original designs reproduced in* Cinqualbre, *Jean Prouvé: La Maison tropicale.* Guilloux, "The Maison Tropique: A Modernist Icon or the Ultimate Colonial Bungalow?" 10.
37. Cinqualbre, *Jean Prouvé: La Maison tropicale.*
38. For example, Barry Bergdoll and Peter Christensen, *Home Delivery: Fabricating Modern Dwelling* (New York: The Museum of Modern Art, 2008); Touchaleaume, *Jean Prouvé: Les Maisons Tropicales*; Alexander Vegesack (von) ed. *Jean Prouvé: The Poetics of the Technical Object* (Weil am Rhein: Vitra Design Museum, 2005).
39. Manthia Diawara, "Maison Tropicale" (Portugal 2008).
40. Alastair Gordon, "Out of Africa, a House for a Kit Bag," *The New York Times* 2004.
41. Steve Rose, "La Maison Tropicale Is One Hot House: Jean Prouvé's Fantastic Retro Prefab Has Landed by the Thames. Don't Miss Having a Nose Around . . .," *The Guardian*, 2008.
42. Interview of the author with Bernard Toulier; ICOMOS, "Heritage at Risk 2001–2002: Shared Colonial Heritage".
43. Toulier, *Brazzaville-la-Verte: Inventaire Général des Monuments et Richesses Artistiques de la France*; Toulier, *Brazzaville Decouvertes.*
44. Ibid.
45. Interview of the author with Toulier.
46. Ibid.
47. Ibid.
48. Phillippe Joussee and Patrick Seguin, *Jean Prouvé* (Paris: Galerie Enrico Navarra, 1998).
49. Rubin, "Jean Prouvé's Tropical House: Preservation, Presentation, Reception." 117.
50. *Francoise—Claire Prodhon* in Joussee and Seguin, *Jean Prouvé.*
51. Gordon, "Out of Africa, a House for a Kit Bag."
52. Joussee and Seguin, *Jean Prouvé.*
53. Rubin, "Jean Prouvé's Tropical House: Preservation, Presentation, Reception."
54. Nicolai Ourousoff, "The Best House in Paris," *The New York Times*, 2007.
55. Ibid.
56. David Armstrong, "House Proud," http://www.forbes.com/free_forbes/2006/0410/112.html?partner=yahoomag.
57. Interview of the author with Robert Rubin.
58. Gordon, "Out of Africa, a House for a Kit Bag."
59. Steve Rose, "House Hunting: Eric Touchaleaume Has Been Called the Indiana Jones of Furniture Collecting. Steve Rose Meets Him," *The Guardian*, 2008.
60. Touchaleaume, *Jean Prouvé: Les Maisons Tropicales.*
61. Gordon, "Out of Africa, a House for a Kit Bag."
62. Touchaleaume, *Jean Prouvé: Les Maisons Tropicales.*
63. Amelia Gentleman, "Bullet Holes Extra: A Classic of Modern Design Has Been Saved from Squatters, Snipers, and the Congolese Jungle," *The Guardian*, 2004.
64. Interview of the author with Robert Rubin.

65. Rose, "House Hunting: Eric Touchaleaume Has Been Called the Indiana Jones of Furniture Collecting. Steve Rose Meets Him."

66. Interview of the author with Robert Rubin.

67. Simon Hewitt, "Out of Africa," http://www.blouinartinfo.com/news/story/268281/out-of-africa.

68. Gordon, "Out of Africa, a House for a Kit Bag."; Armstrong, "House Proud".

69. Rubin, "Jean Prouvé's Tropical House: Preservation, Presentation, Reception."

70. Robert Rubin, "Maison Tropicale: Jean Prouvé," in *Home Delivery: Fabricating Modern Dwelling*, ed. Berry Bergdoll (New York: Museum of Modern Art, 2008).

71. Cinqualbre, *Jean Prouvé: La Maison tropicale*.

72. Touchaleaume, *Jean Prouvé: Les Maisons Tropicales*.

73. D. J. Huppatz, "Jean Prouvé's Maison Tropicale: The Poetics of the Colonial Object," *Design Issues*, Fall (2010). 1.

74. William L. Hamilton, "From Africa to Queens Waterfront, A Modernist Gem for Sale to the Highest Bidder," *The New York Times*, 2007.

75. See the catalogue accompanying the exhibition Vegesack (von) *Jean Prouvé: The Poetics of the Technical Object*.

76. Balasz-Properties, "La Maison Tropicale," www.lamaisontropicales.com.

77. Interview of the author with Toulier.

78. Kaye Alexander, "A Visit to Jean Prouvé's Maison Tropicale," *The Architects' Journal* (February 22, 2008) https://www.architectsjournal.co.uk/news/a-visit-to-jean-prouv233s-maison-tropicale/769111.article; Gentleman, "Bullet Holes Extra: A Classic of Modern Design Has Been Saved from Squatters, Snipers, and the Congolese Jungle."; Kaye Alexander, "A City That Sat on Its Treaseures but Didn't See Them," *The New York Times*, 2008; Hamilton, "From Africa to Queens Waterfront, A Modernist Gem for Sale to the Highest Bidder."

79. Interview of the author with Toulier.

80. Rubin, "Jean Prouvé's Tropical House: Preservation, Presentation, Reception."

81. Ibid.

82. Ibid.

83. Ibid.

84. Ibid.

85. Ibid.

86. UNESCO, ICCROM, and CRATerre-EAG, "Africa 2009," www.africa2009.net.

87. Interview of the author with Toulier.

88. Ibid.

89. Rubin, "Jean Prouvé's Tropical House: Preservation, Presentation, Reception."

90. Robert Rubin "Preserving and Presenting Prefab: Jean Prouvé's Tropical House," *Future Anterior* II, no. 1 (2005). 31.

91. Ibid., 38.

92. Interview of the author with Rubin.

93. Interview of the author with Rubin; Cinqualbre, *Jean Prouvé: La Maison tropicale*.

94. Clifford, *The Predicament of Cultures*. 233.

95. Ibid., 222.

96. Benedict Anderson, *Imagined Communities: Reflections on the Origin and Spread of Nationalism*, rev. ed. (London: Verso, 2006). 181.

97. Rubin, "Jean Prouvé's Tropical House: Preservation, Presentation, Reception." 118.

98. Rose, "House Hunting: Eric Touchaleaume Has Been Called the Indiana Jones of Furniture Collecting. Steve Rose Meets Him."
99. Interview of the author with Rubin.
100. Ibid.
101. Price, *Primitive Art in Civilized Places*. 102.
102. Robert Rubin quoted in Gordon, "Out of Africa, a House for a Kit Bag."
103. Price, *Primitive Art in Civilized Places*.
104. Price, *Paris Primitive: Jaques Chirac's Museum on the Quai Branly*. 75–77.
105. International Herald Tribune, "Style Alert Maison Tropicale," http://www.newsletterarchive.org/2007/06/18/175352-IHT+Style+Alert+for+June+19,+2007
106. James Clifford, *Routes: Travel and Translation in the Late Twentieth Century* (Boston: Harvard University Press, 1997). 226.
107. Ibid., 8–9.
108. Clifford, *The Predicament of Cultures*. 232.
109. Interview of the author with Ângela Ferreira.
110. Jürgen Bock, ed. *Angela Ferreira: Maison Tropicale, Portugese Pavillion* (Lisbon/Venice: La Ministério da Cultura, 2007).
111. Diawara, "Maison Tropicale."
112. Interview of the author with Ângela Ferreira.
113. Diawara, "Maison Tropicale."
114. Ibid.
115. Ibid.
116. Ibid.
117. Ibid.
118. Ibid.
119. Clifford, *Routes: Travel and Translation in the Late Twentieth Century*.
120. Interview of the author with Ângela Ferreira.
121. Rubin, "Jean Prouvé's Tropical House: Preservation, Presentation, Reception." 129.
122. Diawara, "Maison Tropicale."
123. Clifford, *Routes: Travel and Translation in the Late Twentieth Century*. 3.
124. Ibid., 229.
125. Ibid., 218.
126. Ibid., 222.
127. Thomas, *Entangled Objects: Exchange, Material Culture and Colonialism in the Pacific*. 4.

7 Many Words for Modern

Negotiating Ethics of
Legitimacy and Responsibility
in Dar es Salaam, Utrecht,
Amsterdam and Accra

In 2001, a group of five Dutch architects founded the NGO ArchiAfrika in the Netherlands. Their aim was "to put (modern) African architectural culture on the world map" and "to maintain an "international exchange of expertise and knowledge within the African continent".[1] To mark its launch, ArchiAfrika in 2005 organized a student workshop and academic conference, *Modern Architecture in East Africa around Independence*. It took place in Dar es Salaam, the capital of Tanzania, and was inspired by the architect Anthony B. Almeida. In 1950, Almeida had been one of the first members of the Royal Institute of British Architects chartered in Dar es Salaam, then the capital of the British protectorate of Tanganyika. As an architect building according to modern principles, Almeida was commissioned to work for the British regime, though he continued to build for the successive independent national governments after Tanganyika's political independence.

During ArchiAfrika's first event, the NGO's interest in the colonial and postcolonial legacy of Almeida's oeuvre led to a debate between European and African participants about whether there is such a thing as an African modern architecture, as well as about the notion of a modern architectural heritage in Africa. The strong debate was inconclusive, formatively affecting ArchiAfrika's subsequent development, as the organization quickly positioned itself more generally in "the field of African architecture, and architecture in Africa".[2] ArchiAfrika proceeded to build a large, interdisciplinary and considerably transnational network that linked individual researchers at universities, at other governmental, intergovernmental and nongovernmental institutions, as well as various businesses. Eventually, this fast growth led to a structural reorganization, including, most important, the NGO's transfer to Africa, which happened in 2013, when the NGO's headquarters moved from Utrecht in the Netherlands to Accra, Ghana. Three years earlier, in 2010, two of ArchiAfrika's original Dutch founders, Antoni Folkers and Berend van der Lans, established a private spin-off to the NGO: African Architecture Matters, now based in Amsterdam. Referring to their personal experience of working as architects in Africa, as well as their experience working with ArchiAfrika, Folkers and van der Lans advertise African Architecture Matters as a consultancy that provides services to "commercial parties, cultural institutions, housing corporations and developers, educational institutes, governmental parties, and NGO's",[3] including ArchiAfrika itself.

In this chapter I focus my inquiry on the case of ArchiAfrika and its initial occupation with Anthony Almeida's modern architectural heritage in Dar es Salaam. Leading up to the foundation of African Architecture Matters, I describe ArchiAfrika's evolution, which I have followed over the course of my multisited anthropological fieldwork. My emphasis is on the intellectual, institutional and personal dimensions and dynamics of ArchiAfrika and African Architecture Matters' practices. I analyze them as relevant problematizations of current norms and forms of scientific knowledge and expertise.

Recent scholarship in the anthropology of science points to important transformations in the authorities and venues of scientific knowledge- and expertise-making today. Scholars particularly note a general reshaping of the position of the modern research university within a global context of national institutional reform, as well as concerning the emergence of transnational research organizations and contract research groups.[4] My interest is in ArchiAfrika and African Architecture Matters's relationship with the modern research university and their common goal to produce scientific knowledge and expertise concerning modern architecture in Africa. I ask how discord and affect in the context of a global heritage assemblage around Anthony Almeida's architecture in Dar es Salaam led to changes in ArchiAfrika's organizational structure, notably its "transfer to Africa" and the ensuing foundation of African Architecture Matters. Furthermore, I would like to find out how personalities shape negotiations of contemporary scientific authority on modern architecture in Africa.

My analysis reveals how ArchiAfrika experienced a crisis of legitimacy and responsibility as a result of its launch event, *Modern Architecture in East Africa around Independence*. Preparing the Dar es Salaam workshop and conference, ArchiAfrika cooperated with Eindhoven's and Delft's Universities of Technology in the Netherlands, the Catholic University of Leuven in Belgium, and the University College for Land and Architectural Studies (UCLAS, now Ardhi University) in Tanzania. When UCLAS officially withdrew its support on late notice, however, ArchiAfrika decided to launch without its local Tanzanian partner. As a consequence of this decision, though, the institutional, as well as the intellectual and personal dynamics of the event left ArchiAfrika with a normative uncertainty about its nascent aims and structure. I argue that this normative uncertainty explains the reorganization of ArchiAfrika after *Modern Architecture in East Africa around Independence*, including the spin-off of African Architecture Matters. Throughout this process, ArchiAfrika and African Architecture Matters can be said to engage in a significant social experiment with contemporary norms and forms of collaboration in the production of scientific knowledge and expertise about modern architecture in Africa. Ultimately, I claim that ArchiAfrika and African Architecture Matters's assumption of a position of scientific authority relative to the modern research university amounts to a problematization of ethics of legitimacy and responsibility.

Ethics of Legitimacy and Responsibility

I base my approach to scientific ethics on Max Weber, who in his famous 1918 lecture *Science as a Vocation* noted that "science today is a vocation organized in special disciplines in the service of self-clarification and knowledge of interrelated facts".[5] Though Weber claims that scientific knowledge and expertise cannot by themselves answer questions of value and morality, modern science can help individuals pursue clarity regarding the meaning of their own conduct.[6] For Weber, science ultimately contributes to an ethos of "self-clarification and a sense of responsibility".[7] In this context, he introduces the notion of an inward calling for science, inner ethics, maintaining that the personal attitude of a legitimate scientist is such that "he engages in science for science's sake and not merely because others, by exploiting science, bring about commercial or technical success and can better feed, dress, illuminate, and govern".[8] Weber reflects critically on the material conditions of science in the early 20th century, providing an analysis of the modern research university as an increasingly capitalist and bureaucratized enterprise that may disappoint and compromise any inner ethics of science.[9]

As Paul Rabinow and others have observed, Weber's analysis of the modern research university in Europe and America remains remarkably true in the 21st century.[10] Still, Weber's view of science and its emphasis on the research university, essentially a product of the 19th century, also require modification, as he neglects the fact that in the early 20th century the scientific mission to invent concepts and to conduct experiments increasingly moved scientists away from the metropolitan university to the periphery of the colonies.[11] The historian of science Helen Tilley also situates changing and contested meanings of modern science in the context of colonialism. Her focus is on the European colonies in Africa, which she claims provided whole scientific diasporas with vital opportunities to develop emerging disciplines such as sociology and anthropology, as well as professional practices such as architecture and urban planning.[12] She explains how at the beginning of the 20th century, many scientific innovations were tested on the African continent, providing scientists with important fields of experimentation.[13] She places Weber's account of modern science in a new light, arguing that crucial to the negotiation of scientific modernity was a certain "Africanization of science"[14] that entailed a decentering of the European research university.

Tilley's primary example is the British African Research Survey. Initiated in 1929, this survey brought together a network of academics, officials and public intellectuals vested not only in modern research universities but also in a broad range of other institutions and systems of patronage, learned societies and disciplinary structures.[15] Tilley uses the African Research Survey to show how national and transnational scientific infrastructures were constituted simultaneously. Furthermore, she indicates how a dynamic interplay emerged between scientific fieldwork and research across metropolitan and colonial contexts, also showing the ways in which this interplay helped to challenge and transform established scientific practices.[16] She claims that, as a result, Africa was placed at the core of an emerging scientific discourse of complexity, interrelations and independence, as well as at the heart of governmental interventions.[17] She speaks of colonial Africa as a living laboratory for scientific research, development experiments and social engineering. Moreover, Tilley believes the continent was a significant field for developing "social criticism, interdisciplinarity and transnational methods, the study of interrelated phenomena and the codification of new areas of ethnoscientific and vernacular research".[18]

According to Tilley, modern science thus for an important part evolved on the African continent in the context of its practitioners' engagement with local ideas and knowledge.[19] Her account of the appropriation of colonial Africa as a "living laboratory" describes what her colleague Steven Shapin calls a social experiment in science, an attempt "to explore what novel configurations of people, space, knowledge, material resources and external support can best bring about wanted intellectual and technological futures".[20]

Shapin, whose interest in the moral history of modern science also draws on Weber, describes how scientists engage in social experiments whenever there is a need to jointly negotiate a range of sometimes conflicting motives.[21] He claims that conflicts about scientific practice and purpose—as well as the people and motivations behind these conflicts—frequently cause fundamental normative uncertainty.[22] A case in point for Shapin's argument is Tilley's analysis of the African Research Survey. Tilley indicates how the negotiation of new norms and forms of scientific knowledge and expertise during colonialism led to increasing normative uncertainty among scientists. She shows how this had the unexpected and unintended effect of initiating a certain epistemic decolonization, although the political will to maintain colonial rule continued well into the second half of the 20th century.[23] Tilley contends that an early-20th-century 'Africanization' of science gradually cast doubts on the legitimacy of established scientific authorities, as well as that of their colonial governments. To her, the appropriation of colonial Africa as a living laboratory consigned to the individual scientist certain responsibilities regarding his or—much less frequently—her relations with local populations.

Of course, this essentially raises a Weberian question about the ethics of science: Who is the legitimate and responsible scientist engaging in research on the African continent? Tilley argues that this question of an ethics of legitimacy and responsibility continues to be relevant as Africa is still often thought of as a laboratory for scientific research and development interventions. One of ArchiAfrika's policy plans, for example, literally considers Africa "a true laboratory" to "approach contemporary architectural issues contributing to the reconsideration and innovation of issues in the African and worldwide context".[24]

Tilley claims that by and large research and policy continues to be driven by extra-African organizations with their own needs and interests.[25] She does not believe that legitimacy and responsibility problems stemming from the colonial period are likely to be settled soon, only that their ongoing dynamics do change when researchers shift their focus to their African interlocutors' concerns.[26] But, what exactly happens when ArchiAfrika (re)appropriates Africa as a "living laboratory" for the production of scientific knowledge and expertise?

A Global Heritage Assemblage around Modern Architecture in East Africa

ArchiAfrika's establishment goes back to five Dutch friends all working as architects in Africa. In 2000, Janneke Bierman, Antoni Folkers, Joep Mol, Belinda van Buiten and Berend van der Lans got together in the Netherlands to reflect on their "fascination with the [African] continent, as well as things seen and done".[27] According to Folkers, the impetus was a realization that

> it is strange that we have all been to Africa; have learned and experienced a lot, but not much is done with it. And now that we are all active in the Netherlands, again—what sticks? How can it be that there is so little attention to the field of architecture in Africa?

Eventually, the groups' discussions led to the conclusion that they "must organize a platform on which to study and discuss African architecture—whatever that may be—and also to disseminate knowledge [. . .]". Hence, in 2001 ArchiAfrika was registered as a not-for-profit foundation under Dutch law. Its proclaimed aims as a non-governmental organization were "to put (modern) African architectural culture on the world map", to establish a "platform for the exchange of news and expertise in this field", and to facilitate "research and projects on the terrain of African architecture and architecture in Africa".[28]

Cofounder Joep Mol remembers a long debate about the definition of ArchiAfrika's profile:

> Very vaguely, our aim was to put African architecture on the map of the world. And that was always an enormous quest: What to do with it? We wanted to build a website, we wanted to organize a conference, we wanted to expand a network, we wanted to do research. Actually, we really had six, seven, eight goals we wanted to reach. For two years we thought about it and talked about it and the bottom line was always: How can we get funding? Then we came to the conclusion that we had to start somewhere concretely. Because, you might want to take all of Africa at the same time, but . . . So, then we got down to asking: what would be an interesting topic to start with?

Antoni Folkers suggested organizing an initial project around the architect Anthony Almeida. Folkers assumed that a concrete project, such as a book or an exhibition about Almeida's modern architecture in Tanzania, would generate attention for ArchiAfrika. According to Folkers, the simple reasoning behind his choice for Almeida was that "everyone of us has been to Tanzania, he's an interesting man, and he's a friend of mine". Besides, he had always wanted to put Almeida in the spotlight.[29]

Anthony B. Almeida was born in 1921 in British Tanganyika's capital Dar es Salaam to parents who had emigrated from Goa. He was educated in colonial India and studied architecture at the J.J. School of architecture in Bombay from 1941 until 1948.[30] Almeida reflects on his background and professional education in a short curriculum vitae:

> [My] architectural studies could be said to have been greatly enriched by the fact that they took place in India, a land uniquely endowed with a rich heritage of ancient architecture, the study of which was given greatest importance. [. . .] At the same time however, [I] was fortunate to have also gained much awareness of the trends of the contemporary architecture being carried out in the West, due to the presence of visiting lecturers who had all studied abroad. These lecturers also provided the school library with their having been read architectural magazines from the west and this in my case resulted in an influencing exposure to the works of such architects as Frank Lloyd Wright, Le Corbusier, Erich Mendelsohn, Alvar Aalto, and South American architects as Oscar Niemeyer.[31]

Almeida claims that these influences informed a principled search for "modern solutions" in his architectural practice.[32] After completing his studies, Almeida was elected Associate Member of the Royal Institute of British Architects. He first gained some work experience in India, after which he returned to Tanganyika and opened an office in Dar es Salaam in 1950.

Initially, the bulk of Almeida's work consisted of commercial and residential buildings for the local Asian business community.[33] Only in 1953 did the British colonial government commission Almeida to design standard types of police posts.[34] Then, in 1954, "after four years of architectural starvation",[35] as he puts it, the Goan community of Dar es Salaam approached him with a major commission to plan a primary school. And although government inspectors apparently criticized his modern design, according to Almeida the completion of the Goan school established his name as an architect and constituted an important turning point in his career.[36] Subsequently, Almeida was approached to plan several other schools:

> In nearly all the cases, I was reminded to carry out the works in the 'modernistic style'. Interestingly, the largest and most prestigious of the school projects was that of the Dar es Salaam Technical College complex for none other than the Government's Education Department which earlier had come close to rejecting my proposal for the Goan community school.[37]

When Tanganyika gained its independence in December 1961 and joined with Zanzibar to become Tanzania in April 1965, Almeida had thus established his reputation as an architect. The newly independent government and its parastatal organizations commissioned Almeida to carry out many works from the 1960s until the 1990s, including several large office buildings, a library and a hospital. Today, well in his nineties, Almeida still engages in smaller-scale architectural projects, because, as he says, "a cowboy will die with his boots on".[38]

Admiration for Almeida and his modern architecture in Tanzania thus led Antoni Folkers to suggest him as a focus for ArchiAfrika's first event. However, after "sometimes heated"[39] discussion, ArchiAfrika's founders decided that any project about Almeida had to be placed in a broader context.[40] They agreed that an exclusive focus on the biography and oeuvre of Almeida was inappropriate and not 'attractive' enough. Furthermore, they wanted to encourage a wider exchange of knowledge and expertise. As a consequence, ArchiAfrika made plans to organize a student workshop and academic conference in Dar es Salaam, where Almeida lives. In 2003, ArchiAfrika compiled a brochure with the title *Modern Architecture in Tanzania around Independence: The Work of Anthony Almeida* in order to convince other parties to become partners in organizing and financing the planned event.[41] This, ArchiAfrika's first publication, announced the following goals for its initial project:

1. Inventory and documentation of the work of the architect Anthony Almeida and his contemporaries in the period around independence;
2. Analysis of his work concerning the role of this work in the development of Tanzanian architecture, its position in relation to the

architecture of the international Modern Movement and the role of this work in the (contemporary and historical) cultural and political context;

3. Appraisal of the studied work from a historical and contemporary perspective.[42]

With the help of the brochure, ArchiAfrika successfully secured institutional support: first in the Netherlands from Eindhoven Technical University and Delft University of Technology and then in Belgium from the Catholic University of Leuven. Later, links were made with the Tanzanian Architects Association and UCLAS in Dar es Salaam, which agreed to provide the venue and participate in the planned workshop and conference.[43]

ArchiAfrika's cooperation with a Tanzanian university was crucial to obtaining funding because many Dutch grant-issuing bodies required proof of a local partner. Ultimately, ArchiAfrika received money from a variety of donors, including the Dutch National Commission for International Cooperation and Sustainable Development, the Homogene Groep Internationale Samenwerking (Homogenous Group International Cooperation), the Prins Claus Fund for Culture and Development, the Humanistisch Instituut voor Ontwikkelingssamenwerking (Humanistic Institute for Development Aid), but also the Vermogensfonds (Private Wealth Fund), Stichting DOEN (the charitable foundation of the Dutch lottery), Fonds voor de Beeldende Kunst en Vormgeving en Bouwkunst (Foundation for the Visual Arts, Design and Architecture), as well as the foundation Diophrathe. There also were a number of corporate and private sponsors, and the participating universities contributed too.

In February 2005, on receiving its first funds, ArchiAfrika launched a website to promote the student workshop and conference. Its homepage invited students to participate in the so-called Almeida Project[44] to help inventory Almeida's architecture in Dar es Salaam. Under the new title *Modern Architecture in East Africa around Independence*, ArchiAfrika also published an online call for papers that broadened the scope of the planned event once more. Academics were now invited to submit contributions on a set of predefined research topics:

1. The rise of Modern Architecture in East Africa in the 1950s and 1960s and its role in the development of local architecture;
2. The position of East African Modern Architecture in relation to the architecture of the international Modern Movement;
3. East African Modern Heritage in its cultural, social and political context.[45]

Two dominant themes emerge here, which would become a source of discord and affect during and after the actual student workshop and conference: the question of a distinct African identity of modern architecture and the notion of a significant modern architectural heritage in Africa.

ArchiAfrika thus developed from an exclusive focus on Almeida's architecture to a wider interest in modern architecture before and after political independence in British East Africa. Folkers claims that this shift in focus was informed by a realization that architectural styles and ideologies hardly changed during the transition from colonial to postcolonial politics:

> One would expect a sort of revolt, or something like that, but that's not what happened. Modernism seems to have been a formal expression as well as an architectural approach, however you want to put it, which was applied on a large scale during the late colonial, as well as the post-colonial regimes. In fact, [modernism] is adopted by every new political power. It is perceived as a very good way to express the newness of the nation. I thought that was interesting.

ArchiAfrika's close examination of Almeida's oeuvre thus already suggested questions about the nature of historical continuities and discontinuities when comparing colonial and postcolonial architecture. In fact, Folkers "knew" that studies of buildings and sites in Northern Africa published by The International Working Party for the Documentation and Conservation of Modern Movement architecture (DOCOMOMO).[46]

The influence of DOCOMOMO looms large over the establishment of ArchiAfrika, not only in the initial project, *Modern Architecture in East Africa around Independence*, but also in the very origins of the NGO. Much like ArchiAfrika, DOCOMOMO started as a small Dutch organization based on a shared interest among friends. Hubert-Jan Henket and Wessel de Jonge brought DOCOMOMO to life in the late 1980s, after which it grew rapidly, developing into a recognized network of experts and raising awareness about modern architectural heritage.[47] By now, it regularly advises governments and intergovernmental organizations such as ICOMOS and UNESCO. For ArchiAfrika then, DOCOMOMO was an inspiration. This is no surprise, considering all of ArchiAfrika's five founders very personally participated in DOCOMOMO's development: Berend van der Lans was a student assistant to Wessel de Jonge, while Belinda van Buiten worked for Hubert-Jan Henket. Janneke Bierman recently assumed the position as chair of the Dutch chapter of DOCOMOMO and became a partner in Henket's studio. Antoni Folkers explains:

> It is almost self-evident that DOCOMOMO is an example for us; besides the fact that we are very good friends with each other, it

is really sort of natural. But, there is also a series of coincidences. Hubert-Jan Henket built in Dar es Salaam and his wife who is a fashion designer lived with us in Dar es Salaam for a while working with handicapped people on a design project. At the time he also visited [my partner Belinda van Buiten and me]. So, stuff like that. It's all a little bit like a family.[48]

Given this statement, it is also not surprising that ArchiAfrika's initial event *Modern Architecture in East Africa around Independence* bears a certain DOCOMOMO mark.

At the time, DOCMOMO's Hubert Jan Henket explicitly asked ArchiAfrika to focus on the colonial heritage of the modern movement because he hoped to generate local support for his organization.[49] For a long time, DOCOMOMO had been trying to establish national DOCOMOMO chapters on the African continent, but without any real success.[50] Now the NGO hoped that ArchiAfrika's two-week student workshop in Dar es Salaam could fulfill a task otherwise assigned to these nonexisting national chapters: The completion of detailed descriptions of buildings with "the ultimate aim to determine a possible strategy for preservation and valorization of these would-be (or could-be) monuments".[51] Yet in spite of ArchiAfrika's support of the DOCOMOMO agenda, the young NGO set out to establish itself independently. As Folkers points out,

> [t]he interest of DOCOMOMO was clear. They couldn't get a foothold in Africa so they thought: Hey, nice club! [ArchiAfrika] can do something for us . . . We still want to help, but we explicitly do not only want to be a DOCOMOMO Africa-vehicle. That wasn't the idea.[52]

Instead, ArchiAfrika's aim behind the decision to hold a student workshop and an academic conference in Dar es Salaam was to reach out to local stakeholders through sustained "exchange" and "dialogue".[53]

ArchiAfrika's vision met with lot of encouragement, particularly from the university-based European DOCOMOMO community. ArchiAfrika's relationship with its local Tanzanian partner UCLAS, however, gradually deteriorated as a result of what Folkers calls "misunderstandings about expectations".[54] This became especially apparent when, as a prelude to *Modern Architecture in East Africa around Independence*, ArchiAfrika invited officials from UCLAS to visit the universities of Eindhoven and Leuven. Once in Europe, the UCLAS representatives saw a chance to cooperate beyond the scope of an incidental workshop and conference. They asked for a concrete "memorandum of understanding"[55] between the respective universities that ArchiAfrika was in no position to facilitate.

Antoni Folkers explains that while ArchiAfrika thought of *Modern Architecture in East Africa around Independence* as a small initial project, its African partners wanted more:

> They had it the other way around. [They said:] "relationships with highly qualified academics are extremely important for us. We don't really know who's behind ArchiAfrika. Never mind, if only our cooperation with them can serve as a means to cooperation with [the universities]." [. . .] Then, [UCLAS] even introduced as a condition for their support of the project the financing of a PhD project. But, who'd pay for that? [They said:] "Well, that's your problem." Ultimately, they wanted to participate if a PhD position was in it for them. [. . .] But, the costs of setting an African PhD student up here in the Netherlands? [. . .] That's easily €100,000. [ArchiAfrika] couldn't and didn't want to finance this.

Because of these and "a number of other practical difficulties" in reaching conclusive agreements with UCLAS, ArchiAfrika was forced to delay *Modern Architecture in East Africa around Independence* several times.[56]

Ultimately, UCLAS withdrew its institutional support altogether and in affect. Six weeks before the beginning of the two-week student workshop and eight weeks before the scheduled three-day conference, ArchiAfrika was left without a local partner. Folkers recalls that the organizing committee were faced with a difficult decision:

> At the time, we looked at each other: All those preparations behind us! Maybe we can delay for another year and fix this? But, you can imagine that in the meantime we had received all these papers. So then we said: It's a go or no go. And we decided to do it. We decided to organize it on our own. And fortunately we had business contacts in Tanzania whom we could ask for an alternative venue.[57]

In July 2005, a company guesthouse in need of renovations replaced the UCLAS campus and accommodated ArchiAfrika's event in Dar es Salaam. But the withdrawal of local institutional support still created an obvious problem for the NGO. And when ArchiAfrika assumed legitimacy and responsibility for *Modern Architecture in East Africa around Independence* without a Tanzanian partner, they were asked what Folkers calls the "mean" question: If ArchiAfrika wanted to facilitate a global heritage assemblage around modern architecture in East Africa based on exchange and dialogue, "who's waiting for it; what's the demand from Africa?"[58]

Negotiating Legitimacy and Responsibility

According to Folkers, "the question concerning demand from Africa was and still is an important question" for ArchiAfrika.[59] Before the launch of

Modern Architecture in East Africa around Independence, ArchiAfrika presupposed an African demand for assistance in research of architecture on the continent, but they also emphasized that there was a demand from the West.[60] As Folkers puts it, ArchiAfrika wanted to debate with the Tanzanians because they were curious what they had to say.[61] But, while the European participants of ArchiAfrika's student workshop and conference signed up, booked their flights and were looking forward to their stay in Dar es Salaam, UCLAS staff indicates that the NGO's decision to go it alone created a sense of frustration with them.[62] Even Anthony Almeida, who was certainly sympathetic to ArchiAfrika's initial project, was surprised at the NGO's perseverance: "They had the money and they were going ahead. Some here perceived this as kind of arrogant."[63]

In retrospective, ArchiAfrika's Joep Mol admits that

> [t]o give money, to send people. It's such a maze of interests—also mutual interests. It's so complicated to create links. And as newcomers we were possibly a bit naïve in this. Like, we will come here for our project and people will participate.

When the workshop and conference took place in July 2005, local participation turned out higher than expected, even without the institutional support of UCLAS. A recurrent debate about demand from Africa, however, reinforced a sense of discord.

Hilde Heynen, a professor of architectural theory at the Catholic University of Leuven and one of the keynote lecturers of *Modern Architecture in East Africa around Independence*, speaks of "a clash between European expectations and African realities".[64] She writes in her preface to the conference proceedings:

> The group of European students and professors that set out for Dar es Salaam in July 2005 was in for a challenging encounter. [From the beginning,] a certain tension developed within the whole group. This tension had to do with different opinions regarding the correct way of addressing the basic questions that were raised.[65]

For Heynen, these "basic questions" were about nothing less than the relevance of modern architecture in Africa: On one hand, Dutch and Belgian students were asked to provide a historical analysis of buildings during the workshop according to established heritage documentation practices as prescribed by DOCOMOMO.[66] On the other hand, Tanzanian students approached the same buildings from the point of view of their present-day usage and as "urban catalysts"[67] for future development.

Heynen notes a similar discord at the academic conference:

> For the Europeans among the speakers, it was clear that the topic was 'modernist architecture in East-Africa around independence'—meaning that the focus was on a historical period, and that the basic

questions had to do with the valorization today of the buildings that emerged during this recent past. The other speakers more or less stuck to this scheme, too, but it was most telling that the discussions with the audience almost always diverted away from these supposedly central issues.[68]

Heynen describes the event as informed by a "confrontation between different realities and different outlooks upon the world".[69] And indeed, ArchiAfrika raised two major intellectual problems: the problem of a distinct African identity of modern architecture and the problem of modern architectural heritage.

ArchiAfrika engaged with the first problem, the question of identity, when it encouraged research on "the position of East African Modern Architecture in relation to the architecture of the international Modern Movement" and the influence of the rise of Modern Architecture on local architecture.[70] During the workshop and conference in Dar es Salaam, this approach met opposition. Anthony Almeida, for instance, finds ArchiAfrika's characterization of him as one of the first East African architects inappropriate:

> I am not an African! I am an Indian. There is no African architecture. The Kenyan climate is not the same as the bloody Tanzanian. And then, there was no [such thing as the] East Coast before the colonials, before the Omanis when they brought their capital to Zanzibar. So East Africa in this sense had nothing in common. [. . .] There is nothing like East African architecture. You can say architecture in East Africa, all right. That is because at one time Uganda, Kenya and Tanzania were under British rule. So it was British East Africa, at a time. But there is no such thing, or there cannot be such a thing as East African architecture.[71]

Clearly Almeida has a problem with the assumption that his work has a distinct African identity. Calling for more nuance, he refers to the intricacies of his personal colonial legacy and is himself sensitive to the different colonial and postcolonial pasts of his region. He complains about the invocation of a certain identity politics at *Modern Architecture in East Africa around Independence*: "African this, African that. It was all too politicized."[72]

Almeida's irritation appears to have been a common sentiment among the local participants of the Dar es Salaam workshop and conference. This is confirmed by Camilus T. Lekule, a professor of architecture at UCLAS, who said he also grew tired of the discussion. Lekule complains about a "pushy", paternalistic attitude displayed by some of the European participants and accuses them of an arrogant, "you guys have to understand" approach along the lines of "you have to understand: This is your modern African heritage."[73] Though it left Lekule wondering,

"What can we possibly get out of this?" he displays a certain pragmatism, suggesting they "get on with recreating identities, today" instead.[74] He points to the limits of concerning oneself with an 'essential African identity of modern architecture'. Instead, he would like to have talked about what he calls "architecture with values": specific colonial and postcolonial buildings with different cultural histories and futures.[75]

A second problem contributing to the discord was ArchiAfrika's attempt to valorize modern African architecture as heritage. Many European participants took the concept of modern architectural heritage for granted, also as a result of years of personal engagement for DOCOMOMO. Hilde Heynen writes:

> In Europe the ideas and practices of conservation have been established already for a long time (at least since the second half of the 19th century). This made it rather obvious to extend their usage to a more recent heritage such as that of the Modern Movement. In most African countries, on the other hand, and also in Tanzania, the awareness about the need for conservation is far less mature.[76]

At the conference, however, the very idea of modern heritage alienated many local participants. According to Daniel Mbisso, a researcher at Ardhi University (formerly UCLAS), the concept of architectural heritage is generally not very popular at his institution: "The voice of the historic preservation department is quite low and overwhelmed. When you talk about conservation, people think of forests etc., not buildings."[77]

Indeed, given that architectural conservation policy in Tanzania is based on colonial legislation and remains virtually unaltered since 1961, addressing the particular issue of modern architectural heritage was bound to cause confusion.[78] For example, Almeida states,

> See, what I am against is the use of the term 'modern heritage'. I don't see what it is about this one word. They are just going for it because everybody talks of it. Heritage is something that's from the past, handed down to you. How could something that is of the past become modern? Modern is of today. Look in the dictionary what modern means: Of the present. Contemporary is of the present. Modern is of today! [. . .] What is the dictionary meaning of heritage: something of the past. My architecture is not about the past, at all.[79]

Local participants of the workshop and conference similarly criticized ArchiAfrika's approach to Almeida's work as modern heritage as counterintuitive.

Even more significantly, local critics complained about a certain ignorance among the European participants of the problematic dimensions of modern architecture's colonial and postcolonial legacies. Camilus T. Lekule, for instance, laments ArchiAfrika's "approach to modern heritage that ignores what people are about, what the urban environment is all about, here".[80] He contends:

> The locals had the idea that it was too early to talk about modern heritage, but the European participants said: "Look, this is what created development." I would say no: "Look, this is what hampered development!"[81]

According to Lekule, the equations of modern architecture first with colonial and later with postcolonial ideologies of progress and development were too often taken at face value in the discussions. To him, the decay of buildings supposedly "representing progress",[82] which led to calls for their heritage conservation in the first place, is visible proof of the failures to stimulate development through the modern built environment. Consequently, Lekule skeptically reviews assertions that now, in a strange turn, the conservation of modern architecture should be "instrumental to African development".[83] For him, "future development issues" in Tanzania, such as increasing and uncontrolled urbanization, poverty and HIV/Aids are not likely to be answered by a global heritage assemblage around modern architecture in East Africa.[84]

Sharing Lekule's skepticism about the relevance of historic preservation in contemporary Tanzania, Anthony Almeida introduces an analogy: "When does a man need a flower garden in the house? When one has the time and resources to care for it! After all, you cannot eat flowers."[85] Thus, whereas Hilde Heynen emphasizes the significance of a global "transfer of knowledge, of research methodologies [and] of conservation practices"[86] for modern architecture, for Almeida and Lekule these are not the tools that Tanzanian architects practicing in a context of poverty need most urgently today. It is clear to them that any occupation with architecture in present-day Africa "should not end with modern architecture, it should go beyond".[87]

For ArchiAfrika's founders, the institutional, intellectual and personal dynamics of *Modern Architecture in East Africa around Independence* thus led to an experience of normative uncertainty. While the NGO claimed legitimacy and responsibility to represent scientific knowledge and expertise about modern architecture in Africa because "the important voice of Africa" was "lacking"[88] or at least "often not heard enough",[89] ArchiAfrika's single-handed organization and profiling of *Modern Architecture in East Africa around Independence* provoked discord about the meaning and relevance of an African identity of modern architectural heritage, leaving ArchiAfrika's nascent structure and aims in a definite crisis of legitimacy and responsibility.

After ArchiAfrika's Dar es Salaam event, Antoni Folkers reacted to local criticism of the NGO's focus and approach in the conference proceedings, addressing the need for ArchiAfrika to "shift in focus from 'how to treat modernist buildings today' to 'how to build today'.[90] Accordingly, ArchiAfrika aimed to work more generally on "the unlocking and scientific study of African architecture". In the aftermath of *Modern Architecture in East Africa around Independence*, the NGO assumed that besides raising "awareness of the value of the (modern) African heritage and its architectural identity [. . .] this can probably contribute to help solve some of the contemporary worldwide architectonic issues on for example sustainability and cultural identity".[91] Nowadays, ArchiAfrika also wishes to establish an "international exchange of expertise and knowledge within the African continent", which it claims "to date, leaves a lot to be desired".[92]

Those phrases are taken from ArchiAfrika's most recent policy plan for the period between 2009 and 2012, which features a number of reinterpreted "core tasks".[93] The first of those is to organize projects. In 2006, for instance, ArchiAfrika started *The African House Project* together with Delft University of Technology and Stichting Africa Naast de Deur (foundation Africa Next Door). This project is designed to "gain more awareness and in-depth knowledge about the dwelling culture of the African diaspora in Southeast Amsterdam".[94] Extending over several years, it brings together activists and researchers from the African diaspora as well as European participants in a workshop and in the making of an exhibition and a documentary.

ArchiAfrika's second self-assigned core task is to continue the organization of conferences and workshops. In 2006, for example, ArchiAfrika co-organized a conference entitled *African Architecture Today* in Kumasi, Ghana. Then, ArchiAfrika in 2007 launched the first event of its ongoing *African Perspectives* series in Delft, the Netherlands. Events in this series are scheduled biannually and thus far were held in Pretoria in 2009 and in Casablanca in 2011. They combine academic debate about the themes of urban development, built cultural heritage, building in Africa, the African diaspora, and African architecture with art exhibitions, movie screenings, talks, exercises and performances.[95] For ArchiAfrika, the "target of *African Perspectives* is to draft an agenda for structural cooperation based on issues that will emerge from the days spent together".[96] And the NGO considers *African Perspectives* events "meeting points for everybody interested and concerned with the topic".[97]

ArchiAfrika's third core task, maintaining a website and publishing a an e-mail newsletter, closely corresponds with its ambition to create open spaces for the exchange and "exploration"[98] of knowledge and expertise. This online presence is meant to constitute a virtual open space. Throughout, ArchiAfrika bridges the dominant language divide on the African continent by conducting all digital communication bilingually in English and French. Furthermore, ArchiAfrika's homepage since 2008 features an online database and search engine covering the field of African architecture.[99] It considers its website and e-mail newsletter "pillars of the organization" that are supposed to lead visitors "to relevant information, places, organizations, treasuries, and people".[100]

The final core task ArchiAfrika specifies is to facilitate partnerships. Although the NGO emphasizes its independence, it embraces partners in order to approach architecture "from a broad cultural and social perspective".[101] Among ArchiAfrika's regular institutional partners are different non-governmental, governmental and intergovernmental organizations, as well as private and corporate actors. Most significant, however, ArchiAfrika positions itself in relation to the modern research university. It currently cooperates with a number of universities such as the University of Pretoria, the Kwame Nkrumah University of Science and Technology in Kumasi, the Universidado Eduaerdo Mondlane in Maputo, the Ecole Supérieure d'Architecture in Casablanca, Ardhi University in Dar es Salaam and the Technical University of Delft. Thus, ArchiAfrika is building a far-reaching, transdisciplinary network.

Ultimately then, ArchiAfrika's reformulated targets form a pragmatic attempt to rectify the discord experienced during *Modern Architecture in East Africa around Independence*. ArchiAfrika's pragmatism is also evident in the final product that was meant to round off its launch event. Based on the results of the Dar es Salaam student workshop and the academic conference, ArchiAfrika had first planned to publish an academic book exclusively about Anthony Almeida. They cancelled the book project in reaction to the conference's discussion and debate, and instead supported the making of a documentary, produced by ArchiAfrika's cofounder Joep de Mol and directed by Jord den Hollander.

This film, *Many Words for Modern: A Survey of Modern Architecture in Tanzania*, is exclusively based on interviews with local participants of Modern Architecture in East Africa around Independence as well as with Tanzanian experts from the fields of architecture, urbanism and development. Along with footage of modern and contemporary buildings, the documentary reflects on current problems related to the urban environment of Dar es Salaam as identified by the local interviewees. Producer Joep Mol describes the raising of awareness about Tanzanian concerns in Europe and Africa—the film was first screened on Tanzanian TV—as the primary objective of the documentary, claiming this is "more important than any heritage inventory of the modern built environment".[102]

After *Modern Architecture in East Africa around Independence*, ArchiAfrika is careful not to be pinned down on the issue of modern architectural heritage in Africa. Yet even if ArchiAfrika reacts like that to what Antoni Folkers called the "mean"[103] question about demand from Africa, the NGO remains entangled with the specific modern heritage of an early-20th-century Africanization of science in its goal to produce scientific knowledge and expertise about African architecture. This becomes evident in ArchiAfrika's 2009 policy plan, which declares: "the predominantly one-way transfer of Western knowledge has to be coupled with

African expertise brought to Europe and the rest of the World".[104] And ArchiAfrika projects that

> during the period 2009–2012 the emphasis will lie on consolidation of the structure and on our African partners taking the role of co-production of the activities. The aim is that in the subsequent four-year period of 2013–2016 the organization will mostly be carried by the African members of ArchiAfrika.[105]

In order to resolve the normative uncertainty ensuing from its launch event, ArchiAfrika linked traditional scientific authorities and venues with new and relatively unestablished actors and sites on the African continent, thereby conducting a social experiment negotiating norms and forms of producing scientific knowledge and expertise. ArchiAfrika's final move in attempting to reconcile a crisis of legitimacy and responsibility was to announce its transfer to Africa.[106]

Laboratory/Collaboratory

When ArchiAfrika considered Africa a "true laboratory"[107] for what I call its social experiment in the production of scientific knowledge and expertise concerning architecture, the NGO hoped that a transfer to Africa would allow it to go beyond occasional collaboration with its partners on the continent.[108] In this respect, it is interesting to look at Paul Rabinow's understanding of 'collaboration' in scientific knowledge and expertise making. For Rabinow, scientific collaboration entails a common definition of problems, as well as an interdependent division of labor. Collaboration is not the same as "cooperation", which instead is based on "demarcated tasking on distinct problems and objects, with occasional if regular exchange".[109] Following Rabinow's definition, ArchiAfrika's event *Modern Architecture in East Africa around Independence* was at best an exercise in cooperation because the NGO *presupposed* the problems of a distinct African identity of modern architecture, as well as of modern architectural heritage in Africa. Afterward, however, ArchiAfrika began to question its own dominant practices of inquiry in an effort to contribute to "the reconsideration and innovation of issues in the African and worldwide context".[110] These days, ArchiAfrika experiments with new collaborative modes to produce scientific knowledge and expertise; it wants to create a globally distributed research network based on a "genuine exchange of ideas". Speaking with Rabinow, ArchiAfrika seems to want to engage a scientific "collaboratory".[111]

Besides ArchiAfrika's transfer to Africa, now more or less complete as its headquarters have moved to Accra in September 2012, another concrete example is one of the NGO's recent projects, launched when they were still based in Utrecht: the ArchiAfrika Expertise Centre on

African Architecture, an initiative which follows the bequest of the German architect Dr. Georg Lippsmeier's research library to ArchiAfrika in 2007. Since the late 1960s, Lippsmeier had run an "Institut für Tropenbau", for which ArchiAfrika's cofounders Antoni Folkers and Belinda van Buiten managed the Dar es Salaam office between 1987 and early 1994. During Lippsmeier's practice in 'the tropics', he collected a library of over 3,000 titles and 4,000 images. After Lippsmeier's death, his heirs donated this collection to ArchiAfrika. ArchiAfrika housed the archive in its Utrecht headquarters and founded the *Dr. Georg Lippsmeier Library Fund* for the purpose of making the multimedia archive accessible "to the Africans".[112] ArchiAfrika considered Lippsmeier's library a stepping-stone toward the institutionalization of a collaborative hub in research and expertise based on a rotational system of so-called library godfathers; researchers from ArchiAfrika's international university partners were to work on specific themes and problems related to the contents of the archive.[113] ArchiAfrika would then organize all resources accordingly and make them globally available through its online search engine project.[114]

Yet ArchiAfrika's ambitious plan to establish such a collaborative center of expertise failed in the wake of the NGO's transfer to Africa. When ArchiAfrika reorganized in order "to be steered by its network members" and announced it was moving its headquarters to the African continent, it decided to abandon the goal of an *ArchiAfrika Expertise Centre on African Architecture* and to keep the Lippsmeier library in the Netherlands. Mainly this was because Antoni Folkers and Berend van der Lans, ArchiAfrika's two founders most actively involved with the NGO's day-to-day activities as director and secretary, regarded the financial circumstances for managing the *Dr. Georg Lippsmeier Library Fund* to be best in the Netherlands.[115] They also believed, again mostly because of their worry for discontinuous funding, that ArchiAfrika's "internationalization" complicated the material safeguarding of the library.[116] Eventually Folkers and van der Lans offered to take over the management of the Lippsmeier library on their own account.

Since their cofoundation of ArchiAfrika, Folkers and van der Lans had been driving forces behind the NGO's many initiatives, including the *Dr. Georg Lippsmeier Library Fund*. Their voluntary commitment to ArchiAfrika was engendered by idealism and they did not receive any compensation for their work. Over time, however, this engagement began to put a considerable strain on their architectural practices. Therefore, when ArchiAfrika chose to appoint a new board to procure the NGO's transfer to Africa in 2010, Folkers and van der Lans decided to manage the transition, including the exploitation of the Lippsmeier library, by setting up another not-for-profit spin-off, African Architecture Matters, through which they now also pay themselves compensation for their work.[117]

Folkers and van der Lans's objective for African Architecture Matters, which is registered as a Dutch foundation and has moved from Utrecht to Amsterdam in 2013, was to enable them to continue their support to ArchiAfrika in a financially sustainable manner. They advertise African Architecture Matters as a consultancy bureau, with the Lippsmeier library as one of its most important assets. Their website states that

> [a]fter years of experience in Africa, both in design practice and in architectural debate and research, the founders of African Architecture Matters offer a knowledge and service centre concerning African architecture.[118]

In effect, what Folkers and van der Lans did for ArchiAfrika so far, namely, "initiate, support and facilitate projects in the field of architecture, with an affiliation to African architecture", now describes their role as directors of African Architecture Matters.[119] They no longer work under the exclusive auspices of ArchiAfrika. Instead, they continue their mission to establish a collaborative center of knowledge and expertise based on the Lippsmeier library solely through African Architecture Matters. Folkers and van der Lans have thus become scientific entrepreneurs: through African Architecture Matters, they aim to provide their services to "commercial parties, cultural institutions, housing corporations and developers, educational institutes, governmental parties, and NGO's",[120] explicitly including ArchiAfrika. The latter has even contracted African Architecture Matters to manage its international secretariat.[121]

All this brings with it problems of legitimacy and responsibility. Though ArchiAfrika's policy plan announces the "reinforcement and extension" of its web-based community, from which "individuals will emerge as champions to take up the role of establishing ArchiAfrika on the ground",[122] it at the same time asserts that

> [b]ecause ArchiAfrika's roots and the relevance of the subject to the future of Western architecture, an important part of the expertise and research will remain in the Netherlands. The exchange activities will be performed by several parties in equal cooperation. However, the Dutch branch [African Architecture Matters] will play a permanent part in supporting the project organization and in fundraising.[123]

In this respect, African Architecture Matters somewhat relativizes ArchiAfrika's transfer to Africa. Folkers and van der Lans envision that African Architecture Matters would assist "ArchiAfrika with co-ordination and management of the global network". This very network, however, invariably becomes a service for sale by African Architecture Matters, whose website offers clients "an infrastructure for the organization of activities in Africa; network, facilitation, management, coordination".[124]

In a way, African Architecture Matters thus reappropriates ArchiAfrika's social experiment in making scientific knowledge and expertise.

To a certain extent, this reappropriation is reminiscent of colonial appropriations of Africa as a living laboratory. The early-20th-century colonial scientists' engagement with African's ideas and knowledge led to the emergence of new scientific networks, as well as to the transformation of established scientific infrastructures. ArchiAfrika is currently expanding its network on the African continent, but it still struggles with global realities of doing science in the 21st century. African Architecture Matters's control of ArchiAfrika's database from the Netherlands exemplifies a certain marginalization of scientific infrastructures on the African continent, as well as skewed relationships between Europe and Africa. Though African Architecture Matters's founders wish to contribute to a genuine exchange of ideas between European and African researchers, their Dutch consultancy firm is proof of the limits of both local expansion and global reach. Through African Architecture Matters, Folkers and van der Lans unilaterally claim authority over the production of "valuable knowledge regarding architectural & urban developments that take place on the continent",[125] boldly assuming legitimacy and responsibility for the "comprehensive" dissemination of scientific knowledge and expertise "for practical, educational and scientific use".[126]

This is particularly interesting and relevant against the backdrop of ArchiAfrika's original crisis, a crisis essentially based on normative uncertainty around the question, who now has the legitimacy and responsibility—as well as the resources—to use Africa as a living 'laboratory' or a living 'collaboratory'. Although Folkers and van der Lans maintain that, for African Architecture Matters, "dialogue as a means for an *exchange* [emphasis added] of knowledge lies at the core of activities",[127] they effectively *offer* scientific knowledge and expertise as based on years of personal experience in Africa.[128] Emblematically, African Architecture Matters's website states that in the provision of services, ArchiAfrika's "extensive network of architects and experts on African architecture, a community with over 1.900 members" will "be actively involved if *required* [emphasis added]";[129] ultimately though, Folkers and van der Lans are the ones who decide if and when such involvement is required. Arguably, they attempt to defuse the normative uncertainty resulting from ArchiAfrika's growing organization and representational complexity through focusing on what Steven Shapin describes as "the personal, the familiar and the charismatic".[130]

African Architecture Matters's dismissal of ArchiAfrika's normative uncertainty confirms Shapin's insight that "people matter more than ever" in contemporary science. Without doubt, Folkers and van der Lans's engagement in ArchiAfrika is driven by genuine idealism. Nevertheless, their scientific entrepreneurship through African Architecture Matters illustrates certain structural dynamics in the production of scientific knowledge and expertise that currently assign Africa and Africans a marginalized place in the world. In this respect, it is worth going back to Shapin, who, reflecting on the institutional landscape of science today, notes that

> universities have changed, most specifically in the institutional configurations in which interdisciplinary scientific, medical and engineering research gets done, but industry, non-profit research institutes and the form of associations between all of these have changed ever faster. And new forms and sites continue to emerge—various sorts of contract research organizations, "virtual companies", globalized research groups and the like.[131]

African Architecture Matters's existence as a Dutch consultancy indicates that such new forms and sites of knowledge and expertise often emerge outside of Africa, even when they explicitly concern the African continent. And certainly to the extent that African Architecture Matters is an offshoot of ArchiAfrika, Folkers and van der Lans depend on being "part of the basic infrastructure"[132] of Dutch research funding; they receive support from a range of powerful institutions in the production of scientific knowledge and expertise, and these types of institutions are weak or maybe even nonexistent in much of postcolonial Africa.

A good example of the structural dynamics of making scientific knowledge and expertise in relation to Africa, as well as the way 'people matter', is Antoni Folkers's PhD thesis at Delft University of Technology in 2011. As founding director of both ArchiAfrika and African Architecture Matters, Folkers personally represents relevant dynamics in the production of scientific knowledge and expertise concerning architecture in Africa. His friendship with Anthony Almeida particularly proved to be formative for the definition of the subject of modern architecture in Africa as an open field of research, leading as it did to ArchiAfrika's launch event, *Modern Architecture in East Africa around Independence*. Consequently, when Folkers received his doctorate for a book with the title *Modern Architecture in Africa*, this calls attention to the blurry fault lines between his activism for ArchiAfrika, what Shapin would call his "scientific entrepreneurship" through African Architecture Matters, as well as his relationships with the modern research university.[133]

Folkers's starting point for *Modern Architecture in Africa* is the "position of contemporary African architecture within the modernist project".[134] He attempts to link what he calls "the previously separate worlds of traditional, locally rooted architecture with the modernist project in Africa":[135]

> Africa has never played a significant role in the debate on architecture. The general public knows little about African architecture, or

architecture in Africa. There is a handful of books about the great richness of traditional African architecture, but apart from Udo Kultermann's work, there has been little attention paid since World War II to the idea of introducing modern western architecture to Africa, let alone to the identity and the position of African architecture in the global, over-all debate concerning architecture—a subject very few serious thinkers would risk seriously researching.[136]

Relying on his own experience and information based on interviews, Folkers takes on this risk, inviting his readers to follow his "journey made over the last twenty-five years and to share [his] thoughts as a 'reflexive practitioner'."[137]

In *Modern Architecture in Africa*, he speaks of a "longing to travel to Africa" going back to his early youth: "It began with a desire for warmth and the exotic, followed by the wish to do something to improve the difficult situations in which most Africans live."[138] According to Folkers, 40 percent of the African population live in cities, where living conditions are "uncertain and worrying"[139] Previous, more utopian solutions to this issue, Folkers claims, are no longer valid as we have "moved on from the modernist faith in the closed technical systems and planning techniques that were applied to control urban developments in Africa" in the past.[140] Instead, he implies that new solutions could be found in ArchiAfrika's social experiment in the production of scientific knowledge and expertise. Folkers states that now

> there is a growing attention to local experiments in which a spontaneous, more modest and open viewpoint takes the lead. Architects, urban planners, social scientists, politicians, artists, business people, and religious leaders seek each other out in order to learn from each other and to collaborate on various projects.[141]

Indeed, Folkers's participation in ArchiAfrika's social experiment must be considered a major source of inspiration for his book.[142] He discusses, for example, the debates during ArchiAfrika's Dar es Salaam conference and workshop, criticizing the orthodox DOCOMOMO approach to modern architecture in Africa that emphasizes the need of historical documentation and conservation:

> It would be regrettable if the joyful modernism of the 1950s and 1960s were to disappear, but Africans should be the first to decide what to do with their heritage, and Western institutions will have to agree with their vision and approach.[143]

Folkers emphasizes that concepts such as shared, mutual, or common heritage, which were devised "in order to encourage African participation in the care of monuments" are not very convincing, and that "we should drop these labels and return to the straightforward name 'colonial heritage' ".[144] He believes that "the Africans have been occupied with more pressing matters than restoring old buildings that, for the most part were not even designed by Africans".[145]

His expertise, Folkers claims, is not that of an architectural historian or professional preservationist of modern heritage; instead, he bases his knowledge and expertise about modern architecture in Africa on his personal experience of working together with locals. In this respect, Folkers research for *Modern Architecture in Africa* transcends conventional boundaries between academia, NGO and consultancy. A decade after Folkers's cofoundation of ArchiAfrika and immediately following his establishment of African Architecture Matters, his doctorate officially acknowledges him as a scientific authority and expert in the field of modern architecture in Africa.

Yet Folkers's PhD also indicates how contemporary norms and forms of scientific practice are, as Shapin would have it, "implicated in and harnessed to socio-economic and political processes"[146] that structurally assign Africa and Africans a marginalized place in the world. The valorization of Folkers's book with a Dutch PhD degree thus represents the heterogeneity of the contemporary scientific landscape. Actually, Folkers had not even intended to submit *Modern Architecture in Africa* as a dissertation, but because the Dutch state reimburses its universities for the delivery of diplomas, Delft University of Technology could claim money in return for issuing Folkers a PhD. The university had to spend only fractions of the costs of salary and expenses of a regular PhD candidate on Folkers, who made an independent living as an architect and consultant for African Architecture Matters. So when Delft University of Technology funded Folkers to do some traditional research abroad and urged him to defend his book as a PhD thesis, it 'regained' at least some of the investments it had made in its cooperation with ArchiAfrika in the years before.[147]

Folkers's academic career therefore reveals skewed relations between Europe and Africa. If you will recall, ArchiAfrika and its European university partners lacked the funds to honor the Tanzanian request of a PhD position for a Tanzanian student made in connection with the organization of *Modern Architecture in East Africa around Independence*. Ultimately, this contributed to the withdrawal of local institutional support for ArchiAfrika's student workshop and academic conference in Dar es Salaam, as well as to ArchiAfrika's fundamental crisis of discord and affect. The nominal costs of Folkers's Dutch doctorate could thus symbolically stand for ArchiAfrika's original crisis of legitimacy and responsibility revolving around demand from Africa. After all, it is likely that independent researchers from the African continent experience more difficulties than the Dutchman Folkers in gaining access to institutional and personal networks, not to speak of the necessary material resources.

In a foreword to *Modern Architecture in Africa*, the architectural historian Namndi Elleh praises Folkers for his "architectural study conducted during a pilgrimage to a continent in which he was a stranger".[148] Elleh describes Folkers as a charismatic "new voice to the discourse of modern architecture in Africa",[149] arguing that

> [*Modern Architecture in Africa*] is singular and entertaining to read because the ideas it contains developed naturally with Folkers. And, in turn, Folkers grew with the ideas during his practice and the lectures, conferences and workshops he and his colleagues—fellow members and founders of ArchiAfrika—have hosted in and beyond the continent on the subject of modern architecture in Africa.[150]

Furthermore, Elleh writes that "despite his status as an outsider, Folkers is uniquely qualified to bring this beautiful and accessible study of Modern Architecture in Africa to the public, and to scholars and students of architecture".[151] Yet perhaps Folkers could successfully produce *Modern Architecture in Africa* and acquire a PhD based on it not despite but *because* of his status as a European stranger and outsider. Arguably, what Folkers calls his "natural development" and his intellectual "growth" resulted from a certain reappropriation of Africa as a true and living laboratory.

Nevertheless, Folkers's engagement did enable ArchiAfrika to contribute valuably to a global negotiation of scientific authority and to developing a vision of a 'true' collaboratory between European and African scientists. Today, ArchiAfrika's homepage features a "Become an Expert" function, inviting visitors to share their personal contact information and engage other members in discussion and debate. Effectively then, ArchiAfrika now takes a social-network approach to its organizational structure. Its website and online newsletter are designed to encourage the sharing of agency in the construction of scientific knowledge and expertise on architecture in and of Africa.

Yet Africans remain disconnected from relevant infrastructures of scientific knowledge and expertise making, and African Architecture Matters's preliminary control of ArchiAfrika's database from Europe as well as Antoni Folkers's PhD trajectory are two specific examples of how this disconnect seems hard to shake. Of course, the fact that much of the African continent is literally disconnected from broadband Internet may be a more consequential impediment to the inclusion of more local researchers in the production of contemporary science than African Architecture Matters's compromise of ArchiAfrika's transfer to Africa. But, Berend van der Lans's and Antoni Folkers's reliance on virtues of inquiry and knowledge exclusively based on their personal experience as European architects working in Africa—although well intentioned—problematizes scientific ethics of legitimacy and responsibility, respectively.

Conclusion

In this chapter, I have traced the intellectual, institutional and personal dynamics of producing scientific knowledge and expertise about modern architecture in Africa, today. My study describes the emergence and transformation of the non-governmental organization ArchiAfrika, including the launch of its branch-off African Architecture Matters. In ArchiAfrika's beginnings, the NGO's original Dutch founders referred to their legitimacy and responsibility "to put (modern) African architectural culture on the world map" and to maintain an "international exchange of expertise and knowledge within the African continent"[152] because "the important voice of Africa"[153] is lacking or at least "often not enough heard".[154] In the process, I have shown, this imbued ArchiAfrika's emergent organizational structure and aims with a particular "normative uncertainty"[155] regarding 'demand from Africa'.

My analysis particularly reveals how, during ArchiAfrika's initial student workshop and academic conference in Dar es Salaam, a certain preoccupation with an African identity of modern architectural heritage locally resulted in discord and affect. As a result, ArchiAfrika experienced a crisis of legitimacy and responsibility, realizing that predefined problems and their significance can no longer be taken for granted, as they can "fruitfully be contested".[156] Consequently, the NGO began what can be understood as a social experiment with contemporary norms and forms of making scientific knowledge and expertise about architecture in and of Africa. And, in effect, ArchiAfrika tackled the Weberian question, "Who is the legitimate and responsible scientist engaging in research on the African continent?" by planning its own move to Africa.

Ultimately, ArchiAfrika developed innovative participatory approaches to the production of scientific authority. By relating unconventionally with the modern research university, the NGO challenged traditional institutional configurations, as well as moral claims to knowledge and expertise.[157] Nnamdi Elleh even refers to ArchiAfrika as facilitating "the future of African architecture in the making":[158]

> We often hear the comment, 'history is in the making', a statement which suggests that an on-going event might impact the way people, especially historians, may look at the events being witnessed today in the distant future. The objectives of ArchiAfrika to 'put modern and contemporary architecture on the world map and offer a platform for the exchange of news, expertise and development in the field' is making and guaranteeing the future of the profession on the continent. ArchiAfrika is making history because [. . .] the organization has effectively brought practitioners, scholars, students, engineers and the general public together for the purposes of facilitating research,

understanding and dissemination of information on modern and contemporary African architectural practices around the world.[159]

Indeed, ArchiAfrika has started a search for new "modes of collaboration"; its ambition has been to facilitate "global" negotiations of scientific authority. However, as I have shown, skewed postcolonial power relations structurally still tend to—despite many good intentions—exclude or at least impede Africans from partaking.

This becomes apparent in what Shapin would call Berend van der Lans's and Antoni Folkers's 'scientific entrepreneurship' through African Architecture Matters, specifically in their personal pursuit of ArchiAfrika's original plans for a collaborative center of expertise revolving around the Dr. Georg Lippsmeier library, as well as their effective control of much of ArchiAfrika's social network. Moreover, Folkers's PhD research—a simultaneous result of his work as an independent European architect working in Africa, his activism for ArchiAfrika and his consultancy for African Architecture Matters—shows that the African continent remains significantly disconnected from most relevant scientific infrastructures. That the Dutchmen Berend van der Lans and Antoni Folkers can reappropriate Africa as their personal living laboratory indicates how difficult it remains to turn against the historical tendency that Africa remains "local", and "the global originates outside Africa".[160] My analysis furthermore confirms Steven Shapin's argument that, in science, personal networks, as well as "the characteristics and virtues of familiar people now, matter more than they have for many years and that this mattering concentrates in just the intellectual and institutional configurations from which the most consequential changes of late modernity emerge".[161]

In the end, ArchiAfrika's "social experiment" in the negotiation of scientific knowledge and expertise is a case in Shapin's point and a source of hope for the future. When ArchiAfrika planned its own move to Africa, it engaged a particular "modern heritage": early-20th-century science's 'Africanization', which was problematically intertwined with colonial appropriations of the African continent as a living laboratory. In fact, ArchiAfrika is concerned with a normative uncertainty caused by the realization that there are 'many words'—many interpretations and appropriations—for modern. For instance, the documentary *Many Words for Modern* tried to rectify the discord resultant of ArchiAfrika's Dar es Salaam event *Modern Architecture in East Africa around Independence* by promoting the Swahili translation of the term modern architecture: *usanifu mayengo asiria*, which means "research of new building". Indeed, ArchiAfrika appeals for global collaboration in research in and on Africa, last but not least to tackle its fundamental normative uncertainty as an NGO originally founded by five Dutch architect friends sharing the experience of working on the African continent.

Ultimately, however, ArchiAfrika and African Architecture Matters's normative uncertainty will not be resolved before Africans become equal partners in global negotiations of scientific authority.[162] For now, Archi-Afrika's social experiment, even as it is muddled by African Architecture Matters, is a relevant problematization of scientific ethics of legitimacy and responsibility. Yet it remains to be seen whether this will eventually facilitate the establishment of an effective scientific collaboratory between European and African researchers. In any case, ArchiAfrika and African Architecture Matters have introduced an important experimental ethos to the making of scientific knowledge and expertise concerning architecture in Africa; Paul Rabinow's urge to "stop worrying, start experimenting"[163] captures it well.

Notes

1. ArchiAfrika, "Policy Plan 2009–2012," (Utrecht, 2009). 7–8.
2. Ibid.
3. ArchiAfrika, "Homepage," www.archiafrika.org
4. Paul Rabinow, *French DNA: Trouble in Purgatory* (Chicago: The University of Chicago Press, 1999). 13; Rabinow, *Making PCR.* 57; 62; Steven Shapin, *The Scientific Life: A Moral History of a Late Modern Vocation* (Chicago: University of Chicago Press, 2008). 264–265.
5. Weber, "Science as a Vocation." 130; I am also drawing on Rabinow's analysis in Rabinow, *Anthropos Today: Reflections on Modern Equipment.* 101.
6. Ibid., 130.
7. Ibid.
8. Ibid., 116.
9. Ibid.
10. Rabinow, *Anthropos Today: Reflections on Modern Equipment.* 99.
11. Ibid., 101.
12. Helen Tilley, *Africa as a Living Laboratory: Empire Development and the Problem of Scientific Knowledge* (Chicago: University of Chicago Press, 2011). 8.
13. Ibid., 314ff.
14. Ibid.
15. Ibid., 4; 6.
16. Ibid., 12.
17. Ibid., 317ff.
18. Ibid., 27.
19. Ibid., 6.
20. Shapin, *The Scientific Life: A Moral History of a Late Modern Vocation.* 264.
21. Ibid.
22. Ibid.
23. Ibid., 322.
24. ArchiAfrika, *Policy Plan 2009–2012.* 10.
25. Tilley, *Africa as a Living Laboratory: Empire Development and the Problem of Scientific Knowledge.* 323; Helen Tilley, ed. *Ordering Africa: Anthropology, European Imperialism and the Politics of Knowledge* (Manchester: Manchester University Press, 2007). 12.
26. Ibid., 12.

27. Interview of the author with Mol.
28. ArchiAfrika, "Mission Statement," (Utrecht, 2001).
29. Interview of the author with Folkers.
30. Pieter Burssens, "Anthony B. Almeida: Modern Architecture in Tanzania between 1950 and 1975: Architecture Serving Colonial and Post-Colonial Politics?" Thesis submitted to obtain the degree of civil engineer-architect, Leuven, 2005. 44.
31. Interview of the author with Almeida.
32. Ibid.
33. Burssens, "Anthony B. Almeida: Modern Architecture in Tanzania between 1950 and 1975: Architecture Serving Colonial and Post-Colonial Politics?" Thesis submitted to obtain the degree of civil engineer-architect," 44.
34. Anthony Almeida, "Curriculum Vitae," (2010).
35. Ibid.
36. Interview of the author with Almeida; Almeida, "Curriculum Vitae."
37. Ibid.
38. Interview of the author with Almeida.
39. Interview of the author with Mol.
40. Interviews of the author with Mol; Folkers.
41. Interview of the author with Mol.
42. Justine Timmermans, "Stageverslag: Het Almeida Project," (2009).
43. Interview of the author with Folkers.
44. Timmermans, "Stageverslag: Het Almeida Project."
45. Quoted in Ibid.
46. Interview of the author with Folkers.
47. Both were practicing architects and part-time researchers at TU Delft at the time.
48. Interview of the author with Folkers.
49. Ibid.
50. Heynen, "The Intertwinement of Modernism and Colonialism: A Theoretical Perspective." 9.
51. Ibid.
52. Interview of the author with Folkers.
53. Ibid; ArchiAfrika, "Mission Statement."
54. Interview of the author with Folkers.
55. Ibid.
56. Interview of the author with Mol.
57. Interview of the author with Folkers.
58. Ibid.
59. Ibid.
60. Ibid.
61. Ibid.
62. Interviews of the author with Lekule; Mbisso.
63. Interview of the author with Folkers.
64. Heynen, "The Intertwinement of Modernism and Colonialism: A Theoretical Perspective." 9–10.
65. Ibid.
66. Ibid; Interview of the author with Folkers.
67. Heynen, "The Intertwinement of Modernism and Colonialism: A Theoretical Perspective."
68. Ibid.
69. Ibid., 10.
70. Compare the original call for articles in Timmermans, "Stageverslag: Het Almeida Project."
71. Interview of the author with Almeida.

72. Ibid.
73. Interview of the author with Lekule.
74. Ibid.
75. Ibid.
76. Heynen, "The Intertwinement of Modernism and Colonialism: A Theoretical Perspective." 10.
77. Interview of the author with Mbisso.
78. Interview of the author with Richard Besha.
79. Interview of the author with Almeida.
80. Interview of the author with Lekule.
81. Ibid.
82. Interview of the author with Mbisso.
83. Interview of the author with Lekule.
84. Ibid.
85. Interview of the author with Almeida.
86. Heynen, "The Intertwinement of Modernism and Colonialism: A Theoretical Perspective." 10.
87. Interview of the author with Lekule.
88. ArchiAfrika, "Annual Report," (Utrecht, 2007).
89. ArchiAfrika, "Policy Plan 2009–2012." 7.
90. *Folkers in* ArchiAfrika, (paper presented at the Conference Modern Architecture in East Africa Around Independence, Dar es Salaam, 2005). 17.
91. Ibid., 8.
92. ArchiAfrika, "Policy Plan 2009–2012." 7–8.
93. ArchiAfrika, "Annual Report."; ArchiAfrika, "Policy Plan 2009–2012."
94. ArchiAfrika, "Policy Plan 2009–2012." 20.
95. ArchiAfrika, "African Perspectives: Conference Programme," (Delft, 2007).
96. Ibid.
97. ArchiAfrika newsletter April 2010.
98. ArchiAfrika, "Policy Plan 2009–2012." 8.
99. Ibid., 10.
100. Ibid., 10.
101. Ibid.
102. Interview of the author with Mol.
103. Interview of the author with Folkers.
104. ArchiAfrika, "Policy Plan 2009–2012." 7.
105. Ibid., 24.
106. Ibid.
107. Ibid., 10.
108. Ibid., 24.
109. "Wikipedia.org: Paul Rabinow".
110. ArchiAfrika, "Policy Plan 2009–2012." 10.
111. Rabinow, *The Accompaniment*. 143–144.
112. Anne-Katrien Denissen, *Kick Off Meeting: ArchiAfrika Expertise Centre on African Architecture, Memo* (Utrecht: ArchiAfrika, 2008).
113. Ibid; interviews of the author with Mol; Folkers; van der Lans.
114. Ibid.
115. Interview of the author with van der Lans; even after ArchiAfrikas's "transfer to Africa" the NGO's main sources of funding continue to be the original Dutch donors, e.g. the Prins Claus fund and Stichting Doen.
116. Interview of the author with van der Lans; Interview of the author with Folkers.

117. Berend van der Lans, personal communication with the author.
118. ArchiAfrika, "Homepage".
119. Ibid.
120. Ibid.
121. Ibid.
122. ArchiAfrika, "Policy Plan 2009–2012." 24.
123. Ibid.
124. ArchiAfrika, "Homepage".
125. Ibid.
126. Ibid.
127. Ibid.
128. "African Architecture Matters: Homepage," www.aamatters.nl.
129. Ibid.
130. Shapin, *The Scientific Life: A Moral History of a Late Modern Vocation*. 5.
131. Ibid., 265.
132. ArchiAfrika, "Policy Plan 2009–2012." 15.
133. Shapin, *The Scientific Life: A Moral History of a Late Modern Vocation*. 232.
134. Antoni Folkers, *Modern Architecture in Africa* (Nijmegen: SUN, 2010).
135. Ibid.
136. Ibid., 13.
137. Ibid., 13–14.
138. Ibid., 11.
139. Ibid., 144.
140. Ibid., 147.
141. Ibid., 148.
142. Folkers reacted to an early draft of my chapter as follows: "ArchiAfrika did play an important part in the making of my book, but not a major part. I had already written the first sketch of the book in 1999–2002 that was based on previous writing in a series of private cahiers over the period 1984–1999 ('Discretio '—published by myself) and the writing of the book Modern Architecture in Africa based on Discretio (the concept was ready in 2007) happened parallel to the development of ArchiAfrika, thus providing me with a sort of 'final check' a mirroring of what I had concluded and written over a long period to the growing knowledge and network gathered through ArchiAfrika."
143. Folkers, *Modern Architecture in Africa*. 345.
144. Ibid., 343.
145. Ibid.
146. Shapin, *The Scientific Life: A Moral History of a Late Modern Vocation*.
147. Interview of the author with Folkers.
148. Nnamdi Elleh, "Foreword," in *Modern Architecture in Africa* (Nijmegen: SUN, 2010). 5.
149. Ibid.
150. Ibid., 7.
151. Ibid., 7.
152. ArchiAfrika, "Policy Plan 2009–2012." 7–8.
153. ArchiAfrika, "Annual Report."
154. ArchiAfrika, "Policy Plan 2009–2012." 7– 16.
155. Shapin, *The Scientific Life: A Moral History of a Late Modern Vocation*. 5; 16; 264.
156. "Wikipedia.org: Paul Rabinow".
157. Shapin, *The Scientific Life: A Moral History of a Late Modern Vocation*. 6.

158. Elleh, "Foreword."
159. Ibid; ArchiAfrika, "Policy Plan 2009–2012." 5.
160. Tilley, *Ordering Africa: Anthropology, European Imperialism and the Politics of Knowledge*. 3.
161. Shapin, *The Scientific Life: A Moral History of a Late Modern Vocation*. 4–5.
162. ArchiAfrika, "Policy Plan 2009–2012."
163. Rabinow, *Making PCR*. 166.

Part III

8 Synthesis

Contemporary Politics, Technologies and Ethics to the Rescue of Modernity

> Two tasks: To defend the new against the old, and to link the old with the new.
>
> *Friedrich Nietzsche, 1873*[1]

So far, I have analyzed how the issue of modern architectural heritage on the African continent is given form as an urgent anthropological problem in global heritage assemblages. I have taken my description of cultural heritage practices under the current conditions of globalization as a basic starting point to inquire into the norms and forms of human existence today. My analysis has carved out global heritage assemblages as domains in which human relations are subjected to political, technological and ethical reflection and debate. I have shown how (1) a global heritage assemblage around the modern architecture and urban planning of Asmara asserts politics of sovereignty and security as problematic modern practices, (2) a global heritage assemblage around the *Maisons Tropicales* contests technologies of authenticity and value problematizing of modern things, and (3) a global heritage assemblage around East African modern architecture negotiates ethics of legitimacy and responsibility regarding problematic classifications of the modern.

To reinvoke Paul Rabinow, my research indicates how global heritage assemblages are "real". I illustrate how they have forms and effects, as well as how they include affects. Thus, as Rabinow would put it, while the global heritage assemblages that I describe "differ from what has been traditionally understood as 'a thing' or 'an object' by being composed of heterogeneous parts that retain, as they are combined and recombined into new interrelations, to a degree, their original properties," they certainly "make some things and events possible and others improbable".[2] My inquiry yields access to the actuality and urgency of an extended unstable problem space around the modern as opened up by the institutionalization of an "African modern heritage", thus signaling the latent transformation of a dominant apparatus of modernization.

Together with my diagnostic and genealogical concept work as featured in Part I of this book, my analyses in Part II indicate how the cultural heritage practices I focus on each in their own right struggle with problems that invariably stem from their legacies in broader projects of colonialism and modernization. What I have not yet done, however, at least not explicitly, is to reflect on how, as an anthropologist, I am myself an integral part of the specific global heritage assemblages that constitute the objects of my study. Speaking with Stephen Collier, it remains for me to demonstrate concretely how my conception of global heritage assemblages serves as "an alternative tool for the development of a critical global knowledge, though one that diverges from the standard fare of relativizing cultural analyses, sociological reductions to structures of power, or political economic analyses of hegemony that have dominated discussions of globalization".[3] In other words, I need to explain how I mean to contribute to an anthropology of the contemporary through a relevant structuring and restructuring of global forms.[4]

Spaces of Experience/Horizons of Expectation

Based on my diagnosis of how the issue of modern architectural heritage constitutes a fundamental problematization of modernity incipient in the construction, deconstruction and reconstruction of the Crystal Palace, my genealogical pathway has revealed how an intertwining of modern architecture and heritage preservation practices as part of a powerful apparatus of modernization has gradually complicated ideas of progressive cultural change. I have shown how the notion of modern heritage creates tensions between preservation and development, between past and future. Ultimately, these tensions culminate in the institutionalization of modern architectural heritage in Africa, emerging as an actual and urgent anthropological problem. My pathway thus illustrates how the emergence of an 'African modern heritage' marks the destabilization and latent transformation of a dominant logos of 'modernity-as-culture' into an assemblage of hetero-logoi around the notion of 'alternative cultural modernities'.

Effectively then, my diagnostic and genealogical concept work in Part I of this book identifies the reproblematization of progressive modernity at stake in the issue of modern architectural heritage on the African continent that is so emblematic of a certain crisis of coevalness. In the middle of the 19th century, the Crystal Palace—the first building ever to be placed on any preservation agenda as modern heritage—pointed to a crisis of diachronicity as the site and source of cultural disquiet. As I have shown, this particular crisis took the form of an opposition between tradition and modernity. Now, however, at the beginning of the 21st century, such a crisis of diachronicity is replaced by a crisis of coevalness, which produces a renewed sense of cultural disquiet that is no longer reliant on the opposition between tradition and modernity but, rather, fueled by a conspicuous *pairing* of tradition and modernity.

I have explained this shift toward a crisis of coevalness with altered conceptions of 'the cultural' in and as 'the modern'. Through the institutionalization of modern architectural heritage on the African continent, teleological accounts of cultural change as progress and development toward a universal modern civilization are fundamentally questioned. In its place fall different stylized configurations of the modern, grouped together in a contingent problem space around modern temporality. Indeed, plural conceptions of modernity as cultural diversity, including conceptions of 'traditional living cultures' in Africa, make for a situation in which not only the new becomes the old—the definition of modern heritage—but also one in which all of a sudden the old becomes coeval with the new. Thus, while the crisis of diachronicity as represented by the Crystal Palace originally made the issue of modern heritage appear as a simple paradox, the present crisis of coevalness evident in appeals to an African modern heritage indicates the emergence of a complex heterodoxy against the idea of modernity as an epochal culture.

This particular problematization of progressive modernity closely resembles Paul Rabinow's concept of the contemporary. Rabinow takes up the contemporary as an ethos instead of a period, as a moving ratio rather than a perspective, which allows him to view tradition and modernity not as opposed, but as paired. As he puts it, "tradition is a moving image of the past, it is opposed not to modernity, but to alienation". Accordingly, Rabinow's contemporary is "the moving ratio of modernity, moving through the recent past and the near future in a (non-linear) space that gauges modernity as an ethos already becoming historical".[5] And therefore, as an assemblage of hetero-logoi of the modern, the contemporary resituates historical consciousness in what Reinhart Koselleck would refer to as a field of tension between spaces of experience and horizons of expectation.

Indeed, in his *Futures Past* Koselleck claims that it is the "tension between experience and expectation which, in ever changing patterns, brings about new resolutions and through this generates historical time". As an example, he mentions the structure of a prognosis compared to that of a diagnosis. Koselleck maintains that the substantial probability of a prognosis is not initially founded in one's expectations since one can also expect the improbable. This is why, according to Koselleck, the diagnosis, which is made on the basis of data of experience, has precedence. He notes that in this way the space of experience is open toward the future and draws the horizon of expectation out of itself. In Koselleck's words, "[e]xperiences release and direct prognoses." Nevertheless, he states, "the previously existing space of experience is not sufficient for the determination of the horizon of expectation". For him, the mutual relation between experience and expectation is not static; instead, they "constitute a temporal difference in the today by redoubling past and future on one another in an unequal manner".[6] Significantly then, Koselleck observes that, consciously or unconsciously, the interchanging renewal of connections between experience and expectation "has itself a prognostic structure", from which he derives "a characteristic feature of historical time, which can at the same time make plain its capacity for alteration".[7]

Precisely this capacity for temporal change is at play in Rabinow's conception of the contemporary, in which particular kinds of tension between the recent past and near future generate a historical consciousness that cannot be limited to progress and development. On closer inspection, the idea of modern progress reduces the temporal difference between experience and expectation to a single concept, and this entails that a dominant logos of modernity appears stabilized as increasing and accelerating divergence of the limits of experience and expectation. The contemporary destabilizes the modern as an assemblage of hetero-logoi instead. Again, speaking with Koselleck, if a formula for the temporal structure of modernity sustains a potential 'utopian surplus' along the lines of 'the lesser the experience, the greater the expectation', the contemporary produces a hybrid temporality that includes at least the *possibility* of reinstating another relation: "the greater the experience, the more cautious one is, but also the more open is the future".[8]

Rabinow has noted that, in important ways, the contemporary comes after the modern. Yet what he presents as contemporary temporality is no opposite of modern temporality. The contemporary does not 'develop' modern time further (or else modern heritage would really denote a paradox), but it does mark time in a more complicated, heterodox way: It problematizes conceptions of unilinear progress and development, as well as the knowledge and ways of knowing it informs. In denoting "uncertainty" or a particular "loss of familiarity" with "previous ways of understanding, acting, relating", as an assemblage of hetero-logoi of the modern, the contemporary problematizes the telos of modernity.[9]

Essentially, this is what it means to inherit the modern today: In the contemporary, the problem of modern heritage entails that an inevitable sense of utopia is lost. If the reconstructed Crystal Palace still hypostasized the past as the radical antinomy between present and future by introducing a need to remember utopias of modern architecture, the emergence of an African modern heritage shows how, to a large extent, the contemporary effectively transcends this need.[10] My analysis of global heritage assemblages around instances of modern architecture and urban planning in Africa actually suggests that the need now is to critically contest respective utopias of the modern, as well as, ultimately, to intervene in these utopias.

States of Emergence

The three exemplary global heritage assemblages I have described in Part II of this book emerge from my analysis as historical spaces of contingency in which global forms are concretely articulated. However, if my inquiry into global heritage assemblages has shown how specific administrative apparatuses, technical infrastructures and value regimes configure old and new elements in contemporary relationships, they primarily and quite consistently appear to take up these elements in a mode of reproduction. I have revealed how (1) a global heritage assemblage around the modern architecture of Asmara is informed by restorative nostalgia for colonial rationalities of government, (2) a global heritage assemblage around the *Maisons Tropicales* is shaped by collecting practices reminiscent of colonial exchanges of objects of art and culture, and (3) a global heritage assemblage around East African modern architecture depends on a certain reappropriation of Africa, not dissimilar from the one of colonial times, as a living laboratory for the production of scientific knowledge and expertise. In effect, my examples of global heritage assemblages remain structured by distinctly modern ideals of sovereignty and security, of authenticity and value, as well as of legitimacy and responsibility; they all seem unable to avoid the reproduction of modern norms and forms.

My analysis of these global heritage assemblages and their struggle with modern politics, technologies and ethics nonetheless also suggests much potential for a restructuring of such global forms. After all, as assemblages of hetero-logoi of 'the modern', my three exemplary global heritage assemblages not only frame the present in modes of reproduction, but they also do also in significant terms of emergence. Indeed, from the global heritage assemblage around the modern architecture of Asmara emerges an alternative to the prevailing 'restorative nostalgia' for modern forms of government: (1) the option to reassert corresponding politics of sovereignty and security based on 'reflective nostalgia'. Similarly, from the global heritage assemblage around the *Maisons Tropicales* emerges an alternative to the dominant modern practices of collecting objects of art and culture: (2) the possibility to recontest applicable technologies of authenticity and value in a cultural 'contact zone'. And, last but not least, from the global heritage assemblage around East African modern architecture an alternative emerges to the reappropriation of Africa as a colonial 'living laboratory' for the development of modern science: (3) the opportunity to renegotiate relevant ethics of legitimacy and responsibility in a 'collaboratory' instead. Insofar as these global heritage assemblages thus destabilize the basic structures of modern expert systems and their colonial legacies, they also create real chances for a necessary restructuring of global forms.

With Paul Rabinow one could say that these global heritage assemblages indicate a need to formulate an 'ethos' of 'the contemporary', that is, to formulate appropriate codes of conduct to deal with 'hetero-logoi' of modernity. Indeed, for Rabinow the contemporary appears to offer an alternative to received norms and forms of modernity that could be more than a compromise of the modern:

> [The contemporary] provides an orientation that seeks out and takes up practices, terms, concepts, forms, and the like, from traditional

sources but seeks to do different things with them from the things they were forged to do originally or how they have been understood more recently. The core idea is that concepts arose from and were designed to address specific problems in distinctive historical, cultural and political settings. When the settings change, and as problems differ, one cannot take these things up once again and simply reuse them without changing their meaning and efficacy. To meet a present problem they need to be reconfigured, modified, rectified, and adjusted.[11]

Accordingly, Rabinow claims that such an ethos of the contemporary would have to be "skeptical about the implicit metaphysics of the avant-garde or the tendency toward nostalgia (or worse) of an unconditional allegiance to tradition"[12] which seems to precisely describe the kind of skepticism that emerges from the global heritage assemblages that I have described.

My analysis of global heritage assemblages thus attests to Rabinow's claim that a revisiting of traditional settings can "provide fertile examples of concepts, forms, and practices from which to begin a process of conceptualization and eventual redesign".[13] My research shows how assemblages of hetero-logoi of the modern open up possibilities for a fundamental restructuring of particular global forms through critical reflection on and debate of modern heritage, be it symbolic, intellectual, institutional or the like. To put it in Stephen Collier's terms, my examples of global heritage assemblages circumscribe "situations in which it becomes necessary for actors to shift between modes of reflection and intervention; when for instance, technical modes of reflection and action break down, and ethical or political reflection—or alternative frames of technical response—emerge in their stead".[14]

Now the purpose of my analysis of global heritage assemblages has quite explicitly been to gain analytical and critical insight into global forms by examining how specific heritage actors reflect on them or call them into question.[15] Aside from that, however, my role as an aspiring anthropologist of the contemporary also requires me to engage in more than just implicit self-reflection on how the discipline of anthropology is—just like me—part and parcel of the global heritage assemblages that I set out to analyze. As in important ways my position as an observer of the contemporary has been from within my respective objects of inquiry, I have to acknowledge the historical, as well as the current, intertwinement of my academic discipline with the global forms under observation.

From its beginnings in the 19th century, the discipline of anthropology has always been—and continues to be—involved in the formulation of administrative apparatuses, technical infrastructures and value regimes. Whereas it early on informed colonial governmental rationalities, today it influences governmental, intergovernmental and nongovernmental organizations that promote nation building and development through, for example, cultural heritage preservation. Likewise, anthropologists were and are drivers behind collections of objects of art and culture, and they continue to issue authoritative claims to scientific knowledge and expertise about 'the cultural'. As a result, when my analysis of global heritage assemblages identifies rather fundamental problematizations of relevant politics, technologies and ethics, these problematizations also concern my own practices of anthropological research or mode of inquiry.

In this context, it is important to note how the Foucaultian concept of problematization entails that the analyst has at her disposal several possible ways of responding to "the same ensemble of difficulties".[16] According to Rabinow's reading of Foucault, then, the primary task of the analyst should not be to directly proceed toward intervention and the repair of a problematization but, rather, to *understand* and diagnose what makes a set of responses to the problem at hand "simultaneously possible".[17] Rabinow claims that Foucault's own work was also "meant both as a diagnostic and as a means of making problematizations more visible, available and open to remediation".[18] And this indeed is what Foucault seems to have had in mind when he stated, "The diagnostic establishes that we are difference, that our reason is the difference of forms of discourse, our history is the difference of times."[19]

Ultimately then, my inquiry into the anthropological problem of an African modern heritage is meant as a critique in Foucault's terms. It is not intended as "a matter of saying that things are not right as they are"; instead, I present my diagnosis and analysis of respective problematizations of modernity as "a matter of pointing out on what kinds of assumptions, what kinds of familiar, unchallenged, unconsidered modes of thought the practices that we accept rest".[20] I have attempted to engage in what Foucault refers to as "a movement of critical analysis in which one tries to see how the different solutions to a problem have been constructed; but also how these different solutions result from a specific form of problematization". As Foucault maintains, "it then appears that any new solution that might be added to the others would arise from current problematization, modifying only several of the postulates or principles on which one bases the responses one gives".[21]

In Rabinow's interpretation, Foucault "implied that such knowledge would provide assistance in assembling something better; not just a refusal, but a critique".[22] And this is what I have aimed to do with this book: present an anthropological critique of how things are (and could be) done differently in global heritage assemblages today. My analysis was geared at what Rabinow describes as

> the dynamic and mutually constitutive, if partial and dynamic, connections between anthropos and the diverse, and at times inconsistent, branches of knowledge available during a period of time; that

claim authority about the truth of the matter; and whose legitimacy to make such claims is accepted as plausible by other such claimants; as well as the power relations within which and through which those claims are produced, established, contested, defeated, and disseminated.[23]

I thus not only criticize the arbitrariness, contingency and powerful effects of specific administrative apparatuses, technical infrastructures and value regimes as they concern the issue of modern architectural heritage in Africa, but my inquiry into respective global heritage assemblages also points to emergent challenges, as well as the opportunities to reassemble the very practices of anthropological research.[24]

Whereas my analysis suggests that the discipline of anthropology should move away from *restorative* nostalgia for its inherited apparatus of concepts, I show how it would do well to embrace a *reflective* nostalgia for its conceptual modern heritage in 'the contemporary'. In turn, this may yield a better understanding of the residual, the dominant and the emergent in 'the cultural' today. Moreover, I argue that anthropology should continue to acknowledge and critically reflect on how its research practices are situated in ongoing and powerfully charged historical and political relationships. For this purpose, and in order to delimit the dimensions and dynamics of 'the cultural' under current conditions of globalization, anthropology could transcend a methodological focus on the national by engaging its disciplinary modern heritage in a transnational "contact zone".[25] Finally, my research indicates how a continuing reinterpretation of the scientific ethics of fieldwork could benefit from the notion of a multisited 'collaboratory', which should entail redesigning of anthropological inquiry in terms of a 'social experiment' that would respect all participants as equally knowledgeable epistemic partners.[26]

Having placed myself amidst the relationships of contending logoi of the modern in global heritage assemblages, I find myself back amid anthropology's problems in 'the contemporary'. As a matter of fact, because my anthropological inquiry is concerned with a critical understanding of the political, technological and ethical dimensions and dynamics of the cultural in the here and now, I must reckon with the circumstance that such an analytical understanding is itself intricately bound to the cultural in a synthetic state of emergence; it is itself a political, technological and ethical practice that is subject to alteration in the contemporary.[27] Hence, by inquiring into how different administrative apparatuses, technical infrastructures and value regimes inherit modernity today, I observe the contemporary as a structured site of inquiry and simultaneously offer it as restructured mode of inquiry; I describe clustered elements and stylized configurations of the modern in emergent states of declustering, reconfiguration and alternate stylization—contemporary politics, technologies and ethics to the rescue of modernity.

Demands of the Day

In 1960, UNESCO engaged in a 'rescue operation' to save ancient Nubian monuments from the construction of the Aswan High Dam, an archetypical modern development project on the African continent. Rather than taking modernization as an exclusive peril to cultural heritage, however, UNESCO's International Campaign to Save the Monuments of Nubia actually introduced 'culture' and 'the past' as tools for modern development in their own right. From the Nubia campaign thus emerged a notion of world heritage as stimulating progress and development, which amounted to a certain breach of self-evidence concerning classifications, practices and things modern; the emergence of a notion of world heritage problematized progressive modernity.

With the present study I have tried to unravel the vagaries of this fundamental problematization of modernity in the issue of modern architectural heritage. Building on a diagnosis of how this issue is already incipient in the construction, deconstruction and reconstruction of the Crystal Palace in the 19th century, I have presented its genealogical pathway, as well as analyzed its most recent manifestation in the anthropological problem of modern architectural heritage on the African continent. Indeed, one of my main claims remains that contemporary heritage practices cannot adequately be understood globally without studying Africa as a historically and socially constructed category and 'place in the world'.

This claim leads me back to UNESCO's 'global strategy' for a representative, credible and balanced World Heritage List, and particularly to the organization's worry about Africa's underrepresentation. While UNESCO began its World Heritage Programme with the prominent appeal to preserve an ancient African heritage in Egyptian and Sudanese Nubia, today UNESCO's explicit objectives also include preserving as world heritage Africa's more recent, modern heritage in the form of modern architecture and urban planning; UNESCO has thus set out to 'rescue' an African modernity.

Significantly then, the intergovernmental organization also appeals to the rescue of modern heritage because it claims that to do so would bring development to the African continent—after all, UNESCO recommends the protection of world heritage as an important resource in the fight against poverty and, specifically, in achieving the UN's Millennium Development Goals.[28] Yet UNESCO's invocation of modern architectural heritage for progress and development in Africa amounts to somewhat of a conceptual loop, as my work indicates that the ambition to bring progress and development through preserving the modern built environment is itself a problematic modern heritage.

Indeed, if relevant projects of modern architecture and urban planning from the late 19th and early until mid-20th centuries originally promised comprehensive modernization and a better future—first to the European colonies on the African continent and later to the newly independent, postcolonial nation-states there—it is ironic that now, in the 21st century, the preservation of these very buildings and urban sites should finally manage what they effectively failed to deliver in the first place. My analysis suggests that any concern for modern architectural heritage must come to terms with the problem of what one is to make of those utopian promises of a better future that never came about. Put differently, my research demonstrates how UNESCO's institutionalization of modern architectural heritage in Africa is problematically limited by the question of how to rescue modernity when we have lost its sense of a *better* future through design, when all that remains instead is a certain nostalgia for such a utopian future of the past, however long bygone. This problem is at the heart of the matter of preserving modern heritage, be it specific instances of modern architecture and urban planning on the African continent, or even received administrative apparatuses, technical infrastructures and value regimes—those global forms that also characterize UNESCO itself as an integral part of a residual apparatus of modernization, an apparatus that once was dominant but now emerges destabilized and in a latent state of transformation.

To some extent, UNESCO's struggle for the preservation of modern architectural heritage on the African continent at the same time is a fight for its own identity as a development organization. At the beginning of her term of office in 2009 Irina Bokova, UNESCO's current director general, for instance, felt the need to emphasize the following in her mission statement:

> The constitutional mandate of UNESCO is still relevant in the 21st century, where building knowledge-based societies is an imperative, where culture is crucial to any meaningful debate on development, where science and innovation mark the new era of humanity's future in all social and environmental fields, such as climate change and water, where we need to understand better the deep transformations of our societies, and finally, where dialogue, tolerance and respect for diversity is a humanistic value in itself that should be cherished.

Furthermore, Bokova stated that she was more confident than ever before that "notwithstanding UNESCO's universal mandate, Africa's development needs [. . .] should continue to be a strong priority".[29]

In this context too, then, my research indicates how the notion of African modern heritage amounts to an urgent anthropological problem; its powerful currency with organizations such as UNESCO essentially means that ongoing and often problematic practices of modernization matter more than corresponding theories of progressive modernity, not to mention the ways these theories can be criticized.[30] Nonetheless, with Paul Rabinow I have to say that the issue of modern architectural heritage in

Africa begs the question: "How can we get from progress to motion?"[31] My study shows that, as a fundamental anthropological problem, the notion of African modern heritage implies a need to acknowledge that reducing modern temporality to a single concept—progress—has failed. I have revealed how in its stead a contingent, historical problem space has opened in which global inequalities can neither be situated in a distant or not so distant past, nor can their solution any longer be postponed to a distant or not so distant future.

As Rabinow claims, "worldviews concerned with progress and decadence as essential elements of a totalizing figure should be allowed to retire into the past, to take their place as historical memories". He believes that "by relinquishing them we will enable reason to better confront contemporary problems".[32] And, of course, Rabinow is not alone in perceiving the necessity for such a restructuring of global forms. One of the many social scientists that have issued similar calls for change is Helga Nowotny, who in her book *Insatiable Curiosity: Innovation in a Fragile Future* has—quite aptly given the topic of my study—noted the following:

> Modernity is no longer the program that provides answers to prefabricated utopias, even if the building blocks that it once contributed to furnish institutions and societal structures are still present and usable. Nor does modernity answer any longer to explicit or implicit expectations: the majority of its promises have been fulfilled, even if differently from what was expected. It still functions as a substitute for a belief in progress that has collapsed under its own hubris and the illusions it created for itself. But modernity must continue to create itself out of itself, and to this end a future is needed that is radically open and uncertain.[33]

With regard to these observations then, it only remains for me to sum up concretely how I imagine the present book to contribute to such a critical global knowledge of 'motion' in the here and now.

Above all, I have explained how progressive modernity has ceased to be understood as an epochal and spatially bounded culture. Through my account of emergent assemblages of hetero-logoi of "the modern", I have situated the destabilization and latent transformation of a dominant logos of modernization in a global contemporary. However, my research indicates that "today, there exists neither a logos adequate to understanding this globalizing *oikeumene* nor a means of regulating its volatility", which is why I have attempted to contribute to an anthropology of the contemporary by presenting various means of observing and analyzing how different logoi are currently being assembled into contingent forms.[34]

Accordingly, I have shown how a pragmatically oriented historical perspective on the present can unravel problematic practices, classifications and things modern.[35] My anthropological inquiry into global heritage assemblages around instances of modern architecture and urban planning on the African continent has framed specific politics of sovereignty and security, technologies of authenticity and value and ethics of legitimacy and responsibility as urgent problematizations of modernity. My study describes an ethos of modernity already becoming historical, a circumstance, which—I have argued—yields a number of rather complex problems in the contemporary. But, in spite of the very complexity of those problems, I want to conclude this book by contending that they could well be subsumed under a single, if not simple, question: How to preserve change?

First of all, my work indicates that this critical question lies at the heart of the issue of modern architectural heritage today, mainly because it directly relates to the principle of "intentional transitoriness" often presented as a defining feature of ideologies of modern architecture and urban planning.[36] My pathway has cited DOCOMOMO's claim that the principle of intentional transitoriness "is now an important part of our cultural heritage and therefore deserves conservation".[37] In this respect, the NGO already proposes an answer to the question of how to preserve change; its mention of transitoriness as the most significant inheritance of the Modern Movement in architecture and urban planning results in the advocacy of conservation through 'stylistic restoration'.

However, DOCOMOMO's appeal to a stylistic restoration of the modern built environment presupposes an authoritative interpretation of the *nature* of desirable change. Therefore, the NGO's critical contestation of and intervention in dominant heritage practices—practices that form a kind of 'cult of heritage'—effectively turns the question of how to preserve change into a question of how to *direct* it. Ultimately then, my analysis suggests that this particular variation of dealing with modern heritage is problematic, especially considering DOCOMOMO's conspicuous reference to the preservation of instances of modern architecture and urban planning as 'living heritage'. After all, the NGO took as a major legitimization for the institutionalization of modern architectural heritage what it called "the Modern Movement's continuing and vital role in meeting social needs",[38] which is why its approach to stylistic restoration inevitably resort to promises of unilinear progress and development and respective theories of 'modernity-as-culture'.

Nevertheless, as I have reflected on in this book, recent appeals to cultural diversity have come to embrace different ideals of cultural change, for instance along the lines of 'alternative–cultural–modernities'. One example is UNESCO's 2001 *Universal Declaration of Cultural Diversity*, which asserts that "cultural diversity widens the range of options to everyone; it is one of the roots of development, understood not simply in terms of economic development, but also as a means to achieve more satisfactory intellectual, emotional, moral and spiritual existence".[39] In this context, the question of how to preserve change receives a different connotation, turning into a question of how to avoid falling back on teleological accounts of modernity, the conservation or stylistic restoration of which must be deemed undesirable today. After all, teleological accounts of modernity have proved to go wrong—and the apparent need to preserve modern architectural heritage is a pretty good example thereof.

Although the telos of modernity appears lost, there may still be hope for solutions to actual problems of 'development'. But besides the fact that one can call them something different now, one must be aware of the dangers of failure. Take target 5a of the UN Millennium Development Goals: "Reduce by three quarters the maternal mortality ratio" by 2015. According to the United Nations, "an estimated 287,000 maternal deaths occurred in 2010 worldwide, a decline of 47 per cent from 1990, but levels are far removed from the 2015 target". Although these figures do show some improvement, they still imply that a woman dies from—largely preventable—childbearing-induced complications roughly every two minutes. Furthermore, the United Nations notes that "the maternal mortality ratio in developing regions is still 15 times higher than in the developed regions".[40]

According to the US government, "a highly disproportionate number of maternal deaths occur in Sub-Saharan Africa",[41] a situation that has hardly seen any improvement over the years. In the latest statistics, African countries exclusively fill the first 19 ranks, Chad topping the list with a horrifying 1,100 deaths out of 100,000 births. To mention only the countries that play a role in this book: Niger ranks 13th with a ratio of 590/100,000; the Republic of the Congo is 15th with a ratio of 560/100000; Tanzania, 23rd with a ratio of 460/100,000; and Eritrea, 43rd with a ratio of 240/100,000 (to compare, the Netherlands ranks 170th with a ratio of 6/100,000). Deplorably, the distribution of these maternal mortality statistics indicates that some problems remain, urgently requiring solutions. And it is almost irrelevant whether you call them "development" problems, problems of a "global status" or otherwise.

As my concern in writing this book has also been to answer the question of how to preserve change in the study of change—that is how to critically contest and intervene in some of the main tenets of a rather modern 'cult of anthropology'—my excursion into the problem of maternal mortality reminds me of Max Weber, who would say that "from this we want to draw the lesson that nothing is gained by yearning and tarrying alone, and we shall act differently. We shall set to work and meet the 'demands of the day', in human relations as well as in our vocation."[42] As Weber observed, the human sciences are condemned to be perpetually in motion—"nowhere do we have any point to rest"[43]—underlining some of the relevant problems in and of the contemporary as they emerge from my study. How to meet the vocational requirements of the discipline of anthropology from within the European academy is one problem; how to care for a newborn human being in the face of maternal death is another problem of a different magnitude, wherever you are. Although if your location is on the African continent, the odds remain that this matters greatly and negatively, a condition that can absolutely not be allowed to last. Whatever the case may be, let us cultivate new global forms of collaboration—different cults of expertise—to meet these and other urgent demands of the day and to accept our mutual responsibilities to care for our modern heritage—to link the recent past with the near future and the near future with the recent past.

Notes

1. Quoted in Rabinow, *Marking Time: On the Anthropology of the Contemporary*. 101.
2. "Anthropological Research on the Contemporary: bios-technika".
3. Collier, "Global Assemblages." 400.
4. Ibid., 400.
5. Rabinow, *Marking Time: On the Anthropology of the Contemporary*.
6. Koselleck, *Futures Past: On the Semantics of Historical Time*. 262–263.
7. Ibid.
8. Ibid. 274; 269.
9. Foucault quoted in Rabinow, *Anthropos Today: Reflections on Modern Equipment*.
10. Terdiman, *Present Past: Modernity and the Memory Crisis*. 52.
11. Rabinow, *The Accompaniment*. 110–111.
12. Ibid.
13. Ibid.
14. Ong and Collier, *Global Assemblages: Technology, Politics, and Ethics as Anthropological Problems*. 14.
15. Ibid., 14.
16. Rabinow in Ong and Collier, *Global Assemblages: Technology, Politics, and Ethics as Anthropological Problems*. 43.
17. Ibid.
18. Rabinow, *The Accompaniment*. 90.
19. Foucault, *The Archeology of Knowledge and the Discourse on Language*. 131.
20. Foucault quoted by Rabinow in Ong and Collier, *Global Assemblages: Technology, Politics, and Ethics as Anthropological Problems*. 55.
21. Michel Foucault, "Polemics, Politics, and Problematizations: An Interview," in *The Foucault Reader*, ed. Paul Rabinow (New York: Vintage, 2010 [1984]). 389–390.
22. Rabinow, *The Accompaniment*. 88.
23. Rabinow, *Marking Time: On the Anthropology of the Contemporary*. 4.
24. Rabinow in Ong and Collier, *Global Assemblages: Technology, Politics, and Ethics as Anthropological Problems*. 51.
25. Clifford, *Routes: Travel and Translation in the Late Twentieth Century*. 218.
26. Faubion and Marcus, *Field Work Is Not What It Used to Be*. 30.
27. Rabinow, *Anthropos Today: Reflections on Modern Equipment*. 3.

28. Barillet, Joffroy, and Longuet, *Cultural Heritage and Local Development: A Guide for Local African Governments*. 9.
29. Irina Bokova, "Mission Statement—UNESCO in a Globalised World: New Humanism for the 21st Century," UNESCO, http://www.unesco.org/new/fileadmin/MULTIMEDIA/HQ/BPI/EPA/images/media_services/Director-General/mission-statement-bokova.pdf.
30. Dreyfus and Rabinow, *Michel Foucault: Beyond Structuralism and Hermeneutics*. 125.
31. Rabinow, *Anthropos Today: Reflections on Modern Equipment*. 122.
32. Ibid., 133.
33. Nowotny, *Insatiable Curiosity: Innovation in a Fragile Culture*. 135.
34. Rabinow, *Anthropos Today: Reflections on Modern Equipment*. 15.
35. Dreyfus and Rabinow, *Michel Foucault: Beyond Structuralism and Hermeneutics*. 125.
36. ISC/Registers, "The Modern Movement and the World Heritage List: Advisory Report to ICOMOS." 50.
37. Ibid.
38. Ibid.
39. UNESCO, "Universal Declaration on Cultural Diversity". Compare article 3.
40. UN, "The Millenium Development Goals".
41. "Wikipedia.org: Maternal Death," http://en.wikipedia.org/wiki/Maternal_death.
42. Weber, "Science as a Vocation."
43. Joachim Radkau, *Max Weber: A Biography* (London: Polity Press, 2009). 257.

Appendix

List of Interviews

1. Antoni Folkers, director ArchiAfrika, Utrecht, 17.3.09
2. Konrad Melchers, former chief editor *e1ns Entwicklungspolitik*, Berlin, 24.3.09
3. Omar Akbar, urban curator, former director Bauhaus Dessau, Berlin, 25.3.09
4. Mekonnen Mesghena, director department of Migration, Citizenship and Intercultural Democracy, Heinrich Böll Foundation, Berlin, 25.3.09
5. Christoph Melchers, architect, organizer travelling exhibition Arbate Asmara, Tübingen, 26.3.-27.3.09
6. Lodovico Folin-Calabi, consultant UNESCO World Heritage Center, Paris, 8.4.09
7. Uschi Eid, German member of parliament, phone interview, 28.5.09
8. Naigzy Gebremedhin, former director CARP, Bologna, 5.6.09
9. Robert Rubin, financier and collector, Paris, 19.6.09
10. Maristella Casciato, former chair DOCOMOMO International, phone interview, 22.7.09
11. Ângela Ferreira, artist, Lisbon, 18.8.09
12. Edward Denison, heritage consultant, London, 21.8.09
13. Lazare Eloundou-Assomo, director Africa Section UNESCO World Heritage Center, Paris, 27.8.09
14. Bernard Toulier, senior heritage consultant French Ministry of Culture, Paris, 27.8.09
15. Michael Baer, historic preservationist/tourist, Asmara, 6.1.10
16. Tedros Kebbede, travel guide Travelhouse International, Asmara, 8.1.10
17. Marisia Pechaczek, cultural attaché Dutch embassy, Asmara, 8.1.10
18. Mike Shute, construction works consultant for British Council, Asmara, 10.1.10
19. Peter Herzel, European Commission delegation to Eritrea, Asmara, 10.1.10

20. Yozef Lipsikal, director Eritrean national museum, Asmara, 11.1.10
21. Giorgio Vicenzi, consultant European Commission delegation to Eritrea, Asmara, 11.1.10
22. Ronald McMullen, American ambassador, Asmara, 12.1.10
23. Klaus-Peter Schick, German ambassador, Asmara, 12.1.10
24. Marco Lapuda, consultant Italian embassy, Asmara, 12.1.10
25. Romain LeChequer, head cultural affairs French embassy, Asmara, 13.1.10
26. Afwerki, consultant Alliance Francaise, Asmara, 13.1.10
27. Samuel Zerom, consultant World Bank, Asmara, 14.1.10
28. Zemeret Yohannes, information minister, member of politburo Peoples Front for Democracy and Justice, Asmara, 14.1.10
29. Angus Bjarnason, director British Council, Asmara, 14.1.10
30. Medhanie Maria, director urban planning Department of Infrastructure, Asmara, 13.1.10
31. Anthony Almeida, architect, Dar es Salaam, 18.1.2010
32. Daniel Mbisso, lecturer in architecture Dar es Salaam University, 20.1.2010
33. Richard Besha, lecturer in architecture Dar es Salaam University, 20.1.2010
34. Dr. Camilus T. Lekula, lecturer in architecture Dar es Salaam University, 20.1.2010
35. Roxanne Hakim, senior heritage consultant World Bank New Delhi, phone interview, 11.2.10
36. Jürgen Bock, director Maumaus Lisbon, phone interview, 12.2.10
37. Dr. Christopher Young, heritage consultant English Heritage, phone interview, 25.2.10
38. Arlene Fleming, senior heritage consultant World Bank Washington, phone interview, 4.3.10
39. Joep Mol, architect, producer Many Words for Modern, Den Bosch, 8.3.2010
40. Ron van Oers, director UNESCO Modern Heritage program, phone interview, 15.4.10
41. Berend van der Lans, African Architecture Matters, Amsterdam, 21.9.2010

Participant Observation/Site Visits

1. ArchiAfrika conference African Perspectives, Delft, 6.-8.12.2007
2. Exhibition of André Balasz's *Maison Tropicale* in front of the Tate Modern, London, 29.3.08
3. Design Museum London, Jean Prouve furniture, retrospective exhibition, 29.3.08
4. Exhibition of Robert Rubin's *Maison Tropicale* on display at the Centre Pompidou, Paris, 8.4.09

5. ArchiAfrika board meeting, Utrecht, 16.4.09
6. Opening of the travelling exhibition Asmara: Secret Modernist City, Bologna, 4.6.-5.6.09
7. Asmara, 6.1.-17.1.2010
8. Dar es Salaam, 17.1.-23.1.2010
9. Architecture Association of Tanzania board meeting, Goan institute, Dar es Salaam, 21.1.2010
10. ArchiAfrika book presentation *Mtoni Palace*, Amsterdam, 15.4.2010
11. ArchiAfrika book presentation Modern Architecture in Africa, Delft, 27.4.2010

Bibliography

"Abu Simbel: Now or Never." *UNESCO Courier*, 1961.

"African Architecture Matters: Homepage." http://www.aamatters.nl.

Alexander, Kaye. "A Visit to Jean Prouvé's Maison Tropicale." *The Architects' Journal*, 2008, https://www.architectsjournal.co.uk/news/a-visit-to-jean-prouv 233s-maison-tropicale/769111.article.

Almeida, Anthony. "Curriculum Vitae." 2010.

AlSayyad, Nezar, ed. *Forms of Dominance: On the Architecture and Urbanism of the Colonial Enterprise*. Aldershot: Avebury, 1992.

Amit, Vered, ed. *Constructing the Field: Ethnographic Fieldwork in the Contemporary World*. London: Routledge, 2000.

Anderson, Benedict. *Imagined Communities: Reflections on the Origin and Spread of Nationalism*. Rev. ed. London: Verso, 2006.

"Anthropological Research on the Contemporary: Anthropos-Lab." http://www.anthropos-lab.net.

"Anthropological Research on the Contemporary: Bios-Technika." http://www.bios-technika.net.

Appadurai, Arjun. "Disjuncture and Difference in the Global Cultural Economy." *Public Culture* 2, Spring (1990): 1–22.

———, ed. *Globalization, Millennium Quartet*. London: Duke University Press, 2001.

———. *Modernity at Large: Cultural Dimensions of Globalization*. Minneapolis: University of Minnesota Press, 1996.

———. *The Social Life of Things*. Cambridge: Cambridge University Press, 1986.

"Appeal Launched on 8 March 1960 by Mr. Vittorino Veronese, Director General of Unesco." http://www.itnsource.com/shotlist//RTV/1960/03/08/BGY503240109/?s=buries.

ArchiAfrika. "African Perspectives: Conference Programme." Delft, 2007.

———. "Annual Report." Utrecht, 2007.

———. "Homepage." http://www.archiafrika.org.

———. "Mission Statement." Utrecht, 2001.

———. "The Intertwinement of Modernism and Colonialism: A Theoretical Perspective." Paper presented at the Conference Modern Architecture in East Africa Around Independence, Dar es Salaam, 2005.

———. "Policy Plan 2009–2012." Utrecht, 2009.

Armstrong, David. "House Proud." http://www.forbes.com/free_forbes/2006/0410/112.html?partner=yahoomag.

Balasz-Properties. "La Maison Tropicale." http://www.lamaisontropicales.com.

Barillet, Christian, Thierry Joffroy, and Isabelle Longuet, eds. *Cultural Heritage and Local Development: A Guide for Local African Governments.* CARTerre-ENSAG/Convention France, UNESCO, 2006.

BBC. "Eritrea 'Rounds up Draft-Dodgers'." http://news.bbc.co.uk/2/hi/africa/323436.stm.

Bergdoll, Barry, and Peter Christensen. *Home Delivery: Fabricating Modern Dwelling.* New York: The Museum of Modern Art, 2008.

Berman, Marshall. *All That Is Solid Melts into Air: The Experience of Modernity.* London: Verso, 1983.

Birch, Dinah. *Ruskin and the Dawn of the Modern.* Oxford: Oxford University Press, 1999.

———. *Ruskin's Myths.* Oxford English Monographs. Oxford: Clarendon, 1988.

Blake, Peter. *Form Follows Fiasco: Why Modern Architecture Hasn't Worked.* Atlantic Monthly Press Book. Boston: S.l.: Little Brown, 1977.

Bock, Jürgen, ed. *Angela Ferreira: Maison Tropicale, Portugese Pavillion.* Lisbon/Venice: La Ministério da Cultura, 2007.

Bokova, Irina. "Mission Statement—UNESCO in a Globalised World: New Humanism for the 21st Century." UNESCO, http://www.unesco.org/new/file admin/MULTIMEDIA/HQ/BPI/EPA/images/media_services/Director-General/mission-statement-bokova.pdf.

Boym, Svetlana. *The Future of Nostalgia.* New York: Basic Books, 2001.

Breglia, Lisa. *Monumental Ambivalence: The Politics of Heritage.* Austin: The University of Texas Press, 2006.

Burssens, Pieter. "Anthony B. Almeida: Modern Architecture in Tanzania between 1950 and 1975: Architecture Serving Colonial and Post-Colonial Politics?" Thesis Submitted to Obtain the Degree of Civil Engineer-Architect, Leuven, 2005.

Casciato, Maristella. "Editorial: Modern Architecture in Africa." *DOCOMOMO Journal Special Edition* (2005): 1.

Celik, Zeynep. *Urban Forms and Colonial Confrontations: Algiers under French Rule.* Berkeley, CA: University of California Press, 1997.

Centre-Pompidou. "Jean Prouvé: Maison Tropicale, Prototype De Brazzaville, 1953." http://www.centrepompidou.fr/Pompidou/Musee.nsf/Docs/ADFA69 FCEF2DD1D0C12576E7002D8B96?OpenDocument&salle=1N5TERSUD= salle&Key=1N5&L=1.

Choay, Francoise. *The Invention of the Historic Monument.* Cambridge: Cambridge University Press, 2001.

Choay, Francoise, and Denise Bratton. *The Rule and the Model: On the Theory of Architecture and Urbanism.* Cambridge, MA: MIT Press, 1997.

Cianci, John, and Peter Nicholls. *Ruskin and Modernism.* Basingstoke: Palgrave, 2001.

Cinqualbre, Olivier, ed. *Jean Prouvé: La Maison Tropicale.* Paris: Centre Pompidou, 2009.

Clifford, James. *The Predicament of Cultures.* Cambridge: Harvard University Press, 1988.

———. *Routes: Travel and Translation in the Late Twentieth Century.* Boston: Harvard University Press, 1997.

Collier, Stephen J. "Global Assemblages." *Theory, Culture, Society* 23 (2006): 399–401.

Collingwood, W. G. *The Life and Work of John Ruskin.* 2nd ed. London: Methuen & Co., 1893.

Commission, EU. *European Commission Delegation to Eritrea: Policy Plan National Heritage Programme.* 2009.

———. *European Commission Delegation to Eritrea: Terms of Reference National Heritage Programme.* 2009.

———. "The European Consensus on Development." http://ec.europa.eu/europeaid/what/development-policies/european-consensus/.

Crinson, Mark. *Empire Building: Orientalism and Victorian Architecture.* London: Routledge, 1996.

———. *Modern Architecture and the End of Empire.* Aldershot: Ashgate, 2003.

de la Torre, Marta. *Assessing the Values of Cultural Heritage.* Los Angeles: The Getty Conservation Institute, 2002.

Denison, Edward, Naigzy Gebremedhin, and Guang Yu Ren. *Asmara: Africa's Secret Modernist City.* London: Merrell, 2003.

Denison, Edward, and Guang Yu Ren. "Africa's Secret Modernist City." http://www.theglobalist.com/StoryID.aspx?StoryId=4115.

———. "Supporting Africa's Secret City." http://www.theglobalist.com/StoryID.aspx?StoryId=3761.

Denissen, Anne-Katrien. *Kick Off Meeting: Archiafrika Expertise Centre on African Architecture, Memo.* Utrecht: ArchiAfrika, 2008.

Di Giovine, Michael A. *The Heritage-Scape: UNESCO, World Heritage and Tourism.* Lanham: Lexington Books, 2009.

Diawara, Manthia. "Maison Tropicale." 58 minutes. Portugal, 2008.

Drew, Jane, and Maxwell Fry. *Tropical Architecture in the Dry and Humid Zones.* Malabar, FL: Robert E. Krieger Publishing Company, 1982.

Dreyfus, Hubert L., and Paul Rabinow. *Michel Foucault: Beyond Structuralism and Hermeneutics.* Chicago: University of Chicago Press, 1983.

Duer, Kreszentia. *Culture and Sustainable Development: A Framework for Action.* Washington, DC: The Worldbank, 1999.

Elleh, Nnamdi. "Foreword." In *Modern Architecture in Africa.* Nijmegen: SUN, 2010.

"Executive Summary of the Strategic Urban Development Plan for Asmara," edited by Department of Infrastructure, Asmara, 2006.

Fabian, Johannes. *Time and the Other: How Anthropology Makes Its Object.* New York: Columbia University Press, 1983.

Falzon, Mark-Anthony, ed. *Multi-Sited Ethnography.* Farnham: Ashgate, 2009.

Faubion, James, and George E. Marcus, eds. *Field Work Is Not What It Used to Be.* Ithaca: Cornell University Press, 2009.

Ferguson, James. *The Anti-Politics Machine: 'Development,' Depoliticization, and Bureaucratic Power in Lesotho.* Minneapolis: University of Minnesota Press, 1994.

———. *Expectations of Modernity: Myths and Meanings of Urban Life on the Zambian Copperbelt.* Berkeley: University of California Press, 1999.

———. *Global Shadows: Africa in the Neoliberal World Order.* Durham: Duke University Press, 2006.

Folkers, Antoni. *Modern Architecture in Africa.* Nijmegen: SUN, 2010.

Foucault, Michel. *The Archeology of Knowledge and the Discourse on Language.* London: Tavistock, 1971.

———. *The Birth of Biopolitics: Lectures at the Collège De France*. Vol. 5, London: Macmillan, 2010.

———. "Polemics, Politics, and Problematizations: An Interview." In *The Foucault Reader*, edited by Paul Rabinow. New York: Vintage, 2010 (1984).

———. *Remarks on Marx: Conversations with Duccio Trombadori*. New York: Semiotexte, 1991.

———. *Security, Territory, Population: Lectures at the Collège De France*. Vol. 4, London: Macmillan, 2007.

Frampton, Kenneth. *Modern Architecture: A Critical History*. New York: Oxford University Press, 1980.

Fuller, Mia. *Moderns Abroad: Architecture, Cities and Italian Imperialism*. London: Routledge, 2007.

Gaonkar Parameshwar, Dilip. *Alternative Modernities*. Durham: Duke University Press, 2001.

Garrigan, Kristine Ottesen. *Ruskin on Architecture: His Thought and Influence*. Madison, WI; London: University of Wisconsin Press, 1973.

Gay, Peter. *Modernism: The Lure of Heresy*. New York: W.W. Norton, 2010.

Gebremedhin, Naigzy, ed. *Asmara: A Guide to the Built Environment*. Asmara: CARP, 2003.

Gentleman, Amelia. "Bullet Holes Extra: A Classic of Modern Design Has Been Saved from Squatters, Snipers, and the Congolese Jungle." *The Guardian*, 2004.

———. "A City That Sat on Its Treasures but Didn't See Them." *The New York Times*, 2008.

"The Getty Conservation Institute: 1933 Athens Charter." http://www.getty.edu/conservation/publications_resources/research_resources/charters/charter04.html.

Giedion, Sigfried. *Space, Time and Architecture: The Growth of a New Tradition*. Cambridge, MA: Harvard University Press, 1974.

Gordon, Alastair. "Out of Africa, a House for a Kit Bag." *The New York Times*, 2004.

Guilloux, Tristan. "The Maison Tropique: A Modernist Icon or the Ultimate Colonial Bungalow?" *Fabrications* 18, no. 2 (2008): 6–25.

Gupta, Akhil, and James Ferguson, eds. *Anthropological Locations: Boundaries and Grounds of a Field Science*. Berkeley: University of California Press, 1997.

Hamilton, William L. "From Africa to Queens Waterfront, a Modernist Gem for Sale to the Highest Bidder." *The New York Times*, 2007.

Hannan, Lucy. "Desert War of Rusty Weapons and Sophisticated Words." *The Independent*, 1999.

Hassan, Fekri A. "The Aswan High Dam and the International Rescue Nubia Campaign." *African Archeological Review* 24 (2007): 73–94.

Henket, Hubert-Jan, and Hilde Heynen. *Back from Utopia: The Challenge of the Modern Movement*. Rotterdam: 010 Publishers, 2002.

Hewitt, Simon. "Out of Africa." http://www.blouinartinfo.com/news/story/268281/out-of-africa.

Heynen, Hilde. "The Intertwinement of Modernism and Colonialism: A Theoretical Perspective." Paper presented at the ArchiAfrica: Conference Modern Architecture in East Africa around Independence, Dar es Salaam, Tanzania, 2005.

———. "Transitoriness of Modern Architecture." In *Modern Movement Heritage*, edited by A. Cunningham. London: E.FN Spon, 1998.

Hobsbawm, Terence, and Terence Ranger, eds. *The Invention of Tradition.* Cambridge: Cambridge University Press, 1983.

Holston, James. *The Modernist City: An Anthropological Critique of Brasilia.* Chicago: University of Chicago Press, 1989.

Hosagrahar, Jyoti. *Indigenous Modernities: Negotiating Architecture, Urbanism, and Colonialism in Delhi.* London: Routledge, 2005.

Huppatz, D. J. "Jean Prouvé's Maison Tropicale: The Poetics of the Colonial Object." *Design Issues,* Fall (2010): 32–44.

ICOMOS. "The 1931 Athens Charter for the Restoration of Historic Monuments." http://www.icomos.org/en/charters-and-texts/179-articles-en-francais/ressources/charters-and-standards/167-the-athens-charter-for-the-restoration-of-historic-monument.

———. "Experts Meeting Report: Developing an Historic Thematic Framework to Assess the Significance of Twentieth Century Cultural Heritage: An Initiative of the Icomos International Scientific Committee on Twentieth Century Cultural Heritage." http://www.getty.edu/conservation/publications_resources/pdf_publications/pdf/mod_arch_bib_aug11.pdf.

———. "Heritage at Risk 2001–2002: Shared Colonial Heritage." http://www.international.icomos.org/risk/2001/colonial2001.htm.

———. "History of the Venice Charter." http://www.icomos.org/venicecharter2004/history.pdf.

———. "Venice Charter." http://www.icomos.org/charters/venice_e.pdf.

———. "World Heritage List, Advisory Body Evaluation No. 445." http://whc.unesco.org/archive/advisory_body_evaluation/445.pdf.

Inda, Jonathan Xavier. *Anthropologies of Modernity: Foucault, Governmentality and Life Politics.* London: Blackwell, 2005.

"International Working-Party for Documentation and Restoration of Early Modern Architecture: First Newsletter." 1989.

ISC/Registers, DOCOMOMO. "The Modern Movement and the World Heritage List: Advisory Report to Icomos." *DOCOMOMO Journal* 18 (1998): 41–53.

Jokilehto, Jukka. "Definition of Cultural Heritage: References to Documents in History, Revised 15 January 2005." http://cif.icomos.org/pdf_docs/Documents on line/Heritage definitions.pdf.

———. *A History of Architectural Conservation.* Amsterdam: Elsevier, 1999.

———. *The World Heritage List: Filling the Gaps—An Action Plan for the Future.* Paris: ICOMOS, 2004.

Joussee, Phillippe, and Patrick Seguin. *Jean Prouvé.* Paris: Galerie Enrico Navarra, 1998.

King, Anthony D. *The Bungalow: The Production of a Global Culture.* Oxford: Oxford University Press, 1995.

———. *Colonial Urban Development: Culture, Social Power and Environment.* London: Routledge & Kegan Paul, 1976.

———. *Spaces of Global Cultures: Architecture, Urbanism, Identity.* London: Routledge, 2004.

———. *Urbanism, Colonialism, and the World-Economy: Cultural and Spatial Foundations of the World Urban System.* Repr. in pbk. ed. London: Routledge, 1991.

Koselleck, Reinhart. *Futures Past: On the Semantics of Historical Time.* New York: Columbia University Press, 2004.

Kreimer, Alcira, John Eriksson, Robert Muscat, Margaret Arnold, and Colin Scott. *The World Bank's Experience with Post-Conflict Reconstruction.* Washington, DC: The World Bank, 1998.

Kuipers, Marieke C. "Authenticiteit Versus Attrappenkult?" In *Reco.Mo.Mo: Hoe Echt Is Namaak, Hoe Dierbaar Het Origineel?* edited by Sara Stroux, Wido Quist, Frank Foole and Bianca Eikhoudt. Delft: DOCOMOMO, 2011.

Loeffler, Jane C. *The Architecture of Diplomacy: Building America's Embassies.* New York: Princeton Architectural Press, 1998.

Lowenhaupt-Tsing, Anna. *Friction: An Ethnography of Global Connection.* Princeton: Princeton University Press, 2005.

Lowenthal, David. *The Heritage Crusade and the Spoils of History.* London: Viking, 1997.

Luhmann, Niklas. *Art as a Social System.* Stanford: Stanford University Press, 2000.

———. *Observations on Modernity.* Stanford: Stanford University Press, 1998.

———. *Schriften Zu Kunst Und Kultur.* Frankfurt am Main: Suhrkamp, 2008.

Makki, Fouad. "Imperial Fantasies, Colonial Realities: Contesting Power and Culture in Italian Eritrea." *South Atlantic Quarterly* 107, no. 4 (2008): 735–754.

Marcus, George E. "Ethnography in/of the World System: The Emergence of Multi Sited Ethnography." *Annual Review of Anthropology* 24 (1995): 95–117.

———. "Multi-Sited Ethnography: Five or Six Things I Know About It Now." In *Multi-Sited Ethnography: Problems and Possibilities in the Translocation of Research Methods*, edited by Simon Colemann and Pauline Hellerman. London: Routledge, 2011.

Marcus, George E., ed. *Critical Anthropology Now: Unexpected Contexts, Shifting Constitutencies, Changing Agendas.* Santa Fe: School of American Research Press, 1999.

Marcus, George E., and Fred R. Myers, eds. *The Traffic of Culture: Refiguring Art and Anthropology.* London: University of California Press, 1995.

Mayor Zaragoza, Frederico. "The World Decade for Cultural Development." *UNESCO Courier*, November 1988.

Mazzucato, Valentina. "Bridging Boundaries with a Transnational Approach." In *Multi-Sited Ethnography*, edited by Mark-Anthony Falzon. Farnham: Ashgate, 2009.

Miele, Chris. "Conservation and the Enemies of Progress?" In *From William Morris: Building Conservation and the Arts and Crafts Cult of Authenticity, 1877–1939*, edited by Chris Miele. New Haven: Yale University Press, 2005.

———. *From William Morris: Building Conservation and the Arts and Crafts Cult of Authenticity, 1877–1939.* New Haven: Yale University Press, 2005.

———. "Preface." In *From William Morris: Building Conservation and the Arts and Crafts Cult of Authenticity, 1877–1939*, edited by Chris Miele. New Haven: Yale University Press, 2005.

Ministry of Public Works, DUD. "Final Strategic Urban Development Plan: Executive Summary." Asmara, Eritrea, 2006.

Mumford, Eric. *The Ciam Discourse on Urbanism, 1928–1960.* London: MIT Press, 2000.

Nowotny, Helga. *Insatiable Curiosity: Innovation in a Fragile Culture.* Boston: MIT Press, 2010.

O'Kane, David, and Tricia Redeker-Hepner, eds. *Biopolitics and Militarism and Development: Eritrea in the Twenty-First Century*. New York: Berghahn, 2009.

Ong, Aihwa, and Stephen J. Collier, eds. *Global Assemblages: Technology, Politics, and Ethics as Anthropological Problems*. London: Blackwell, 2005.

Ourousoff, Nicolai. "The Best House in Paris." *The New York Times*, 2007.

Pakenham, Thomas. *The Scramble for Africa: White Man's Conquest of the Dark Continent from 1876–1912*. London: Avon Books, 1992.

Paz, Octavio. *Children of the Mire: Modern Poetry from Romanticism to the Avant-Garde*. Cambridge, MA: Harvard University Press, 1991.

Pels, Peter, Birgit Meyer, and Peter Geschiere, eds. *Readings in Modernity in Africa*. London: International Africa Institute, 2008.

Pevsner, Nikolaus, and Richard Weston. *Pioneers of Modern Design: From William Morris to Walter Gropius*. rev. ed. New Haven: Yale University Press, 2005.

Picciotto, Robert. "Cultural Properties in Policy and Practice: A Review of World Bank Experience." In Policy 23369, edited by Operations Evaluation Department. Washington, DC: The World Bank, 2001. http://documents.worldbank.org/curated/en/310631468762018373/pdf/multi0page.pdf

Pol-Droit, Roger. *Humanity in the Making: The Intellectual History of Unesco*. Paris: UNESCO, 2005.

Price, Sally. *Paris Primitive: Jaques Chirac's Museum on the Quai Branly*. Chicago: Chicago University Press, 2007.

———. *Primitive Art in Civilized Places*. Chicago: Chicago University Press, 1989.

Rabinow, Paul. *The Accompaniment*. Chicago: University of Chicago Press, 2011.

———. *Anthropos Today: Reflections on Modern Equipment*. Princeton: Princeton University Press, 2003.

———. *French DNA: Trouble in Purgatory*. Chicago: The University of Chicago Press, 1999.

———. *French Modern: Norms and Forms of the Built Environment*. Chicago: University of Chicago Press, 1989.

———. *Making Pcr*. Chicago: University of Chicago Press, 1996.

———. *Marking Time: On the Anthropology of the Contemporary*. Princeton: Princeton University Press, 2008.

———. *Reflections on Fieldwork in Morocco (30th Anniversary Edition)*. Berkeley: University of Berkeley Press, 2007.

Rabinow, Paul, and Gaymon Bennett. *Designing Human Practices: An Experiment with Synthetic Biology*. Chicago: Chicago University Press, 2012.

Rabinow, Paul, George E. Marcus, James D. Faubion, and Tobias Rees, eds. *Designs for an Anthropology of the Contemporary*. London: Duke University Press, 2008.

Radkau, Joachim. *Max Weber: A Biography*. London: Polity Press, 2009.

Redeker-Hepner, Tricia. *Soldiers, Martyrs, Traitors, and Exiles: Political Conflict in Eritrea and the Diaspora*. Philadelphia: University of Pennsylvania Press, 2009.

"Reporters without Border: World Press Freedom Index 2010." http://en.rsf.org/press-freedom-index-2010,1034.html.

Riegl, Alois. *Der Moderne Denkmalkultus, Sein Wesen, Seine Entstehung*. Vienna: Kessinger, 2010.

Rose, Steve. "House Hunting: Eric Touchaleaume Has Been Called the Indiana Jones of Furniture Collecting. Steve Rose Meets Him." *The Guardian*, 2008.

———. "La Maison Tropicale Is One Hot House: Jean Prouvé's Fantastic Retro Prefab Has Landed by the Thames. Don't Miss Having a Nose Around . . ." *The Guardian*, 2008.

Rubin, Robert. "Jean Prouvé's Tropical House: Preservation, Presentation, Reception." In *Jean Prouvé: La Maison Tropicale*, edited by Olivier Cinqualbre. Paris: Centre Pompidou, 2009.

———. "Maison Tropicale: Jean Prouvé." In *Home Delivery: Fabricating Modern Dwelling*, edited by Berry Bergdoll. New York: Museum of Modern Art, 2008.

———. "Preserving and Presenting Prefab: Jean Prouvé's Tropical House." *Future Anterior* II, no. 1 (2005): 30–39.

Ruskin, John. *The Seven Lamps of Architecture*. New York: Dover Publications, 1989.

Said, Edward W. *Culture & Imperialism*. Reprinted ed. London: Vintage, 1994.

———. *Orientalism*. Penguin History. Repr. / ed. London: Penguin Books, 1995.

Sassen, Saskia. *Losing Control? Sovereignty in an Age of Globalization*. New York: Columbia University Press, 1996.

———. *Territory, Authority, Rights: From Medieval to Global Assemblages*. Princeton: Princeton University Press, 2006.

Save-Soderbergh, Torgny, ed. *Service for Life: State Repression and Indefinite Conscription in Eritrea*. New York: Human Rights Watch, 2009.

———. *Temples and Tombs of Ancient Nubia: The International Rescue Campaign at Abu Simbel, Philae and Other Sites*. London: UNESCO, Thames and Hudson, 1987.

Shapin, Steven. *The Scientific Life: A Moral History of a Late Modern Vocation*. Chicago: University of Chicago Press, 2008.

Smith, Laurajane. *Uses of Heritage*. London: Routledge, 2006.

"Spab: The Manifesto." http://www.spab.org.uk/what-is-spab-/the-manifesto/.

"The Speech of H.R.H. The Prince Albert, K.G., F.R.S., at the Lord Mayor's Banquet, in the City of London, October 1849." http://pages.zoom.co.uk/leveridge/albert.html.

Stoczkowski, Wiktor. "Claude Lévi-Strauss and Unesco." *UNESCO Courier*, 2008.

Terdiman, Richard. *Present Past: Modernity and the Memory Crisis*. Ithaca: Cornell University Press, 1993.

Thomas, Nicholas. *Entangled Objects: Exchange, Material Culture and Colonialism in the Pacific*. Cambridge: Harvard University Press, 1991.

Tilley, Helen. *Africa as a Living Laboratory: Empire Development and the Problem of Scientific Knowledge*. Chicago: University of Chicago Press, 2011.

———, ed. *Ordering Africa: Anthropology, European Imperialism and the Politics of Knowledge*. Manchester: Manchester University Press, 2007.

Timmermans, Justine. "Stageverslag: Het Almeida Project." 2009.

Touchaleaume, Eric. *Jean Prouvé: Les Maisons Tropicales*. Paris: Galerie 54, 2006.

Toulier, Bernard. *Brazzaville Decouvertes*. Itinaires Du Patrimoine. Saint-Herblain: Imprimerie Le Govic, 1996.

———, ed. *Brazzaville-La-Verte: Inventaire Général Des Monuments Et Richesses Artistiques De La France*. Brazzaville/Nantes: Centre Culturel Francais, 1996.

Tournikiotis, Panayotis. *The Historiography of Modern Architecture*. Cambridge: MIT Press, 1999.

———. "Modernism and the Issue of Otherness." *DOCOMOMO Journal* 36, Other Modernisms: A Selection from the DOCOMOMO Registers (2007): 5–9.

Treiber, Magnus. "Trapped in Adolescence: The Postwar Urban Generation." In *Biopolitics, Militarism and Development: Eritrea in the Twenty-First Century*, edited by David O'Kane and Tricia Redeker-Hepner. New York: Berghahn, 2009.

Tribune, International Herald. "Style Alert Maison Tropicale." http://www.news letterarchive.org/2007/06/18/175352-IHT+Style+Alert+for+June+19,+2007.

UN. "The Millenium Development Goals." http://www.un.org/millenniumgoals/.

———. "Security Council Resolution 1907, December 2009." http://www.dfat. gov.au/un/unsc_sanctions/eritrea.html.

———. "World Food Programme: Report on Eritrea." http://www.wfp.org/count ries/eritrea.

UNESCO. "1972 Convention Concerning the Protection of the World Cultural and Natural Heritage." http://whc.unesco.org/en/conventiontext/.

———. "African Cultural Heritage and the World Heritage Convention—Report of the First Global Strategy Meeting 1995, Harare." UNESCO, http://whc. unesco.org/en/events/594/.

———. "Expert Meeting on the "Global Strategy" and Thematic Studies for a Representative World Heritage List." http://whc.unesco.org/archive/global94. htm—debut.

———. "Global Strategy for a Representative and Balance World Heritage List." http://whc.unesco.org/en/globalstrategy/.

———. "Records of the 8th Unesco Conference in Montevideo, 1954." http:// unesdoc.unesco.org/images/0011/001145/114586E.pdf.

———. "Report of the Working Group Set up at the 11th Session of the World Heritage Committee, 1988." Sc-88/Conf.001/02.

———. "Tentative World Heritage List Entry: The Historic Perimeter of Asmara and Its Modernist Architecture." http://whc.unesco.org/en/tentativelists/2024/.

———. "Universal Declaration on Cultural Diversity." http://unesdoc.unesco. org/images/0012/001246/124687e.pdf—page=67.

———. "World Heritage: Challenges for the Millennium." http://whc.unesco. org/documents/publi_millennium_en.pdf.

———. "World Heritage Committee: Operational Guidelines 2001." http://whc. unesco.org/archive/opguide11-en.pdf.

———. "World Heritage List Entry: Brasilia." http://whc.unesco.org/en/list/445.

UNESCO, ICCROM, and CRATerre-EAG. "Africa 2009." http://www.africa 2009.net.

Vale, Lawrence J. *Architecture, Power, and National Identity*. London: Yale University Press, 1992.

van Oers, Ron. *Meeting on Modern Heritage for Africa: Asmara, Eritrea, 4–7 March 2004*. Paris: UNESCO, 2004.

———, ed. *World Heritage Papers 5: Identification and Documentation of Modern Heritage*. Paris: UNESCO.

Vegesack (von), Alexander, ed. *Jean Prouvé: The Poetics of the Technical Object*. Weil am Rhein: Vitra Design Museum, 2005.

"Victory in Nubia." *UNESCO Courier*, 1964.

Visscher, Jochen, and Stefan Boness. *Asmara: The Frozen City*. Berlin: Jovis, 2006.

Weber, Max. "Science as a Vocation." *Daedalus* 87, no. 1, Science and the Modern View (1958): 111–134.

Wesemael, Pieter van, and George Hall. *Architecture of Instruction and Delight: A Socio-Historical Analysis of World Exhibitions as a Didactic Phenomenon (1798–1851–1970)*. Rotterdam: 010 Publishers, 2001.

Wharton, Annabel Jane. *Building the Cold War: Hilton International Hotels and Modern Architecture*. Chicago, IL: University of Chicago Press, 2001.

"Wikipedia.Org: Maternal Death." http://en.wikipedia.org/wiki/Maternal_death.

"Wikipedia.Org: Paul Rabinow." http://www.wikipedia.org.

Wolfensohn, James D. *The Challenges of Globalization: The Role of the World Bank/Address to the Bundestag*. Berlin, Germany: The World Bank Group, 2001.

Worldbank. "Implementation Completion and Results Report on a Learning and Innovation Loan to the State of Eritrea in the Amount of Sdr 4.0 Million (Us\$ 5 Million Equivalent) for a Cultural Assets Rehabilitation Project," edited by Conflict and Social Development Unit (AFTCS) Fragile States, Eritrea Country Department, Washington, DC, 2008.

Woud, Auke van der. *Ciam: Volkshuisvesting, Stedebouw = Ciam: Housing, Town Planning*. Het Nieuwe Bouwen Internationaal. Delft: Delft University Press, 1983.

Index

For Product Safety Concerns and Information please contact our EU
representative GPSR@taylorandfrancis.com
Taylor & Francis Verlag GmbH, Kaufingerstraße 24, 80331 München, Germany

www.ingramcontent.com/pod-product-compliance
Ingram Content Group UK Ltd.
Pitfield, Milton Keynes, MK11 3LW, UK
UKHW020940180425
457613UK00019B/486